The Ideological and Political System of Banselism

The Ideological and Political System of Banselism

by

Royard Halmonet Vantion

(Ancheng Wang)

atmosphere press

Published by Atmosphere Press

Cover design by Ronaldo Alves

atmospherepress.com

This book is dedicated to:

The entire human civilization, including the seven point five billion supreme persons in the early 21st century

as well as the future evolution species of the whole human civilization

regardless of whoever they might be, what country they come from, which social group they belong to.

Contents

Part Two: For High-Welfare States

Part Three: For Developing Countries

Part Four: For China

Part Five: For War-Time States

Part Six: For India

Part Seven: For Central African Countries

Volume Three: The Banselistic Philosophical System

Part One: The Origin

Part Two: The Intersection Between the Banselistic Philosophy and The Historical Materialism

Part Three: The Intersection Between the Banselistic Philosophy and The Objective Idealism

Part Four: The Intersection Between the Banselistic Philosophy and The Subjective Idealism

Volume Four: The Banselistic Educational System

Volume Five: The Banselistic Anthropology

Introduction

The Ideological and Political System of Banselism describes a new ideological system, which includes the political system it corresponds to. It does not go against capitalism, socialism, or communism. In the vast majority of cases, it does not initiate violent revolutions (see Volume 3, Part 2, Chapter 1: The Theory of Atomic Evolution, for details), in order to protect humanitarianism to the maximum extent by avoiding injuries or deaths. Social democracy, for example, which advocates the transformation of capitalist states into socialist states through gradual reform, also refrains from violent revolution. This example shows that ideology does not necessarily mean the creation of violent revolutions, and similarly, in the vast majority of cases, the new ideological system described in this book does not initiate violent revolutions, including armed revolutions.

Unlike the third technological revolution, automation will replace all mechanized laborers over time. In 2018, Sami Atiya, director of the Discrete Automation and Motion Control business unit of the Swiss ABB Group, noted in an interview held by Forbes that robots are growing at 13-14% per year and are being added in almost all industries. The World Economic Forum also suggested in a BBC interview in 2021 that millions of routine or manual jobs will be replaced by technology by 2025, with the greatest impact on the lowest-paid and lowest-skilled workers. Meanwhile, the renewal energy technology is being improved and the energy technology conditions needed for large-scale automation will be in place: According to the news published by the University of New South Wales in Australia on 8 December 2014, a solar energy conversion system developed by this university has successfully converted more than 40% of the light that hits the solar system into electricity, "We hope to see this local innovation take the next step from prototype to pilot-scale demonstration. Ultimately, more efficient commercial solar power plants will make renewable energy cheaper, thereby increasing its competitiveness" said Ivor Frischknecht, CEO of the Australian Renewable Energy Agency (ARENA). This example shows that as the renewable energy technology continues to develop, the price of it will fall and when its price level reaches a certain value, the renewable energy technology will become available on a large scale, which will in turn enables automation to be applied on a large scale.

Nonetheless, once given opportunity, everyone can be retrained, including all those who are replaced by automation. According to the UK Parliament's report "Upskilling and Retraining the Adult Workforce" published on 29 April 2021, automation is reducing the number of manual jobs in the UK and is increasing the number of jobs almost only in high-skilled jobs. Retraining those displaced by automation and enabling them to work in higher-skilled jobs, including high-tech jobs, will be the key measure to resolving this future structural unemployment; also, as the World Economic Forum added in a BBC interview in 2021, millions of people will need to be reskilled to cope with the changes in employment caused by automation.

The British scholar Ernest Gellner has mentioned in his book *Nation and Nationalism* (pp.24-25) that society is egalitarian because it is mobile. Such a measure would strengthen the class mobility of society as never before, helping all working-class members to transform themselves into cutting-edge innovative or creative talents and thus improve their economic situation, thus defending egalitarianism more effectively.

According to Marxism, the economic base determines the superstructure, and such a change in the economic base necessarily implies an improvement in the ideological and political system. For countries with a socialist market economy, including China, this can even help the transition to scientific communism more effectively in the long run (see Volume 2, Part IV: For China for more details).

This book is therefore primarily concerned with the changes and developments in the ideological system, political system, and philosophical systems caused by automation.

The book is divided into five volumes. The first volume is devoted to the general content of the ideological and political system of Banselism, which is applicable to all countries in the entire world. The first part of the first volume deals with the economic and institutional aspects of this ideological and political system, which includes measures and policies to combat the economic problems that automation can cause: inflation, structural unemployment including technological unemployment, and so forth. The second part of Volume 1 deals with the conditions required for the implementation of this ideological and political system, such as the large-scale use of automation. At the same time, the second part of the volume also describes the historical inevitability of the implementation of this ideological and political system by stating the inevitability of the conditions being triggered.

Nevertheless, countries with different ideologies will have different national contexts. Accordingly, different forms of government will need to adopt specific and special policies and measures to implement the Ideological and Political System of Banselism in accordance with their local circumstances. The second volume therefore addresses the different policies and measures needed to implement this ideological and political system in countries with different ideologies.

At the same time, each of the different ideologies has a unique and distinct philosophical system. Thus, the third volume of this book elaborates on the philosophical system in the ideological and political system of Banselism.

However, the general lack of self-control of young children and citizens under the age of 16, as well as their general lack of critical thinking and vulnerability to deceptive information, will prevent non-adult citizens from being turned directly into banselistic students without relevant training. But again, because of the dramatic changes in social conditions at this time, there would be correspondingly dramatic changes in its educational system. Hence, the fourth volume of this book explains the new educational system for citizens up to the age of 16.

The fifth volume of this book aims at demonstrating the non-confrontational nature of this ideological and political system in relation to the idea of objective idealism, including religious theology, by describing the evolutionary trends of the future human race, although the Ideological and Political System of Banselism strongly emphasizes and recognizes direct innovation or creation in the field of natural science. The same is true as if Newton and Einstein believed in the existence of God, the University of Oxford uses 'Dominus Illuminatio Mea (The Lord is my light)' as its motto, and Harvard University has erected a statue of God on its campus. But even so, all human beings still must strengthen and develop their own initiative in order to succeed.

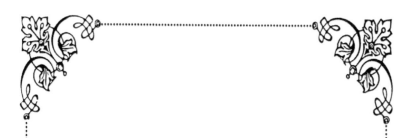

Volume One:

The Specific Definition

Part One:

The Basic Content

Chapter One:

The Student Class

In the *The ideological and political system of Banselism*, the technology of Artificial Intelligence (AI) is applied on a large scale, which replaces all the employed that are not compulsorily required to use innovation and creativity at all and completely do not use them during the process of working. Accordingly, the concept 'student' is divided into three types, which are the examination-oriented student, the Banselistic student, and students.

To begin with, we explain the term 'the exam-oriented student'. This refers to the student who is trained under the educational systems of the stratified education, the exam-oriented education, or the quality-oriented education. Also, this kind of learner is compulsorily required to pass written examinations and the university entrance examination, thereby gaining the qualified diplomas, whose definition is the kind of diploma that enables its owner to find the job which relatively satisfies his or her wants.

Next comes the Banselistic student. This kind of student does not receive education under any kind of educational system whereby the exam-oriented student obtains educations. Also, the Banselistic student does not receive the qualified diploma, and this kind of student develop their skills and ability by making full use of educational resources.

The working class[1] occupies the highest percentage of the population in society, which is far greater than that of other classes. While the population of the teaching staff is far less than that of the proletariat. The working class, accordingly, is not able to become the examination-oriented student. Instead, they will change into Banselistic students.

The Banselistic student has superiority and advancement. To begin with, this kind of student is highly focused: What differs from the examination-oriented student is that this kind of student can avoid the restriction coming from their vulnerable fields on their development to a great extent, making their knowledge directly develop their advantaged fields. Apart from that, the strategies of this kind of student have a great pertinence and flexibility. Without the limitations coming from the educational systems whereby the examination-oriented student obtains education, the Banselistic student is able to adjust development strategies flexibly according to their specific situation, thereby improving their learning efficiency, which maximizes their ability. Moreover, the strategies made by this kind of student are highly scientific: The amount of knowledge in the world is constantly increasing, while the constant increase of knowledge and the limitation of an individual's memory requires the improvement in the pertinence of education to strengthen the division of labor and cooperation. Meanwhile, as there is a considerable amount of knowledge within the same filed that requires interdisciplinary knowledge for individuals to master, the flexibility of the Banselistic students' developmental strategies means these students are able to flexibly carry out interdisciplinary and cross-disciplinary learning according to their own specific conditions, so that they will not only reach the cutting-edge level in their advantageous fields and subjects, but will also build up a wide range of advantages in different disciplines and fields. In these advantages, a large number of knowledge reserves and the corresponding thinking mode of these different disciplines and fields are included, which is conducive to the cultivation of the Cross talents[2].

Meanwhile, to analyze the banselistic student and the exam-oriented student in more depth, the following two fictional examples (i.e., the daily life of a banselistic student and the daily life of a test student), will be used to give an insight into the banselistic student under the ideological and political system of Banselism and the exam-oriented student in the early 21st century wherein the Banselism had not been implemented respectively:

Let us assume that Friedrich Noah Stahle is a banselistic student who was previously a German manual worker in an engine factory. After automation had been introduced on a large scale, his position was replaced by artificial intelligence (e.g., robots). However, he did not lose his job at this time. He found that all he had to do was to download the software developed by the German authorities on a smart electronic device (e.g., a mobile phone) and upload the progress of his new innovative outcome (e.g., the latest manuscript of his book or other kinds of innovative project) to it in order to ensure that his income was not lower than it had been before he was replaced by AI (for more details, see Volume One, Part

One, Chapter Seven: The basic welfare system).

Thus, Friedrich Noah Stahle can write his book while sitting in a Viennese café and drinking coffee: because he only has to upload his manuscript to the software developed by the German federal government to earn his daily bread; he can learn whatever he wants to learn, instead of being forced to learn whatever the school requires him to learn and whatever the school tests him to learn; he is no longer bound by the examination system; he no longer has to be afraid of being late, he no longer has to be pushed by his boss, he no longer has to work overtime, because at this point he is more like a freelancer; he no longer has to go to work, although he gets as much as he would have got if he had gone to work - he just has to upload the latest piece he has written to the software that the government has developed (for which this article is categorized as 'the class mobility'). He can sleep as long as he wants, and he can visit wherever he wants to go because wherever he is, he can upload his latest progress to this government-developed software. His life is free and comfortable but meaningful because he is making a major contribution to the art of human literature—he is writing a work of science fiction literature that has both commercial and literary value.

As his reading of narrative texts increased and his research in the field of literature deepened, his field of study gradually touched on psychology (narrative texts need to conform to the preferences of the reader, hence it has a strong link with psychology) and then on the natural sciences (psychology is closely related to the natural science disciplines, including neuroscience, which in turn has strong links with chemistry and mathematics). As a result of his increased reading of science fiction texts, he acquired a great deal of knowledge of the natural sciences; he discovered new partial equations; he discovered new treatments; he discovered new energy technologies. At this point he had already become a T-shaped talent[3]: he was both deeply involved in literature and had a vast knowledge of related fields such as mathematics - he was both a specialist and a generalist. He read and wrote the manuscript over and over again; he incorporated these new discoveries into his manuscript of science fiction literature and allocated several years to write his work. However, after completing his work, he went to hundreds of publishers over several years and was constantly rejected, but he continued to improve his work based on the feedback he received from the rejections. Finally, a publisher located in Florida agreed to publish his work: by this time, he had completed his class mobility and had become a member in the banselistic class (see next chapter for more details). By this time, he was both a specialist and a generalist, and at the same time created innovative and creative results: he had thus evolved into a cross talent. A few years later he even made a name for himself: his work was made into a film by Hollywood and won an Oscar, making Friedrich an overnight success and earning him a considerable amount of royalties as a direct result of the film.

By contrast, Gorman, an examination-oriented student in the early 21st century, had to sleep less than eight hours per day on average, which was the same as secondary school students in many developing countries in the early 21st century. In common with many developing countries in the early 21st century, Gorman had to do his best to avoid being admitted by irregular universities and low-ranking schools. Otherwise, he would be faced with low incomes and high costs of living, heavy, boring, and mechanical repetitive work and longer working hours. He must also compete with the overcrowded pool of candidates for the very limited resources available at the major universities, otherwise he is, in most cases, doomed to mediocrity or even poverty. Like the education systems of many developing countries, he has little freedom to choose what he wants to study, and he has to study whatever the school asks him to study and whatever the school tests him on, regardless of whether it is appropriate for his own development; like many students in developing countries in the early 21st century, Gorman's personal freedom is severely restricted and confined by the school's cumbersome and bizarre rules: He was not allowed to fall in love freely (this applies only to developing countries with large remnants of feudalism), he is not allowed to carry smart electronic devices, he is not allowed to dye his hair. As is the case in many developing countries' education systems, Gorman must concentrate on improving his national ranking of his overall grade, as universities in developing countries are in most cases based almost exclusively on test scores (note that in most developed countries, including the UK and the U.S., the candidate's curriculum vitae also plays a relatively important role in university admissions, although the overall grade was still highly significant). As a result, like most students in developing countries, he had studied extremely hard for years with no academic achievements and his CV was still unfortunately blank despite his hard work (note: the vast majority of Oxbridge and Harvard undergraduate offer holders have extremely extensive CVs with a wealth of academic achievements that cannot be matched by students from major universities in developing countries). Even if Gorman had been fortunate enough to achieve academic success, he would not have been admitted directly by a major university as a result, and would have been buried by this educational system as long as the candidate did not score enough points (note that the systems in these developing countries have undergone decades-long reforms, but have still not evolved into those of Europe and the United States, which means that the education systems in these developing countries will definitely not be able to reform to the extent that developed countries such as the United Kingdom and the United States did in the early 21st century). Moreover, once Gorman failed his university entrance exams, he would not be able to repeat his studies, and even if he was lucky enough to do so, the cost of doing so would be prohibitive.

In general, the banselistic student is superior to the exam-oriented student. Firstly, the massive spread of banselistic students would guarantee equality of opportunity in access to education, which is conducive to the defense of egalitarianism and democracy. Democracy is based on two major premises: firstly, that all people are equal, and secondly, that those with special skills must serve the common people (Miller. D. 2003). Since society is egalitarian because it is mobile (Gellner. E. 1983), and the mass popularization of banselistic students is conducive to guaranteeing equal opportunity for citizens to progress to higher education, it follows that the mass popularization of banselistic students is more conducive to defending democracy than the mass popularization of examination-oriented students, as it is more conducive to guaranteeing the first premise of democracy. At the same time, in contrast to the majority of high-achieving exam-oriented students in most developing countries, who are highly self-interested and aggressive, most of whom grab resources rather than produce them and develop productivity (which directly serves the interests of ordinary people), banselistic students learn with the aim of contributing new knowledge (including the development of science, technology and productivity)—which directly develops productivity and contributes to the development of the economy. This directly develops productivity and serves the common people, fully safeguarding the second prerequisite of democracy, which means that banselistic students can protect equality and democracy more efficiently than exam-oriented students. Banselistic students, meanwhile, are free to choose the content of their studies in accordance with their own circumstances: for example, those banselistic students who study the art of poetry can choose not to take mathematics, and this does not have a significant direct negative impact on the outcome of the distribution of resources in society, but exam-oriented students do not have the flexibility to choose the content of their studies according to their own circumstances: almost all of them still need to learn this subject regardless whether this is suitable for them or not. Given the fact that the society and the market look primarily at areas of strength rather than areas of weakness in talents (e.g., Li Ka-shing's strength is in business skill. His strength is so advanced that he is on the Forbes list of billionaires rather than being poor by not being high-skilled in academic fileds like natural sciences, etc.), the banselistic student will therefore become more superior than banselistic students as the strength of the banselistic student is generally better than that of the exam-oriented student. In addition, the fact that banselistic students directly apply their knowledge to the field of innovation and practical application directly empowers banselistic students to outperform their test-taking counterparts, and the fact that banselistic students are more spiritually fulfilled and physically and mentally healthy than most test-taking students also helps banselistic students outperform exam-oriented students.

However, in the early 21st century, the technology of AI had not been popularized and applied on a large scale, leading to a large quantity of demand for the physical human labor and repetitive human labor, which is why most members in the student class belonged to the examination-oriented students in the early 21st century.

Finally, the concept of the student will be explained in this paragraph. Students are the general name of different kinds of students, such as correspondence students and banselistic students. In this chapter, students are divided into the corresponding students and the banselistic students in the initial stage, when the technology of AI had just been applied on a large scale. While in the middle stage and the late stage, due to the large-scale rise of banselistic students and the mobility of classes, the authority of diplomas has been weakened and even lost. The corresponding students disappear and no longer exist. The conceptual term 'banselistic students' will be abolished and renamed as 'the student' or 'students'.

Notes:

[1] Working class: A term commonly used in mainstream Western class theory in the early 21st century. This social class is made up mainly of manual workers, the members of which are all low-income earners and the vast majority of whom have no higher education. As the 'proletariat' is defined only by the possession of the means of production - as long as the citizen does not possess the means of production, he or she is a proletarian, whereas the mainstream Western class theory of the 21st century uses the relations of production, disposable income and educational background to jointly define the class. The term 'working class' is therefore used in this book.

[2] Cross talents: one of the professional terms in the academic field of education, which refers to the talents who are highly developed and reach the cutting-edge level in a field, owning innovative or creative

[3] T-shaped talent: The T-shaped talent refers to the talents who has studied intensively in his or her field of expertise and has acquired a wealth of knowledge in different fields and disciplines.

Chapter Two:

The Classification of The Social Class and The Social Strata

The social class refers to the people of a relatively large social group consisting of two or more different social stratas that have the same production relations and similar income levels among all individuals, while social strata is a relatively small social group that contains one occupation or more than one different occupation.

The criteria for classifying are different in different historical periods. In this article, the class and the strata are mainly classified according to production relations, income level, military power, and the population size.

To begin with, we explain who the working class and the working strata are. The working class refers to adults who are not employed, or those whose disposable income is below the average level of the economy, and their educational background is not relatively developed compared with that of the average level of the entire society. For instance, the unemployed, beggars, sweepers, waiters, receptionists, low- and middle-income chefs, receptionists, cashiers, low-income repairmen, handymen, low-income factory workers, low-income farmers, low-income company employees, etc., are classified as the members in the working class.

Under the condition of large-scale popularization of automation technology, the working class will be replaced by the AI, and the member of the working class will become the banselistic student, of which most members will become those who are in the social classes that have higher incomes. Because in this case, all manual workers and mechanized mental workers have been replaced by AI, and almost all members of the working class are manual workers or mechanized mental workers, this will unprecedentedly weaken the group size of the working class and make it insufficient to become A class, with all non-employed people being transformed into banselistic students, the working strata, accordingly, will also disappear.

In addition, we explain what the Student Class is. The different categories of learners, including the Examination-oriented Student, the Banselistic Student are classified as members in the Student Class.

Then we come to the middle class and the upper middle class. Middle-income groups, such as middle-income white-collar workers and auto mechanics in developed countries are classified as the members in the middle-class, whose living standards are not lower than the social average. The upper-middle class refers to the social group whose income level is above the social average level but has not yet reached the cutting-edge level. The vast majority of its members obtain material wealth through salary.

In this book, the members of the middle class are further divided into four different social groups based on the position of production relations. They are manual workers, mechanized mental workers, and the individual who works with a certain degree of flexibility or innovative or creative ability, and the entertainment industry workers.

Mechanized mental workers refer to those who do not have flexibility, innovation, or creativity, and only use mechanized thinking, the thinking stereotypes, during the process of production.

For the part of the middle class wherein all the members are manual labors, including auto mechanics in developed countries in the early 21st century, they will be replaced by AI when automation is popularized on a large scale, and they will become the Banselistic Student, whereby they can become the members in other social classes who have more incomes.

What is similar to manual workers is that the mechanized mental workers will also be replaced by AI and therefore become the Banselistic Student, and on this basis, class mobility will occur.

For middle-class people who have received no less than the social average level of education and have a certain degree of flexibility or innovation or creativity, they will be transformed into the Elite class when automation technology is widely popularized. Because when automation technology was widely popularized, the market 's demand for those middle-class people who had not yet been replaced by artificial intelligence and who were not engaged in the entertainment industry would rise sharply. The income of the individuals who used to be the members in the middle class, in this case, will rise into the level that is almost the same as that of the upper-middle class, when the middle class and the upper middle class are both abolished and combine into the Elite

Class. For instance, the educator who works in the middle school. When automation technology is popularized on a large scale, all mechanized labor is replaced by artificial intelligence. At this time, the educated under the vocational education system no longer exist, and they all need to receive higher education to ensure that they are not replaced by AI. Early in the 21st century, in most countries, the vast majority of educated persons were learners of the vocational education. In this situation, the demand for educators in primary and secondary schools (except vocational education) and higher education will increase substantially. In this case, the gap between the income of educators and the upper-middle class has been greatly reduced, which can be illustrated when comparing this example with the financial analysts. Specifically, since at the early stage when automation technology was popularized on a large scale, the growth of market demand was mainly concentrated in the real economy rather than the virtual economy, so that the market demand for the virtual economy and its corresponding talents would not rise sharply. Correspondingly, the income level of most practitioners in the virtual economy industry, including financial analysts, will not rise sharply. In this situation, the level of income and the position in the production relationship of the middle-class people who are not engaged in the entertainment industry, including teachers, who have not been replaced by AI, are becoming almost the same or even totally the same as that of the upper-middle class. Therefore, the middle class and the upper middle class will merge into the same social class whose name is the 'Elite class'. Another example is the manager. When AI is popularized on a large scale, all the mechanized labor is replaced by AI. In this case, companies need to exercise their best to improve product quality to enhance their core competitive advantages. In this way, the complexity of production activities will be increased, and the demand for administrative talents in the labor market will rise sharply, which will reduce the gap between the income of the manager and the upper-middle class members such as financial analysts. As a result, the difference between the middle class and the upper middle class disappears. In this case, they will all be combined into the Elite class.

For the part of the middle class who are engaged in the entertainment industry, they will be transformed into the entertainment industry worker strata, which is also abbreviated as the EIW Strata. The middle class will be eliminated when artificial intelligence technology is popularized on a large scale, because the main body of the middle class is replaced by AI, and a considerable part of the middle-class members are transformed into elites. This makes the population size of the middle class not to be large enough to be a class. Correspondingly, the entertainment industry workers (EIW) are also separated from the above-mentioned middle-class people due to the production relationship and income level, and they will become the EIW.

This book does not classify classes according to their educational background. This is because under the condition of large-scale class movement of the Banselistic Student, the Examination-oriented students are abolished, and the authority of the diploma is unprecedentedly weakened and lost, which directly destroys the role of the diploma. And all the employed are transformed from the Banselistic student. Therefore, the difference in the educational background of all employed persons is directly lost at this time.

So, on to the Elite Class, which includes those who are managers in the employment relationship, where those work in the state agencies are exclusive. Also, the employed who have a certain level of ability to innovate or create and apply a certain degree of innovation or creativity during the process of production wherein a certain degree of flexibility or high flexibility can be found and does not engage in the entertainment industry and do not directly innovate or create material civilization or spiritual civilization, are also classified as members in the Elite Class.

EIW Strata contains all employees who belong to the entertainment industry worker (EIW) Strata. Its internal members only carry out mechanized production or production with a certain degree of flexibility or high flexibility in the entertainment industry and have a chance to invest a certain amount of innovation or creativity into production activities, and do not directly affect material civilization or spiritual civilization. Innovation or creation.

Also, what will be illustrated is the Capitalist Class. The Capitalist Class refers to the social group whose members have capital and means of production, these members also acquire material wealth through investment and capital acquisition instead of receiving salaries. In the employment relationship, the Capitalists are the employer rather than the employee. Accordingly, entrepreneurs, corporate investors (holding no less than 30% of the shares in the enterprise), bank owners, factory owners, farmers, etc., are classified as the capitalists.

For most Western developed countries that do not implement a constitutional monarchy, the alias is the upper class. In this article, for countries that implement constitutional monarchy, the upper class or the Aristocrat class is further divided into the Capitalist Class and the Bureaucratic Class due to the differences in the positions of their internal members in the relations of production.

To explain the Bureaucratic Class: The bureaucratic class refers to all people responsible for maintaining or directly promoting the functioning of state organs and state institutions. Civil servants, members of parliament, representatives of local people's congresses, speaker of parliament, deputies to national people's congress, lawyers, permanent judges, non-permanent judges, supreme judge, president, prime minister, chairperson, diplomat, minister of foreign affairs, police, soldiers, military commanders, military intelligence personnel, members of the royal family and other people who work in state agencies, or legal practitioners are all classified as bureaucratic class.

Lawyers, one of the specific types of legal practitioners, are those who protect the legal rights and legal rights of the prosecutor or the defendant and are members in an important social group that is responsible for embodying the authority of the law, safeguarding or directly promoting justice in state agencies like the local courts or the Supreme Court. In other words, what is the same as other types of members in the bureaucratic class is that lawyers are also responsible for maintaining or directly promoting the operation of state agencies, so they are also classified as members in the Bureaucratic Class.

What will be analyzed in the following paragraphs is the Banselistic Class, whose definition is the social class that directly innovates or creates in the material progress and the cultural and ideological progress. This social class includes inventors, scientists, researchers, high-end technicians, writers, poets, artists, musicians, designers, enlightenment thinkers, and so forth.

Whether the producer has directly innovated or created material civilization or spiritual civilization depends on whether the producer has directly contributed new knowledge to the academic world. This is because direct innovation or creation of material civilization or spiritual civilization will inevitably contribute new knowledge directly to the academic community. Since the elite class and other social classes mainly use knowledge based on changes in actual conditions, rather than directly contributing new knowledge to the academic world, the members of these social classes do not belong to the Banselistic class.

The emergence of this class is historically inevitable. To begin with, the large-scale popularization of artificial intelligence technology is historically inevitable (See Volume One, Part Two, Chapter One: The Automation, for details), which will directly replace all mechanized employment. Under such circumstances, companies will not be able to gain a competitive advantage by increasing the quantity of products, and economies cannot increase the quantity of products to enhance their international competitive advantages. Instead, they can only strengthen their competitive advantages by improving the quality of their products. Therefore, the direct innovation or creation of material civilization and spiritual civilization becomes their most important means to strengthen their competitive advantages, which will greatly increase the demand for talents, or innovative or creative products provided by the banselistic class. Specifically, enterprises and the entire society will have enormously increased demand for the labors or products provided by the Banselistic Class. This will further improve the social welfare system to ensure that all those who are replaced by AI and are in a non-employed state are transformed into the Student Class. And because of the extremely large increase in the demand for talents, innovations or creative products provided by the Banselistic Class, the income level of the Banselistic Class will directly increase extremely sharply. Also, almost only freelancers are included in the Banselistic Class, which means the work done by the class of Banselism does not have mandatory requirements for a diploma, and most of the class of the Banselistic students will transform into the Banselistic Class.

Apart from that, what is different from the middle class and the working class is that the Banselistic Class is not exploited by the Capitalist Class. To begin with, the capitalist needs to stop the exploitation of the Banselistic Class to attract the talents coming from the Banselistic Class to carry out productive activities for them, or to buy the innovative or creative products of the Banselistic Class such as new technologies and other achievements that directly innovate or create material or spiritual civilization through extremely high price levels. Then, the gap between the unit individual strength of the inner members of the Banselistic Class and that of the members of the Capitalist Class is small. Specifically, The Banselistic Class monopolizes the core technology and various other innovative or creative achievements, which enables its members to have the ability to multi-dimensionally restrain the Capitalists. This means that the individual strength of the members of the Banselistic Class is not weaker than that of the Capitalist Class. Also, the group size of the Banselistic Class presents an overwhelming advantage compared with that of the Capitalist Class. In this case, the power of the Banselistic Class has an overwhelming advantage over the power of the Capitalist Class, which means the Capitalist Class does not have the power to exploit the Banselistic Class. All these have become the reasons why the Banselistic Class is not exploited by the capitalist class.

In the middle class, the power of each member is far weaker than that in the Capitalist Class. This is because the middle class does not master the core technology, it can be replaced by artificial intelligence, which is replaceable. Also, the population of the middle class does not occupy a significant advantage compared with that in the Capitalist Class. In this circumstance, the power of the middle class is weaker than that of the Capitalist Class, which enables the capitalist to exploit the middle class.

Apart from that, what will be criticized in the following paragraphs are the alternative methods whereby the Student Class becomes the individual who has more income.

The first solution to be rejected in this book is becoming capitalists. For those students who are willing to become capitalists, they need to have a diploma or sufficient funds and advanced management experience. However, first, the original diplomas of the students of Banselism cannot be changed, updated, or improved; secondly, the original funding conditions of most of the Banselistic Student cannot be greatly improved, which means most of them have not enough funds to become capitalists. Thirdly, although the administrative experience of Banselistic students can be improved, all mechanized laborers, including working-class people and some middle-class people, account for the vast majority of the total population. Therefore, The Banselistic students transformed from them will make the student class the class with the largest proportion of the total population of all classes. If all its members have the will to transform into capitalists, they need sufficient funds to transform themselves. Nonetheless, the enormously demanding requirements for funds will determine that these students cannot obtain enough money to become capitalists. Therefore, only a very small number of Banselistic students can transform into the Capitalist Class.

The second method that will be criticized in this article is letting all those who are not working to obtain education via the educational systems that were frequently applied in the early 21st century. Banselistic students are transformed from the working class and the middle class replaced by AI. The group that needs to receive education is enormously large: the working class is the class that accounts for the largest proportion of the total population of all classes, accompanied with the number of the middle-class people replaced by intelligence, which means the population of those who are not officially employed have an overwhelming advantage over that of the other classes. In this case, if the Banselistic students are trained under the educational system of the early 21st century to obtain job opportunities, the national government needs to establish an enormously large group of educators within the country in a short period of time. That is, the authority must ensure the educators can become an independent social class with an enormously large population if the government wishes the Banselistic Student to gain a diploma. However, the serious shortage of the number of educators will make it impossible for the Banselistic students to undergo class mobility by accepting the education system of the early 21st century because it is impossible for the authority to establish such an extremely large group of educators.

The third solution that will be refuted in this book is exercising the absolute equalitarianism when the automation had just been popularized. To begin with, this will smash the production enthusiasm of all citizens, so that the development of science and technology, economy, and people's livelihood will be brought to a halt, and the administrative efficiency will be greatly reduced due to the smashing of production enthusiasm, which will reduce the material and spiritual wealth of people. The stagnant development greatly hinders the improvement and improvement of their living standards and quality. In addition, the limited resources of the earth will require the continuous expansion of human civilization and the development of the resources of the rest of the planet to meet their wants and needs. Without strong technology and relatively advanced management, human civilization will lack the ability to develop the resources of the rest of the planet, leading to resource exhaustion and so on.

The fourth solution that will be rejected in this book is rioting, which is inefficient to a large extent. First, from the perspective of natural science and technology and market laws, the large-scale popularization of automation is still historically inevitable (see Volume One, Volume Two, Chapter One: The Automation, for details), and automation will still be promoted after the successful violent revolution. Working-class people will continue to transform into Banselistic students. If they continue to choose riots, then the country and society will fall into an infinite cycle of automation-violent revolution-automation, and what is certain is: the material wealth and spirit wealth are declining sharply, the living standards and quality of the public are also declining and declining sharply, and the country's economic development and overall national strength are also declining firmly. Then, individuals cannot start violent revolution to curb the development of automation technology so that the large-scale popularization of automation technology is not conducive to the improvement of the living standards of mechanized laborers. Practitioners of mechanized labor can have no less than their material wealth when engaged in mechanized labor, as well as continuously developing spiritual wealth: because the unprecedented shortening of working hours and the relative abundance of material wealth allow them to pass through, for example, travel, consumption in the place of residence, or other types of recreational activities to improve their living standards and quality, and allow them to flexibly carry out class mobility according to their own specific conditions to directly improve their quality of life. However, using violent revolutions to hinder the development of automation technology is not conducive to drastically shortening their working hours, which cannot increase material and spiritual wealth, and cannot promote them to become individuals who are in the social classes that have more material and spiritual wealth.

In order to further elaborate the relationship between the banselistic student (the student class), the bureaucratic class, the capitalist class and the banselistic class, the following fictitious example will be used:

Suppose that Silvano Dacia is a banselistic student. He has spent over ten years developing a new technology for the production of tea trees and tea leaves through the full use of bio-engineering techniques. He submitted the technology to several different public auditors for review. A few years later, one of the public auditors, located in the southern suburbs, approved the new invention and granted Silvano Dacia a patent for his invention. Unless this inventor died, the patent would be protected by law in perpetuity. At this point, he began trying to find cafes, restaurants and hotels that needed this new technology through an e-commerce platform developed by the government. Coincidentally, Eugenius, a shopkeeper running a café in Paris, was looking for anything interesting to maximize his profits. At this point, Silvano Dacia sold the technology to Eugenius. As a result, Eugenius' café became the only café that was able to produce and sell this new type of tea drink in the entire world. Eugenius' profits were thus boosted by the tea's unique aroma, its medicinal properties (e.g., immunity, acne and cough), its low side effects and its splendid color. His business went from being an obscure catering company to an overnight success. As the inventor of this technology, Silvano Dacia also rose to prominence and made a fortune.

At the same time, the number of cafés, restaurants and

hotels is huge and widely distributed around the world. Thus, Silvano Dacia sold his technology to cafés, restaurants and hotels in many more different countries, which led to an inexhaustible increase in his material wealth.

Thus, in this case, Silvano Dacia, initially a banselistic student, was granted a patent for a legally protected invention after his novel technology in the natural sciences had passed the scrutiny of the officials of the public examination body (i.e., members of the bureaucratic class). At this point Silvano Dacia became a member of the banselistic class. And he sold it to Eugenius through an e-commerce platform developed by the government. According to this chapter, Eugenius owns the café, is a business owner and is the hiring party in the employment relationship, so he is a bourgeois. In other words, here, Silvano Dacia who has now become a member in the banselistic class sells his new technology to the bourgeois Eugenius. This also allowed this capitalist to increase his profits extremely significantly. In turn, Silvano Dacia, a member in the banselistic class, gained even more wealth by selling his technology to even more members in the capitalist class. This improved and enhanced the economic conditions for him, a member coming from banselistic class in an unprecedented and effective way.

Finally, to explain the Multiple Class and the Multiplists. The Multiple class refers to a class with two or more different production relations, while the Multiplists refers to an individual with multiple different types of production relations at the same time, such as lecturers, professors other than law, professors of law, and entrepreneurs who are also innovators of certain technologies, the singer who also writes songs, and so forth. Take law professors as an example: when they act as defenders for the prosecution or the defendant, they are maintaining or directly promoting the operation of state agencies, and they belong to the bureaucratic class; when they conduct academic research or publish papers, they are trying to improve material civilization or spiritual civilization carries out innovative or creative activities and belongs to the class of Banselism; and when they carry out teaching activities, they need to manage students and belong to the elite class. Therefore, law professors belong to the bureaucratic class, the banselistic class, and the elite class.

Chapter Three:

The Basic Content of The Banselistic Economy

Under the Ideological and Political System of Banselism, the high-tech industry, military industries, the cultural creative industry and high-end service industries, commerce and trade, cultural and creative industries, and financial industries will become the economic pillars. With the convergence of the Keynesian economy, a new type of state intervention in the Banselistic economy will be proposed. This chapter will elaborate on the basic content of the Banselistic economy.

To begin with, high-tech industry: After the large-scale popularization of the AI technology, the student including the Banselistic student will become a social class and thereby conduct the strategy of class mobility. When AI replaces all workers that do not apply creativity, enterprises, in this case, can only strength the competitiveness of products by improving the quality of products rather than increase the number of products. In this situation, the enormous demand for improving the quality of products will force the firm to develop technology. Nonetheless, the technical personnel that the Banselistic class can provide to enterprises are relatively limited. According to market dynamic, the relative shortage of the supply of technologically innovative or creative talents and the extremely large demand for technical talents coming from enterprises will greatly increase the income of technical talents and greatly improve their welfare benefits, which will drive a large number of Banselistic students to develop themselves into innovative or creative technical talents. Consequently, the high-tech industry will become one of the pillar industries under the Ideological and Political system of Banselism.

Regarding capitalist countries, this social class has an enormously great demand for the talents and innovative or creative technics provided by the Banselistic class, especially the huge demand for innovative or creative technical talents, and the number of innovative or creative technical talents that the Banselistic class can provide is relatively few, which will lead to the extremely large increase in the income level of innovative or creative technical talents and the great improvement in welfare of these talents, which will stimulate most of the Banselistic students to develop themselves into technical talents, thereby providing a large amount of innovation or creativity technical talents or technics to the capitalist class. Consequently, the high-tech industry will become one of the pillar industries in these capitalist countries.

Also, as far as socialist countries are concerned, to avoid being subjugated by hostile countries that are attempting to conduct the Ideological and Political system of Banselism ahead of the socialist country, these socialist countries will have to conduct the Ideological and Political system of Banselism. In addition, in socialist countries, there is an urgent need for the development of the state-owned economy, and it will guide most of the Banselistic students to become the Banselistic class, and thereby send innovative or creative technical talents to their state-owned enterprises to develop the state-owned economy (see the Volume Two, Part Four, Chapter One: Regarding the state-owned economy, for details). In this situation, the state-owned high-tech industry will become one of the pillar industries of the socialist country.

Apart from that, in terms of the high-welfare state (see Volume Two, Part Two, Chapter One: Supply-side reforms, for details), what is the same as that of the socialist countries is that in response to the implementation of Banselism in the West (See Volume Two, Part One, Chapter One: The reclassification of Western countries, for details.), they will also implement the Ideological and Political system of Banselism to overcome the threat coming from the countries that are promoting the implementation of the Ideological and Political system of Banselism. In addition, a high-welfare country needs to develop its own economy to maintain the adequacy of its original capital accumulation, to maintain and improve the living standards of the individual. Therefore, when automation technology is popularized on a large scale, the high-welfare state will also implement a series of measures to assist the class mobility of the Banselistic student. According to the laws of the market, most Banselistic students will be transformed into the Banselistic class, which will provide a large number of innovative or creative technical professionals for high-tech enterprises, so that the high-tech industry will become one of the pillar industries in the high-welfare state.

The second pillar industry that will be explained in this book is the military industry. After the formation of the

Banselistic class, in order to maintain its own national security, the Banselistic country will create a large number of military technology research and development opportunities for the Banselistic class by setting more military enterprises or establishing military technology research and development institutions. The relatively large number of technical personnel within the Banselistic class will, in turn, promote the development of military technology to a great extent and enable the military industry to become one of the pillar industries. Also, the limitation of the resources including land and raw materials on earth means that it is indispensable to not only gain resources from earth but also develop the intraterrestrial planets, extraterrestrial planets, and extraterrestrial galaxies in order to gain more resources. However, the increase in extraterrestrial expansion also means that the military power in this country needs to be further improved to deal with the threat posed by extraterrestrial civilization to itself. Such demand will further increase the demand for talents in the military industry, thereby increasing the level of income of military technology R&D personnel and improving their welfare benefits, thereby attracting more innovative or creative technology talents to work in relevant military industry enterprises or military technology research and development institutions, which will further consolidate the status of the economic pillar of military technology.

The third industry that will become one of the pillar industries is the high-end service industry. As the Banselistic Class is a social class that directly innovates or creates in the material civilization or spiritual civilization, there are a large number of members in the Banselistic Class who engage in work related to the creative industry, which includes clothing design, the exterior architectural decoration design, the interior decoration design, the architectural engineering design, etc.

For example, the real estate industry, hotels and various offline stores, because the large-scale popularization of AI technology has replaced all workers without creativity, these sectors, in this case, need to promote the continuous improvement of the quality of interior and exterior decoration design in order to expand the market for them, thereby strengthening their competitiveness. This will increase the demand for the products or talents provided by the Banselistic Class, which increases the salary of the talents and the price of the products provided by this social class, stimulating the Banselistic class to provide relevant talents or creative products on a large scale. This therefore makes these sectors, which are a part of the creative industry, to become part of the pillar industries. Meanwhile, because the creative industries directly serve the service industry, for example, the highly developed interior and exterior decoration design will expand the source of customers for hotels, catering offline stores, etc. This will increase the strength of the service industry unprecedentedly, so that the service industry will become one of the pillar industries. Another example is the fashion design industry. The formation of the Banselistic class will produce a large number of fashion designers. Because AI will replace all workers that do not apply creativity, the Banselistic class, in this situation, will make their own products more innovative and creative, which will greatly promote the development of the apparel design industry, enabling it to become one of the pillar industries.

The fourth industry that will become one of the pillar industries is the commerce and trade industry. The Banselistic class is the social class that directly innovates or creates in the material civilization or mental civilization. In most cases, both the material products including the technical innovation and the mental products including the innovative articles or clothing design provided by this social class are highly innovative and creative, which means they are highly competitive as each of these products are differentiated from all other products all around the world. This is highly beneficial for the development of commerce and trade. In addition, the differentiation of this product means that unless the producer is willing to sell the intellectual property, this product cannot be produced by other producers, which also boosts more trade and commerce.

Apart from that, the large-scale use of AI can replace a wide range of brokers to reduce the links of doing commercial activities or trade activities, thereby greatly reducing the cost of commercial and trade activities, which in turn will enable commercial activities and trade activities to be greatly increased. For instance, the forwarding agent. When AI technology is applied on a large scale, the transportation of goods will be operated by artificial intelligence instead of manual forwarding agents. This will reduce transportation costs for producers and consumers, thereby enabling the commerce and trade to become one of the pillar industries. Another example is the sales agent. AI will inevitably replace human labor to sell products in offline stores. Meanwhile, the management of physical stores can also be finished by the remote control of the firm. This prevents enterprises from selling products through sales agents, which reduces the costs for sales. The reduction in cost will further reduce commodity prices, thereby further expanding the market for the producers, which will enable commerce and trade to become the pillar industry.

The fifth industry that will become one of the pillar industries is the Cultural and Creative Industry (CACI). The existence of the Banselistic class will enable the CACI to become one of the pillar industries. First, albeit with the lack of talents in the CACI in the early 21st century, the existence of the Banselistic class will provide a volume of talents who work in the CACI, all of whom are high-skilled and directly serve the CACI, such as the writers, poetry creators, composers, artists, sculptors, and so forth. Secondly, AI replaces all laborers without creativity, including actors, with programming technology and electronics becoming more developed, the costs of running the CACI will be sharply reduced in the short term, thereby greatly promoting the development of the CACI. Thirdly, the replacement of mechanized labor will make the investment in the CACI more cost-effective, thereby attracting investment extremely effectively, which greatly increases the funds for the development of the CACI. This will establish the economic foundation for it to become a pillar industry.

For instance, the film industry. In the early 21st century, the limitation of consciousness and the backwardness of technology determined the high production cost of film and television works and curbed the income of enterprises that rely on the film and television industry as the backbone. The improvement of technology will greatly reduce the production cost of film works in the short term, because a large number of cultural and creative industry workers, including entertainment industry workers, will be replaced, such as film actors. Because at this time, when shooting a movie, only an intelligent computer and programming technicians (high-end technicians), composers, and screenwriters (writers) can complete the shooting of a movie. In the short term, the reduction in the production cost of film works will also increase the quantity of films in the short run. In addition, the innovation and creativity of the Banselistic class will enable them to produce high-quality spiritual products including high quality films. The development of the film industry will be greatly promoted in the short term, thereby driving the cultural and creative industry to become one of the pillar industries. Also, the completion of class mobility will greatly increase the income of most individuals, which will expand the market for films, effectively increasing the income of film producers. Apart from that, due to the rapid increase in the number of films, the film market will be fragmented for different films.

This phenomenon shows that the writers are indispensable for developing the film industry, which is one of the most significant reasons why the income of writers will greatly increase under the Ideological and Political system of Banselism.

In the long run, in order to gain a competitive advantage in the quality of films, companies have to increase their financial investment in film and television works, which includes hiring more professional talents in programming, music, and film screenwriting in order to produce a movie, so that the cost of filming will become the same as that in the early 21st century. But at this time, the income of most individuals is generally high, which means the market for films is widespread, most of the market, in this case, will be dominated by high quality films, which will greatly increase the production of high-quality film and increase the income of these producers.

The finance industry is going to be one of the pillar industries as well. After the class mobility of the Banselistic students, the Banselistic class and the Elite class are formed, which will provide a relatively large scale of innovative and creative talents and professional management talents for the development of the financial industry, which will promote the development of the financial industry to a large extent, enabling this industry to become one of the pillar industries. Meanwhile, the completion of the class mobility of Banselistic students will greatly expand the market of the financial industry because more individuals will be more likely to be involved in the financial field. In addition, the extremely increased development of the real economy will play a decisive role in supporting and promoting the development of the virtual economy, including the financial industry, and this will directly promote the financial industry to become one of the economic pillars.

For instance, the United States. After the formation of the Banselistic class, most of the innovative and creative technical personnel within the Banselistic class will work in places like the Silicon Valley wherein the high-tech enterprises are includeed. Therefore, there are extremely sufficient innovative and creative technical talents in Silicon Valley to enable Silicon Valley to become extremely developed. Also, the development of Hollywood will become extremely developed due to the sharp drop in the production costs of film and television works and the abundance of talent. Then, in this situation, when Wall Street invests in Silicon Valley and Hollywood, the development of its financial industry will rapidly become extremely developed. Consequently, the finance industry will become one of the pillar industries.

Finally, to explain the intersection of the Banselistic economy and the Keynesian economy, wherein the authority carries out some new way of government intervention, including foreign intervention to develop the economy. For instance, the country that is the first to conduct the Ideological and Political System of Banselism can develop its military strength through strong scientific and technological strength and strong intellectual support, after which these countries use military power to force other countries that have not implemented the Ideological and Political system of Banselism to establish corresponding foundations and provide material rewards to the Banselistic class in the Banselistic country. Thus, economic plundering is carried out based on safeguarding the interests of the Banselistic class and not violating humanitarian and human rights, because this method will not cause casualties and does not violate the human rights of the people of the plundered country.

To begin with, this is conducive to effectively reducing the economic burden of enterprises-because the provision of funds for the Banselistic class of other countries can reduce the provision of funds for the Banselistic class of their country; Secondly, after finishing conducting the method mentioned above, the government can set an appropriate amount of intellectual property tax that can be used to increase government revenue.

Chapter Four:

The Banselistic Social Structure

In this article, the 'social structure' merely refers to the relationship between social classes or the relationship between different social stratas. This term was also widely used and applied in academia early in the 21st century.

In the Banselistic society, there are the following five main social classes and one social strata, which are the Banselistic class, the elite class, the capitalist class, the bureaucratic class, the student class and the EIW strata respectively.

To begin with, the social structure of the west (see Volume Two, Part One: for the west, for details), wherein the Banselistic class and the capitalist class will both lie at the top of the entire society. Due to the extreme demand of the capitalist class for the talents or technics provided by the Banselistic class, the substantial increase in the income level of the members of the Banselistic class is the decisive factor that promotes the class migration of the Banselistic students to the

Banselistic class, which means the Banselistic class will not oppress the capitalist class because the capitalist class has the ability to cut off the capital chain. Nonetheless, the Banselistic class monopolizes various core technologies and other types of innovations or creative outcomes, which means this social class has the decisive and irreversible multi-dimensional restraint ability at the core technology level, so the bourgeoisie will not exploit and oppress the Banselistic class. Consequently, the Banselistic class and the capitalist class will become the ruling class together, at the top of the social structure.

Apart from that, the elite class will rank second place in the social structure. The elite class will only assist the capitalist class and the Banselistic class through management or other methods to indirectly promote the innovative or creative achievements of material civilization or spiritual civilization, which enables them to have certain types of capital such as technological capital, but these capitals cannot compete with that of the bourgeoisie or the Banselistic class. Therefore, this class can only constitute a certain restraint and restraining effect on the capitalist class or the Banselistic class, lying in the lower level of the capitalist class and the Banselistic class.

Also, the bureaucratic class will be in the third layer of the social structure. Although a certain number of members in this social class including the military personnel within the bureaucratic class will have a certain restraint effect on the capitalist class and the Banselistic class, and the power of the bureaucratic class is close to that of the elite class because their activities will also involve management activities, but this social class will only below the elite class. Firstly, there are a considerable number of members of the bureaucratic class who belong to the composite class. For example, the military technicians in the Ministry of National Defense belong to both the Banselistic class and the bureaucratic class, which will directly distract the bureaucratic class when the bureaucratic class goes against the rest of the classes. Also, in the West, the capitalist class and the Banselistic class have a decisive control over the bureaucracy. For example, in the field of national defense, the supply of weapons and equipment is directly controlled by private military-industrial enterprises, which gives the capitalist class and the Banselistic class the ability to paralyze the military power of the bureaucratic class.

In addition, in the social structure, the student class will be below the bureaucratic class. When the class mobility has not yet been completed, the student class only owns means of production, such as intelligent communication equipment and experimental equipment. They also possess a certain material production capability. However, the student class does not have an independent source of funds, and its funds only come from the classes provided by the superstructure. Also, the student class, to some extent, is lack of innovation or creativity, which means that their power is weaker than artificial intelligence, so the power of this social class is lower than that of the bureaucratic class.

The student class, nonetheless, is above the EIW Strata in the social structure. To begin with, the Banselistic student consists of the vast majority of the working class and a considerable part of the middle-class member who is replaced by AI, which means the population of this social class is larger than the EIW Strata. Also, there is no specific and compulsory requirement of working hours or learning hours for the Banselistic student, which means the schedule of this social class is highly flexible, enabling it to strengthen the power by generating strategies flexibly on a large scale. On the contrary, for the EIW Strata, most of time is spent in working with only a low creativity or innovation, which obstructs this social class from developing itself by making strategy flexibly, weakening the ability of the vast majority of this social class, thereby reducing the gap between the individual power of members in the student class and that of the EIW strata. In addition, due to the market mechanism, the income of technological innovation talents in the Banselistic class has risen sharply and surpassed the incomes of practitioners in the rest of the industries, which means the vast majority of the student class will develop the technological innovation and creativity. Because this involves the activity in both the material civilization and the mental civilization, the student class will have a certain material production capacity and a certain theoretical research ability. The length of the work time of EIW determines that their material production capacity is generally weaker than that of the student class, which enables the individual strength of the Banselistic students to become greater than those in the entertainment industry.

Meanwhile, the EIW strata is at the bottom of the social structure. However, the EIW strata still has a certain strength in the social structure. To begin with, the influence of the EIW strata in social media and the public opinion has a certain restraining effect on each class. When it confronts the rest of the classes, its appeal is conducive to attract supporters for itself, after which the EIW strata can promote the opposition between its supporters and other social classes by creating relevant public opinion. Also, the population of supporters of the EIW strata is relatively high. For instance, James had over 20 million fans on the Facebook in 2020. Apart from that, a number of the members in the EIW strata has a considerable income. The data released by the Forbes List in 2020 shows that Jordan's total assets were as high as 1.85 billion U.S. dollars, Kobe's total assets are 800 million U.S. dollars, and the retired basketball star O'Neill, known as the 'big shark', has total assets as high as 735 million U.S. dollars. These examples reflect the advantages and strengths of the EIW at the financial level.

Nonetheless, the EIW strata still cannot eliminate the Banselistic class, the capital class, the elite class, and the bureaucratic class through class warfare. To begin with, this social class cannot unite with the student class to go against other social classes because the power of them is weaker than AI before the class mobility is finished, which makes them lose the advantage in population. In addition, the authority of the EIW strata in the field of public opinion is weaker than that of the Banselistic class, the elite class, and the capitalist class, which is mainly because the professionalism, social status, and economic strength of the EIW strata is weaker than these social classes, making its supporter group smaller than the rest of the social classes. In addition, the income of the EIW class is determined by its market, but its market is derived from the rest of the classes, which makes the EIW economically firmly controlled by other classes.

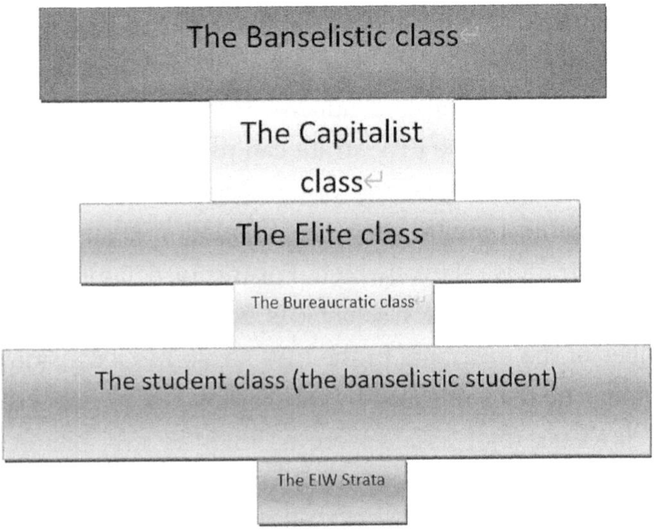

Overall, the social structure of the West will show a multi-T shape (as the diagram above shows). Since all social classes except the student class are generated from the student class, when automation is just being applied on a large scale, the aggregate population of the student class will inevitably be greater than the rest of the social classes, and most of the student class will be transformed into the Banselistic class. Accordingly, the Banselistic class will lie at the top of the social structure, with its population ranking in second place among all classes, which is only slightly less than the total number of the student class. The total number of the capitalists, which is also the center of power, is among all classes. Because each capitalist will correspond to a large number of employees from different classes, for this reason, only a low population can be found in the capitalist class who lie in the upper second tier of the social structure. In this chapter, the number of people corresponds to the length of the graph, which is why the combination of the Banselistic class and the bourgeoisie in the social structure will show a T-shape. Apart from that, among the Banselistic class, there is at least one administrator in each research group, and the capitalist class also has a great demand for the talents in the elite class including the financial analyst, the administrator, the high-skilled seller, which means the total population of the elite class ranks second to that of the Banselistic class. Consequently, the length of the third layer in the upper social structure will be much longer than that of the second layer, which is the capitalist class. The bureaucratic class can review the results of a large number of different research teams consisting of Banselistic-class members and elite-class members, which means the population of the bureaucratic class is relatively low. Also, because all job opportunities that do not require creativity or innovation are replaced by AI, the group size of the bureaucratic class becomes largely limited. Hence, its population will be much smaller than that of the elite class. Consequently, the elite class and the bureaucratic class have a combined T-shaped structure in the social structure. In addition, since every other social class is evolved from the student class, the proportion of the student class in the total population will be greater than that of the rest of the classes. With its power greater than that of the EIW strata and the population larger than that of the EIW strata, the level of the student class will be higher than that of the EIW strata in the social structure and the length of the student class will be longer compared with that of the EIW Strata, forming the T-shaped structure when combining them together. Up to now, combining all the three T-shaped structure mentioned above in accordance with the level of general power of each social class or strata, the multiple-T shaped social structure occurs, which is the social structure of the West under the Ideological and Political system of Banselism.

The second social structure is the social structure of the High-welfare state (See Volume Two, Part Two, Chapter One: For High-welfare States). In the High-welfare state wherein reformist ideas are prevalent and put into practice, the power of the capitalist is effectively weakened. For instance, Sweden. The Swedish Social Democracy Party had been in charge highly frequently since it has been founded and this has weakened the power of the capitalist class efficiently. Consequently, the level of the capitalist class will be below the Banselistic class.

Also, since the capitalist class and the Banselistic class both have a high aggregate demand for the talents provided by the elite class, including the administrator of each scientific research team, the financial analyst, and so forth, the economic advantage of each single person in the elite class (including the administrator of each scientific research team, the financial analyst, and so forth), will be greater than that of the bureaucratic class as they need to hire the talents provided by the elite class rather than that in the bureaucratic class. Apart from that, each research group consisting of the Banselistic class will include at least one talent coming from the elite class, which means the group size of the elite class will be larger than the remaining social classes or stratas. Consequently, the elite class will be below the Banselistic class.

Apart from that, when the Ideological and Political system of Banselism is conducted in the welfare state, the need to supervise the innovative or creative outcomes including the technology, and so forth, will increase the population of the bureaucratic class. Meanwhile, the increased demand for the talents working in the government agency including the ones that supervise the innovative or creative outcomes, will also increase the salary and income of this social class. In addition, the organ of violence, including the National Defense, is directly run and operated by the bureaucratic class, which also strengthens the power of this class. Consequently, the level of this social class will be lower than that of the elite class, lying above the capitalist class in the social structure.

The capitalist class, nevertheless, still holds a relatively large amount of funds and a wide range of capital. The tax that the capitalist class pay in the welfare state is significant for the development of the social welfare system. For instance, Switzerland. According to the data provided by the Hongkong Richful Accountants Service, based on the different taxation in different cantons of Switzerland, the proportion of all taxes in the net profit of a company and its rate of return roughly show the following relationship: when the company's rate of return is 4%, its tax is about 15% to 25%; when its rate of return is

20%, its tax is about 20% to 30%. This shows that the capitalist class is indispensable for developing the welfare state by increasing the government revenue.

Consequently, the power of the capitalist class is greater than that of the elite class and the bureaucratic class as the financial strength of the capitalist class is greater than that of them, while the elite class does not occupy the innovative or creative outcomes including the core technology, and the financial strength of it is weaker than that of the capitalist class. Apart from that, in the economic arena, the bureaucratic class will also be considerably influenced by the capitalist class. Consequently, the level of the capitalist class will be below the elite class and the bureaucratic class, but the general power of this social class will not be far weaker compared to that of the bureaucratic class.

Also, the level of the EIW strata will be below that of the capitalist class and will be above that of the student class. The amount of the resources that the EIW strata can get is firmly controlled and restricted by other social classes as they are the whole market of this social class, which means that the power of this social strata is weaker than that of all other social classes except for that of the student class.

In the short run, under the influence of reformism[1], the willingness of the student class in a high-welfare country to finish the class mobility and produce material and mental products is weakened, and their individual strength is greatly weakened, which directly deteriorates the strength of the student. Consequently, the power of this social class will be weaker than that of the EIW Strata.

In the long run, influenced by factors such as class mobility of a considerable number of the student class and school education, the willingness of students in high welfare states to finish class mobility will generally increase (see Volume Two,

Part Two, Chapter One: Supply-side reforms, for details). Since most of the Banselistic student aim at moving to the Banselistic class, it will be indispensable for most of them to innovate or create in material or spiritual civilization, and there will be a considerable number of activities in it involving material activities such as scientific and technological research and development (R&D). Consequently, their ability to produce material products will be generally improved. Meanwhile, when the Banselistic student is innovating or creating in the material civilization, they will also inevitably directly innovate or create in the spiritual civilization. In this situation, for the Banselistic student, the production capacity for spiritual products will also be greatly improved. Therefore, in the long run, the student class will be above the EIW Strata.

In summary, under the Ideological and Political System of Banselism, the social structure of a welfare state will show an asymmetric hourglass in the short term. This is determined by the corresponding level and length of each class and strata—that is, the size of the group. The group size of the Banselistic class is larger than that of the elite class, and each research team will correspond to at least one elite class, which directly determines that its group size is larger than that of the bureaucratic class because a bureaucratic class can review the results of multiple different team pairs. Also, because the number of bureaucrats is greater than the number of capitalists, the length of the capitalist class is shorter than that of the bureaucratic class. However, since one bourgeoisie corresponds to multiple entertainment industry workers (EIWs), the number of EIWs will be more than that of the capitalists, and the length of the EIW strata will be longer than that of the capitalist class. Apart from that, each class and strata come from the student class, which means the length of the student class is longer than other social classes and strata. At this point, by arranging the corresponding levels of each class and strata, the social structure of a high-welfare country in the short term presents an asymmetric hourglass-because the area of the upper pattern of the hourglass pattern is larger than the pattern below it (as illustrated in the diagram below).

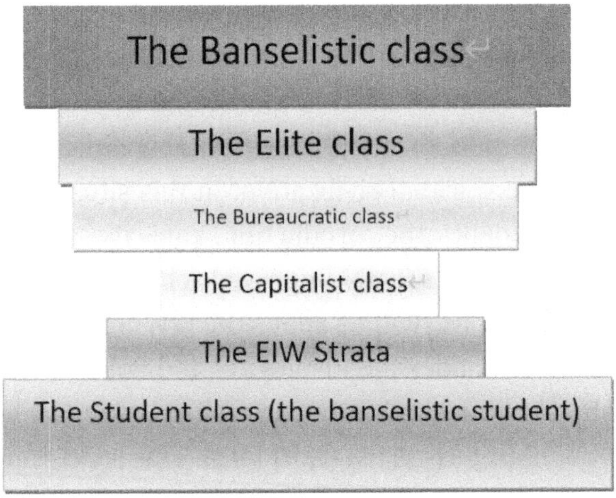

In the long run, its structure will show a double T-shape. Because in the upper part of the pattern, wherein the capitalist class and all other social classes above it can be found, the length of each level decreases gradually from the top of it to the level of the capitalist class. Also, in the lower part of the pattern, which is the same as the level below the capitalist class, the student class is located at the penultimate level, and the length is longer than that of the EIW Strata located at the penultimate level. So far, the double-T social structure has been formed (this is shown in the diagram on the next page).

Thirdly, is the social structure of the mainland of China under the Ideological and Political System of Banselism.

To promote the development of the state-owned sectors, the public-owned economy, the national economy, and the

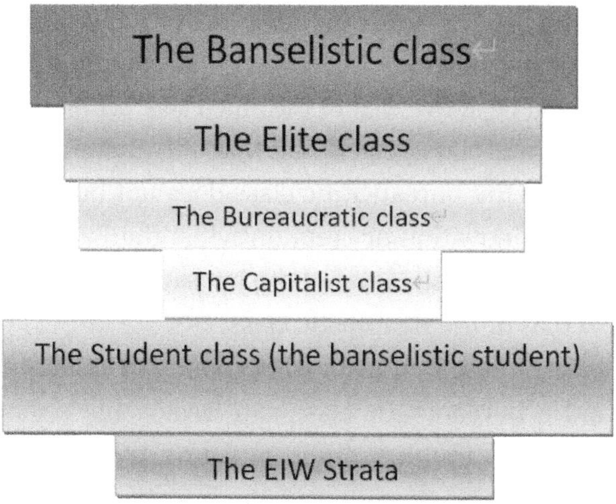

improvement of its overall national strength, the mainland of China will also conduct the Ideological and Political system of Banselism while retaining the political party system implemented in the early 21st century (See Volume Two, Part Four: For China, for details). Under such circumstances, the proletariat will be automatically transformed into the Banselistic student, after which they will directly evolve into the rest of the classes, especially the Banselistic class. Because the class strength of the Banselistic class is greater than that of all other classes, with its group size ranking in the second place, the level of this social class will be at the top of the social structure, with its length second only to the student class.

In addition, the bureaucratic class directly controls state-owned institutions such as the Chinese Academy of Sciences, the Chinese Academy of Engineering, state-owned enterprises, and central enterprises—for example, central enterprises are directly affiliated to the State Council of the People's Republic of China. This social class also controls state agencies, including violent agencies. Apart from that, the continuous expansion of the scale of state-owned enterprises and the need to supervise the innovation and creation will increase the demand for talents provided by the bureaucratic class, which will enhance the strength of the bureaucratic class. Consequently, the level of this class will be above that of the elite class, with the length of the bureaucratic class longer than that of the elite class.

However, the bureaucratic class does not hold the monopoly on the innovation or creation while the Banselistic class does, which means the level of the bureaucratic class will still be below that of the Banselistic class.

Since each research team corresponds to at least one elite class, and a bureaucratic class can review the scientific research results of multiple different teams, the size of the elite class will be larger than that of the bureaucratic class. Also, because the elite class has a managerial role in the research process of various teams, it can directly obtain a certain dividend from the research results, the bonus that is slightly less than the Banselistic class. With its management ability, its individual strength will not be far below that of the bureaucratic class. Therefore, the elite class is below the bureaucratic class, but there will only be a small gap between the power of it and that of the bureaucratic class.

Early in 1949, the socialist revolution had achieved a decisive victory in the mainland of China, after which the monopoly capitalist was replaced by the petty capitalist class, which is the same as the small and medium private business owners in this book. Since the development of private enterprises is also supported by the bureaucratic class, and there are still talents provided by the Banselistic class, the elite class, and the EIW Strata. Consequently, the capitalist class will still have a considerable power and will occupy a position that lies above the EIW strata and student class. However, because each business owner will correspond to multiple talents from other social classes, and state-owned enterprises have achieved decisive victories in the market competition with private enterprises (for details, please refer to the Volume Two, Part Four, Chapter Four: With regard to the state-owned economy). Hence, the group size of the capitalist class is smaller than that of the remaining social classes except for that of the EIW Strata.

What is the same as the west is that the substitutability of the student class determines that this social class will be weaker than all other social classes except for the EIW strata. However, the economic condition of the EIW strata is controlled by other social classes, and regarding the EIW strata, its influence on the public opinion is weaker than that of the rest of the social classes. Also, lacking the flexibility of arranging time to develop new skills compared with the Banselistic student, the power of each single member of the EIW strata is largely weakened, and the relatively low production capacity of material products will determine that the power of the EIW strata is weaker than that of the student class. Meanwhile, the role of the market mechanism will directly determine that its group size is smaller than the rest of the social classes, including that of the student class. Apart from that, because all classes and stratum originate from the student class, the group size of the student class is larger than the rest of the social classes and strata.

Therefore, the social structure of mainland China will show a multi-T shape under the Ideological and Political System of Banselism (as illustrated in the diagram on the next page).

In addition, the Hong Kong SAR will apply the Ideological and Political System of Banselism as well, owing to the demand for financial innovation, and so forth. Because the capitalist class in Hong Kong has absolute dominance and control over almost everything except diplomacy and military affairs, this social class will inevitably continue to be at the top of the social structure map. The capitalist class, however, has

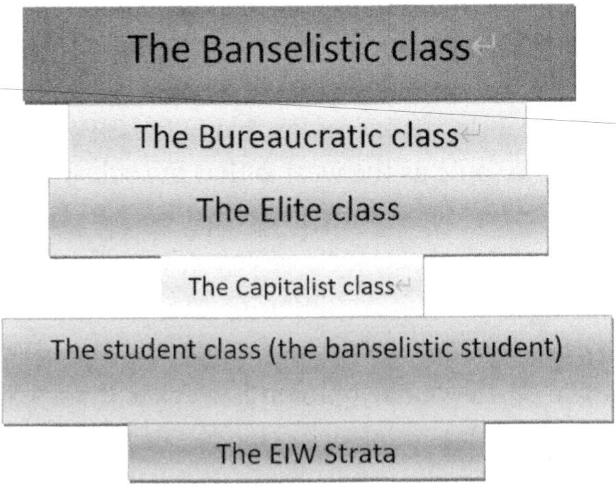

an enormously great demand for the talents provided by the Banselistic class. For example, the demand for editors from news stations, the demand for financial innovative talents from bond companies, the demand for interior and exterior decoration designers, and food remodelers in the catering industry, the demand for decoration designers and AI developers in retail stores as the indoor manual sellers are replaced by AI. This will directly determine that the Banselistic class is also at the top of the social structure map in Hong Kong. Also, the local capitalists' demand for the elite class will be greater than that of other countries and regions, which is also directly determined by its pillar industries. For example, financial companies' huge demand for financial analysts, investment fund groups' demand for investment analysts, real estate industry's huge demand for management talents and sales talents, and re-export trade's demand for sales talents. This means that in Hong Kong SAR, the capitalist class, the Banselistic class and the elite class will all lie at the top of the social structure at the same time. Also, since the capitalist class, the elite class and the Banselistic class all have almost absolute and total control over the HKSAR government, the capitalist class will also lie at the top of the social structure.

The highly centralized control of the capitalist class over material wealth will greatly increase its income from the student class and make more material wealth transfer from the student class to the capitalist class, which will weaken the power of the student class and reduce their influence on the entertainment industry. However, the EIW strata has relatively considerable material wealth, and its influence in the field of public opinion surpasses the student class. Consequently, the level of the EIW strata will be higher than that of the student class in the social structure.

All social classes and strata are derived from the student class, which means the group size of the student class is larger than that of other classes and strata.

Consequently, the social structure of the Hong Kong SAR under the Ideological and Political System of Banselism will show an asymmetrical hourglass shape (this is shown in the diagram below).

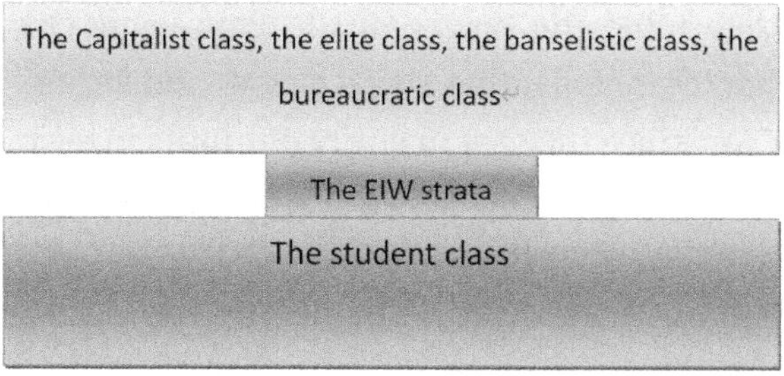

Meanwhile, the Macao SAR will also implement this political system, which is directly determined by its economic structure with gaming and tourism as its economic pillars.

For instance, a large casino. Various amenities within large casinos, including the small casinos, hotels, restaurants, amusement parks, etc. have a huge demand for decoration designers. Although the demand for the decoration design of casinos and other facilities is not long-term, because after the decoration design is completed, there is no need to repeat indoor and outdoor decoration, which will also weaken the power of the Banselistic class to a certain extent. Nonetheless, the Banselistic class will still occupy the top level of the social structure.

Firstly, the catering industry has a huge demand for the talents provided by the Banselistic class for the design of dishes, etc. Secondly, due to the large-scale popularization of automation technology, it will directly make innovative or creative activities the core driving force of economic development. Casinos, the core source of economic wealth in the gambling industry, will also have a huge demand for the Banselistic class. For example, the Banselistic class proposes new forms of gambling, which will strengthen the core competitiveness of the casinos unprecedentedly. Apart from that, the local media still has a huge demand for editors and other talents provided by the Banselistic class, which will directly determine the power of the Banselistic class to be greater than that of all other social classes and strata.

However, since the vast majority of profits in every industry belong to the capitalist class, the capitalist class will also be at the top of the social structure.

In addition, a considerable number of elites, such as casino managers and hotel managers, are required for the operation of related facilities in large casinos. Also, the elite class directly participates in the economic development of the gambling industry and tourism industry more frequently than the Banselistic class, which narrows the income gap between their income and the Banselistic class. Consequently, the elite class will also be at the top of the social structure map.

Meanwhile, as the MSAR government is firmly controlled by the Macau capitalist class, the Banselistic class and the elite class, coupled with the fact that the bureaucratic class has real power in government, the bureaucratic class will thus also be at the top of the Banselistic social structure in Macau.

Apart from that, the student class in the Macau SAR will be above the EIW strata. In addition to the foregoing reasons that the strength of the Western student class under the Ideological and Political System of Banselism is greater than that of the EIW strata, there are mainly the following reasons: Firstly, the loss of talents in Macau's entertainment industry is relatively serious. In the 20th century, since the development of the entertainment industry in Hong Kong and Taiwan has been longer than that in Macau, the income level and welfare benefits of entertainment industry workers in the region are generally better than those in Macau, which stimulates a large number of entertainment industry workers to move to the areas that have been mentioned above. In the early 21st century, the entertainment industry workers in the Macao SAR had generally moved to Hong Kong SAR, Taiwan SAR, and the Mainland of China, which caused a huge loss of entertainment industry workers and greatly reduced the population of it. Also, the serious imbalance in the economic structure of the Macao SAR has severely curbed the development space of the entertainment industry. According to data provided by the Driving Start Engine Consulting (DSEC) in 2018, the gambling industry and the gambling intermediary industry had contributed 50.5% of the total annual GDP altogether that year. Also, The Macau Industry Structure Chart released by the DSEC in 2018 shows: the wholesale and retail, hotel, catering, transportation, storage and communications, leasing, industrial and the construction industry accounts for 39.8% of the GDP altogether, while the remaining 9.7% of

GDP is contributed by the public administration, education, healthcare, and other service industries including entertainment altogether. This reflects the serious imbalance in the economic structure of Macau and severely hinders the development of other types of industries, including the entertainment industry.

Consequently, under the Ideological and Political System of Banselism, the social structure of Macao will be shaped as a hot air balloon. Because of the aging of the population, the aggregate population in the student class is less than the sum of the population of the capitalist class, the Banselistic class, and elite class. According to data released by the DSEC of the Macao SAR, the dependency ratio of Macao's elderly population in 2018 was 19.2%, which reflects the aging population of Macao. Also, because the group at the top of the social structure chart consists of the capitalist class, the Banselistic class, and the elite class, this means that its group size is larger than that of other social classes or stratas, with the student class ranking both the second level and the second largest population. At the bottom of the social structure, the EIW strata can be found, with its group size being the smallest compared with that of other levels. Consequently, a hot air balloon-shaped social structure will be formed (shown in the diagram below).

The social structure of the Taiwan SAR is the same as that of the West.

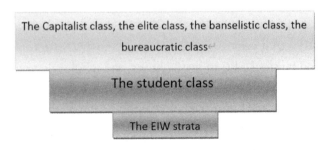

The social structures of the countries and regions mentioned in this article are typical and common types of the banselistic social structure. The remaining special cases will be explained in the second volume.

Notes:

[1] Reformism: This concept refers to a political position that appeals to solve the social contradictions in the capitalist society by perfecting, adjusting, and reforming the capitalist system.

Chapter Five:

The Banselistic Political Structure

Since the power center in each historical period is dominated by different classes, the key supervision and regulation objects carried out in each historical period are different, and these measures for supervision and regulation will directly cause certain changes in the political structure. For instance, before the 19th century, the political center power is generally dominated by the feudal aristocracy and the feudal landlord class globally. Given this situation, western European countries, including the United Kingdom, have adopted a series of measures to supervise and regulate it, such as the United Kingdom's Magna Carta, the 'Bill of Rights' and other restrictions on the power of the monarch. At the same time, Europe's regulation and supervision of the bureaucratic class, including the feudal aristocracy, had also stimulated the United States to use European theoretical grounds and take relevant measures to regulate and supervise the bureaucracy, promoting the formation of the modern American political system. In the 20th century, the center of the political power had been gradually dominated by the capitalist class, and class struggles between the working class, or the proletariat and the capitalist class erupted within the developed Western capitalist countries. Hereafter, trade unions and a large number of social democratic parties were established—for example The British Labor Party, which effectively regulated and supervised the economic activities of the capitalist class, greatly reducing its oppression and exploitation of the working class or the proletariat and caused a significant impact on the western party system. Also, after the formation of the capitalist political system, the sprouting of Banselism that appeared during the first industrial revolution had evolved into the Banselistic strata, after which it evolved into the Banselistic class at the end of the 20th century and the beginning of the 21st century, gradually shifting the center of political power to this social class. When the center of power shifts to the Banselistic class, relevant measures to regulate and supervise their behavior will also be taken, which will also directly lead to changes in the political structure.

To begin with, explain the configuration of the institution used to supervise the Banselistic class.

This institution is an institution that reviews various innovations or creations and is one of the branches of government departments. The department has a large number of branches under its jurisdiction, and the number of branches is determined by the specific population. For instance, China, according to the data released by the State Intellectual Property Office of China in 2017: The number of invention patents in China was 1.382 million, while the data released by the China National Bureau of Statistics in 2018 shows that in 2017, the undergraduate rate in China was 4.43%. The total population was 1.39 billion people, 1.39 billion × undergraduate rate 4.43% = 61.577 million people: in 2017, about 61.577 million people in the mainland of China had a bachelor degree, and 1.382 million patents ÷ 61.577 million ≈ 0.02: according to the development trend in 2017, the number of invention patents per capita in China under the Ideological and Political System of Banselism will reach approximately 0.02. However, what the public needs to notice is that each invention patent may correspond to an individual or a team comprising multiple individuals. In addition, the issued patent is only one form and a small part of intellectual property rights, which means the Ideological and Political System can still boost innovation or creativity highly efficiently. Based on this trend, the total number of patents will approximately be 1.39 billion people × 0.02 = 27.8 million. Also, according to Article 34 of the *Patent Law of the People's Republic of China:* "After the patent administration department of the State Council receives an application for a patent for invention, if it is deemed to meet the requirements of this law after preliminary examination, it shall be announced immediately after the expiration of 1.5 years from the date of application." the number of audit results that can be reviewed by each audit team in a unit time is relatively limited, because the complexity of the audit results will make the time lag of the audit process to be relatively long, and together with the limitation of time, the audit results that can be reviewed by each audit team in a unit time is relatively limited. Assuming that a single invention patent review team can review 10 innovations within 1.5 years, and a building of a single review agency branch can include 240 review teams—about 4 teams on each floor. The agency has more than 60 floors. Therefore, a single the review agency can publish 240×10=2400 invention patent results within 1.5 years. Also, if each first-tier and new first-tier cities can build 3 institutions, and second, third, fourth, and fifth-tier cities can build 6 institutions - because their idle land is generally more than that of first-tier cities, then, 2400 × 3 × (number of first-tier cities (4 cities) + new first-tier cities(19cities)) = 136,800—under such conditions, first-tier and new first-tier cities can review approximately 137,000 invention patents every 1.5 years. Also, 2400 × 6 × The total number of the third, fourth and fifth-tier cities (318) = 4,579,200—under these conditions, a total of 4,579,200 invention patents can be reviewed in these cities every 1.5 years. In this situation, the number of invention patents that can be reviewed in all cities within 1.5 years is 4.716 million.

Moreover, to further increase the number of various intellectual property rights, including invention patents that can be reviewed per unit time, universities will also participate in the review. Assuming that each university can review 15 invention patents within 1.5 years, then, according to the data released by the Ministry of Education of the People's Republic of China on July 9, 2020: There were a total of 3005 universities in China. Given this condition, 3005×15=45075 patents—All universities in China could review approximately 45,000 invention patents within 1.5 years. Also, 4.716 million + 45,000 = 4.761 million - under these conditions, China can review about 4.761 million invention patents within 1.5 years. And 27.8 million ÷ 4.761 million × 1.5 years ≈ 8.8 years. Under such conditions, it only takes about 8.8 years for China to complete the review of all invention patents. Also, compared with Chapter 3 of Part 2 of this volume, the timeline is shorter than that of the time for the class mobility, which means it is feasible to apply the Ideological and Political System of Banselism.

At the same time, since in-depth research in this field will inevitably involve knowledge in other different disciplines, each branch of the institution needs to be equipped with a certain number of auditing talents in a variety of different disciplines.

In addition, lacking relevant supporting laws, regulations, management and standards, the social issues including environmental issues caused by the large-scale innovation and creativity in the mental civilization or the material civilization will be likely to occur more frequently. Consequently, each auditing body, including universities, will be equipped with legislative bodies and relevant legislators. All legislators are responsible for making legislation based on the analysis conclusions of the auditing team. Specifically, in the legislative body located in the auditing body, the legislative acts are directly subject to the analysis results of the auditing team, but the scope of its legislative authority is limited to legislation that innovates or creates results for the institution. When the legal provisions of the legislative body conflict with the central unified legal provisions of the country, the central law shall be obeyed first. This is similar to the legislative system of a considerable number of Western developed countries, wherein although local governments have legislative powers, they still need to obey the laws of the central government.

When the submitter only submits its results to one review team, since the provisions of the legislative body only target for the innovative or creative results reviewed by the review team, it will not conflict with the provisions of other legislative bodies. Nonetheless, when the submitter submits its results to multiple different review teams at the same time, the legislative provisions for the results may conflict. In this case, the submitter is required to abide by the legislative provisions at the top of the timeline for the achievement. Because this will greatly reduce the frequency of law update, which reduces the uncertainty of the law, thereby avoiding the inefficiency caused by the high frequency of law update.

However, since the update of related supporting technologies will eliminate the innovative or creative results that fail to match the latest and best related supporting technologies, it is also inevitable to modify the laws formulated by the review agency so as to enable the innovative or creative result to continue to exist by matching the latest supporting technology. For those Banselistic class members who are willing to modify the law, they can send the original innovative or creative results, the law that had been set earliest, the proposal of the general scope of the corresponding supporting technology and the specific reason for the change of the corresponding technology after the amendment, to any review agency in the professional field involved in the innovative or creative achievement, so that the review agency which receives the material can review and modify the legislative results.

Apart from that, what will be explained is the operation of the auditing agent and the legislature agent equipped with it.

The first example that will be used to illustrate the operation of the audit agency and the legislature in the following paragraphs is the steam engine invented in the first industrial revolution. During the first industrial revolution, steam engines were sold directly to the market almost completely without the review of the auditing agency and the legislation of the legislature. In the short term, this had indeed directly created unprecedentedly huge productivity, enabling capitalism to completely defeat feudalism. However, its lack of regulation and supervision and related supporting laws directly led to its large-scale pollution and destruction of the natural environment, as well as the excessive length of working class and the low income of it.

In the mode of this chapter, the steam engine will be popularized in the following way: When Watt and his partner successfully improve the steam engine, they need to submit the results to relevant institutions or universities for review. And because of its highly destructive impact on the environment, although it will pass the audit, its sales will be strictly controlled by relevant laws and regulations. In this situation, because the capitalist class has a huge demand for the product, and its sales, that is, the supply, is strictly restricted, the price of steam engines will rise sharply, which will not only effectively protect the income of Watt and his partners but also reduce the damage to the environment.

Meanwhile, relevant laws and regulations will be enacted immediately, such as the *Ten Hours Act* passed in 1847, the *Employers liability act of 1880* and the *Clean Air Act* promulgated in 1956. However, these laws will be introduced during the sub-industrial revolution, in accordance with the model of this chapter. In addition, steam engines are only allowed to lift restrictions on sales when relevant technologies to curb environmental pollution are popularized. For instance, calcium-based adhesives and activated carbon, under the model in this chapter, the steam engine must be used in large-scale use of the calcium-based adhesive to lift the sales restriction, or it must be equipped with activated carbon or other anti-pollution technology to lift the sales restriction. In this situation, Britain will still create unprecedented social productivity during the first industrial revolution, but its damage to the environment and exploitation of the working class will be extremely effectively reduced.

When the supporting technologies are updated, for example, when supporting technologies that can reduce environmental pollution more effectively than calcium-based adhesives and activated carbon appear, Watt and Boulton can submit the steam engine technology and the earliest legal provisions issued by the review agency, the first draft of the new law proposed by the submitter to one of the auditing body so as to modify the law targeted at this steam engine—for example, which range of supporting environmental protection technologies should be used in the next steam.

Another example is the Internet companies in Mainland China in the early 21st century. For instance, the e-commerce platform of Meituan. If the delivery staff has the willingness to earn 10,000 yuan a month, their working hours will be extended—more than ten hours a day, and it is highly difficult and unlikely for the driver to maintain an income at the social average level, which can be reflected by the self-immolation of a delivery worker asking for the unpaid salary in Taizhou, China on January 11, 2021. Another example is the 996-work hour system—this working system starts at nine in the morning and ends at nine in the evening, and the half-way break is only one hour or less at noon and evening, which belongs to the prevalent work of Chinese Internet companies in the early 21st century. Also, WeChat, a social software platform, wherein a large number of business managers or business owners used the social software platform to arrange additional tasks during employees' breaks, which resulted in an extension of the actual working hours of employees. These social phenomena reflect the destructive impact caused by the lack of corresponding supporting laws and regulations and management measures for science and technology.

Nonetheless, under the model in this chapter, to begin

with, the income level of blue-collar workers who work eight hours a day (excluding holidays and weekends) will be prohibited from being lower than the average level of white-collar workers. This will be established by law. Secondly, relevant online or offline mandatory vacation regulations will be promulgated on the mainland, and the actual working hours will be the same as in Western countries in the early 21st century. Moreover, in any form, including the Internet, employees will not work during their non-working hours. Sending any work-related information will also be prohibited by legislation. Merely after these three conditions are met at the same time, transportation agents, including Meituan will be authorized to enter the market. The promulgation of these laws and regulations will eliminate companies that have more serious exploitation of employees, and it will also force companies to increase production efficiency, thereby increasing employees' income and shortening employees' working hours while promoting industrial transformation and upgrading. This will increase citizens' sense of happiness and gain, and greatly improve citizens' living standards.

Finally, what will be explained in this paragraph is the impact of the change in the political system. The formation of the political system that supervises and regulates the Banselistic class has the following five main positive impacts. To begin with, this is conducive to screen high-quality talents for enterprises and other institutions. In addition, it can also help the consumer select and choose the high-quality innovative or creative product. Since almost all kinds of products are unique and differentiated, the available choices for consumers will increase, with efficient regulation, the problematic choice for consumers will reduce, creating consumer surplus extremely efficiently. Most importantly, this is also likely to prevent the Banselistic class from exploiting and oppressing other social classes and avoiding Banselistic tyranny. Apart from that, the mode in this chapter is also likely to avoid the negative impact of technology on the environment, thereby saving the arable land, food growth potential, and so forth. Finally, it is helpful to avoid nihilism caused by the lack of supervision and regulation of various innovative or creative behaviors.

Chapter Six:

The Basic Welfare System

When AI technology is popularized on a large scale and automation is implemented, all mechanized laborers, including the vast majority of working-class members and some members of the middle class, that is, most members of the proletariat, will become student class members. In order to avoid riots or civil wars caused by the student class, including the Banselistic students due to insufficient basic living needs and the Gini coefficient beyond the reasonable range of international standards, a basic welfare system will be established.

The basic welfare system refers to the legal form of mandatory establishment in all countries and regions around the world to protect the welfare system of the student class, including that of the Banselistic student. This kind of social welfare system will be inevitably built up owing to its necessity, consisting of the following main content:

To begin with, I will explain the construction of semi-market public housing.

The apartment houses provided to the Banselistic student do not participate in the market competition mechanism. They are government public housing and are provided to the Banselistic students for free to reduce the currency issuance while ensuring their basic living needs, thereby preventing the increase of the inflation rate. Otherwise, assuming that the provision of the public housing to the Banselistic student requires additional fees to be levied on them, the currency circulation will inevitably increase, because the basic living needs of the Banselistic student must be guaranteed so as so finish the class mobility while they do not participate in substantive microeconomic production activities, which in turn will inevitably lead to the increase of inflation. Consequently, the house directly provided to the Banselistic student will not participate in the market mechanism and will not separately levy housing costs from the Banselistic student. The ownership of this type of house belongs to the government, and the Banselistic Student has the right to use it.

These semi-commercial public houses will be equipped with at least one smart electronic device that is also produced by the government. These smart electronic devices will have built-in software for professional knowledge learning and academic research in related fields to assist the student class in gaining the basic educational resources and production materials for class mobility. For example, in Australia in the early 21st century, all legal schools in its territory, including public high schools, private high schools, and noble schools, will equip learners with smart electronic devices, and these smart electronic devices will have relevant built-in software for academic research. One of the advantages of it is that it helps the learner, including the Banselistic student, to get access to infinite knowledge by connecting to the internet. In other words, although the learner merely has a limited memory, the networked electronic device can help the learner get access to the knowledge that he or she wishes to use regardless of whether he or she has succeeded in remembering it. However, on the internet, there is infinite knowledge, which enables the elder manual workers, whose memory has deteriorated, to become the Banselistic student and finish the class mobility after becoming the members in the student class as there is no additional requirement for them to remember knowledge. In addition, for those who choose to study natural sciences or art in professional fields and need to use other related equipment except computers, such equipment is also produced by the government, and the equipment does not participate in the market mechanism. Instead, they will be directly provided to the Banselistic student with a low price or even free of charge by the AI owned by the authority in order to prevent the inflation rate.

In the same semi-commercial building, at least half of the houses will be provided to Banselistic students, and the rest of the houses will be partially commoditized, that is, part of the market competition mechanism—but the government can still directly set the specific price of them regardless of how the market is running. Control is carried out to contain the price of this part of the house, and the ownership of this part of the house also belongs to the central authority, and the purchaser has the right to use it. The housing area of this part of the house needs to be larger than the part of public housing provided to the Banselistic student, and the home environment needs to be better than that of the free public housing provided to the Banselistic student. This part of the house is mainly provided to the corresponding purchasers, such as high-quality talents or normal-skilled local or immigrant talents, etc. This will increase the government total revenue and expand corporate income sources while providing low-cost and medium or high-quality accommodation for relevant talents, and improve the learning atmosphere of the Banselistic student, creating more efficiency of the class mobility.

Take the low-level Western public schools in the early 21st century or the private schools and vocational technical schools in mainland China as examples. Due to the students' low enthusiasm for mastering relevant professional knowledge, their learning atmosphere and academic atmosphere are generally low. However, suppose there are a large number of students with relatively strong learning motivation or relatively strong willingness in academic fields to flow into low-level public schools in the West or private schools and vocational technical schools in mainland China, and this part of the learning motivation is strong, or students with a strong willingness for academic research account for 50% of the total number of students in the school. The learning atmosphere of these schools will be greatly improved, thereby promoting the development and integration of the abilities of these students who are disadvantaged in learning and academic fields. The normal public junior high schools in the coastal areas of mainland China in the early 21st century strongly proved this point: in the coastal areas of mainland China in the 21st century, the top students of their normal public middle schools and the students who were disadvantaged in the field of study and academic are fixedly assigned to the same class and grade, which has become the decisive reason why its academic atmosphere and learning atmosphere are better than those of vocational and technical high schools in the early 21st century in Mainland China. Similarly, the mixed distribution of the semi-commercial housing for the employed and the free public housing for the Banselistic students on the same floor is beneficial to greatly improve the academic atmosphere and the learning atmosphere of the Banselistic student. Meanwhile, a few number of public junior high schools, including the Shenzhen middle school junior department, and so forth, only admitted high-skilled students in the early 21st century, and only mix and distribute excellent students in the same grade. This is similar to the following separate special semi-commercial public housing floor, which is only allocated to sophisticated talents, is also equivalent to high-end commercial housing only allocated to sophisticated talents who are able to pay for the right of using it.

For low quality old commercial housing or low-cost public rental housing provided to former mechanized workers, it needs to be demolished and rebuilt into semi-commercial public housing. However, before this type of house is demolished and rebuilt, it needs to be placed in the corresponding temporary residence; and when it is rebuilt, it needs to be rebuilt in the mode of this chapter—to rebuild it into a semi-commercial public housing.

Except for the special semi-commercial housing, 50% of the accommodation on each floor must be allocated to the Banselistic student, and the other 50% to those who are currently having at least a job. For the Special Commercial Public Housing floor, the area will be different from other normal Commercial Public Housing floors. Specifically, the size of the houses in the Commercial Public Housing floor are larger than that in the normal semi-commercial house—for example, normal semi-commercial houses are only one story houses, while special commercial houses are double story houses, and their home environment needs to be better than conventional semi-commercial houses, which also further stimulates the Banselistic student to finish the class mobility, boosting the long run aggregate supply(LRAS) more efficiently.

Finally, early in the 21st century, the West (see Volume Two, Part One, Chapter One: The reclassification of Western Countries, for details), high-welfare countries (Please refer to volume Two, Part Two, Chapter One: Supply-side reforms, for details), and China already have the infrastructure capabilities to implement the model in this chapter. The infrastructure capabilities of the West, Mainland China, etc. allow them to increase the number of floors and single-story houses to ensure that the houses on each floor are constructed and distributed according to the model in this chapter.

Next, I will illustrate the distribution and allocation of income and resources to the student class. The income distribution of the student class is mainly determined by these two aspects: one is the length of study counted in the system, which may differ from the actual length of study; the second is the process of its innovation or creation of material civilization or spiritual civilization.

Taking the instructional video as an example, pre-recorded courses, including college open courses are classified as 'teaching videos' in this article. 'Teaching videos' are divided into two types, one is free teaching videos, and the other is paid teaching videos. These instructional videos—one form of the concrete manifestations of educational resources, are mainly produced by universities and so on. Completing the free instructional video's corresponding exercises will be shown in the system for less time than the paid instructional video's corresponding exercises; while completing the instructional videos of universities with lower international rankings, the corresponding exercises will be included in the system for less time compared with that of the universities ranked higher than the former. Most public teaching videos produced by colleges and universities need to be charged to maintain the income of colleges and universities while promoting the class mobility of the student class.

The learning time length counted in the system after completing the electronic test questions corresponding to the instructional video is the learning time corresponding to the set of electronic test questions × the correct rate. The numbers after the decimal point are rounded up, and the whole number is finally retained.

For this type of choice: Choice 1, which uses artificial intelligence to remotely supervise the exercises during the examination or assessments. In the early 21st century, artificial intelligence technology was invested in examination proctoring. For example, the college entrance examination in mainland China in 2020 used artificial intelligence technology to do the remote invigilation, a large number of world-renowned universities in Europe and the United States put artificial intelligence technology into invigilation, which includes remote unsupervised examinations for students receiving online teaching. Also, the correction of this type of exercise is automatically conducted by AI or the system. For instance, early in the 21st century, most developed countries and the mainland of China, the multiple-choice and mechanical level fill-in questions were automatically corrected by the system or AI.

The above content belongs to the first choice for the learning behavior of the Banselistic students—complete the corresponding exercises in the instructional video. However, the income of choosing one will be less than that of choosing two, because the activity of choosing one only stays at the mechanical level.

Choice 2 is to carry out direct or indirect innovative or creative activities on material civilization or spiritual civilization, which includes participating in the process of any kind of them. Taking the humanities and social sciences as an example, the second choice of activities includes social research, writing manuscripts, and so forth. When conducting such activities, Banselistic students can upload the progress of the day to the smart electronics equipped in the semi-commercial public housing. The system corresponding to the built-in software of the device directly completes the regular learning time counted in the system on the day. And if the submitted manuscripts or other social research results involve more than 50% of the submitters' results on the day, such as the number of knowledge points and word counts, the student class will be able to receive the excess income of the student class on the day—slightly higher than its daily income before this social class was replaced by artificial intelligence.

Also, taking the natural sciences as another example. Its activities will include, but are not limited to, writing reports, doing new online virtual experiments or offline experiments, etc. The student class can complete the required learning time of the day by completing experiments under manual supervision or artificial intelligence supervision—the experiment process is automatically recorded and uploaded by the system.

For mechanical level experiments, the time counted in the system is only the average of the time counted in the system for completing regular natural science exercises. And the experiment process is automatically supervised by artificial intelligence based on the experiment plan submitted by the experimenter. If the experimenter conducts an experiment that does not conform to the experiment plan during the experiment without authorization, the experiment material will be forcibly collected by the artificial intelligence. If the experimenter refuses to obey the collection of experimental equipment, he or she will receive the administrative or criminal penalties—this approach helps prevent some experimenters from defrauding relevant test equipment for destructive research.

In addition, there is a possibility of safety hazards when conducting some offline experiments in natural sciences. Therefore, for these Banselistic students who use dangerous experimental equipment or raw materials required for academic research, they need to choose online virtual experiments, or alternatively, make a textual description of the experimental program—its content needs to include the experimental steps and the program, the specific time period for the experiment to be manually supervised. After completing the textual description, the Banselistic student should submit it to any auditing body that manages this part of the material. If the text description exceeds the recognition range of AI, then, to begin with, on this day, for this individual, the required length of time for learning will be classified as completed, because this part of the textual description is beyond the mechanical level and is already an innovative activity or creative activity for spiritual civilization. Moreover, in Western developed or sub-developed countries, the copyright belongs to the author, which means this individual will automatically obtain the copyright even if it is not approved by the auditing body.

Also, because the textual description exceeds the mechanical level, the review agency, which is the same as the auditing body, needs to manually review the manuscript. After the review is passed, the Banselistic student can use this part of the natural science experiment materials, and because of the experiment—this material activities, surpassing the mechanical level, will also be carried out under manual supervision and review—the experiment process will be automatically recorded by the system, and after the experiment is completed, it will automatically default to the completion of the class mobility.

The reasons why experiments that exceed the mechanical level require manual supervision are as follows: First, manual supervision and automatic recording of the system can help to avoid academic fraud. Then, if the experimenter does not conduct the experiment under manual supervision but conducts the experiment on his own and describes the experimental phenomenon in text, the review agency will need to consume the corresponding resources again to conduct the experiment again to see if it is factually accurate—this will lead to an increase in social costs. Meanwhile, If the model in this chapter is not adopted, the experimenter can falsely report the experimental phenomenon in the textual description, which will lead to a further increase in social costs.

Except for the reason mentioned above, there is still one reason why it is indispensable to apply the manual supervision: Take some anti-social criminals or anti-human lawbreakers as examples. This group of individuals may defraud the materials needed for destructive academic research through corresponding textual explanations, thereby causing extreme destructive effects.

For this reason, when doing offline experiments, the experimenters need to be approved by the auditors before they can proceed to the next step. If the auditor refuses to proceed to the next step, the AI immediately takes back the experimental materials. If the experimenter carries out the next experimental step without approval, he will be warned by the auditing institution and artificial intelligence. If the warning fails, he will be given administrative or criminal punishment immediately. If the case is extremely serious or urgent, he will be sentenced to life imprisonment or shot on the spot in case of emergency. In countries with the death penalty, he or she can be executed by firing squad in extremely egregious or urgent circumstances—because this part of the research is extremely damaging and needs to be stopped. Thus, this manual supervision also has a positive effect: it avoids the creation of destructive products that are antisocial or antihuman.

For the Banselistic students who are willing to do military research and development (R&D) projects, they need to submit a written application to any auditing body to apply for venues and equipment. After the review is passed, it will be conducted under the manual and real-time supervision of the military and review institutions.

For the natural science research that is completely theoretical, only textual explanations are required. Take Schrödinger's cat as an example. As it was proposed by Schrödinger in 1935: Suppose a cat is confined in a closed container containing radium and chloride. When the radium decays, the bottle containing chloride will be automatically broken due to the trigger of the gear, which will directly lead to the death of the cat. The radioactive radium is in a superposition state of decay and non-decay at the same time, which makes the cat in the airtight container have a superposition state of both life and death. However, the experimenter cannot observe the actual state of the cat by opening the airtight container, because the observation of some particles will cause quantum entanglement between the quantum system and the observer, which will cause the superposition state to collapse into a single state, affecting and changing the experimental results—This can be illustrated by the double-slit interference experiment conducted by Thomas Young in 1801: There were two parallel slits with equal length and width in a plane. When Thomas Young emitted single photons one by one into one of the slits, interference fringes appeared on the detection screen—this had directly reflected the photon's self-interference ability. In order to figure out how it interfered with itself, Thomas Young placed a detector next to the two gaps and continued to emit single photons one by one into one of the gaps. However, the interference fringes on the detection screen disappeared because the observation of the quantum would make the state of it collapse from the superposition into a single state. Therefore, if Schrödinger intended to conduct an experiment, he would not be able to observe the actual result by opening the container.

Experiments that are similar to Schrödinger's cats do not require online or offline virtual experiments. To begin with, all the theories cited have been verified by actual experiments or verified by other experiments; Also, performing offline experiments will not alter Schrödinger's result that has already been deduced by his own thought experiment, as he would not be able to open the container to observe the actual state of the cat.

After the audition is passed, the Banselistic student will become the member in the Banselistic class, who can then directly obtain the stable income whose purchasing power is not lower than the income before he or she is replaced by AI within a certain period of time without learning or academic activities. The income of the Banselistic student will become the income of the Banselistic class. After the expiration of this part of the time limit, they can obtain more income than that of the student class with a shorter study time.

The detection of academic misconduct in various types of manuscripts can be automatically carried out by the AI, the system, or related software, such as the software Turnitin, which was widely used by universities in developed countries in Europe and the United States and universities in the Commonwealth developed economies in the early 21st century, so as to automatically review academic misconduct in academic papers, without manual operation. Meanwhile, in the submitted file, the AI, the system, or relevant software is also responsible for automatically reviewing whether the grammar of these manuscripts is correct, whether the sentence structure is complete, and whether the manuscript contains the academic value that exceeds the mechanical level, that is, whether the AI has the ability to write such manuscripts. After these indicators have been automatically reviewed by the AI, system or relevant software and meet the requirement, the student can submit his manuscript to the manual auditing agency.

The Banselistic student needs to ensure that their daily learning hours accounted in the system during the working day are not less than 7 hours to ensure that their income is not lower than the income before being replaced by AI. According to the data released by the website FindAPHD on December 16, 2020, the average study time of doctoral students should not be less than 35 hours per week. Since most doctoral students have innovative or creative achievements, this chapter takes the data of the average study time of doctoral students. In most cases, except for special holidays and weekends, there are five working days a week. Therefore, 35÷5=7—the banselistic student needs to make sure that their learning hours are not less than 7 hours counted in the system to ensure that the income received by them on that day is not less than that before they were replaced by AI.

Meanwhile, the data provided by the website FindAPHD on December 16, 2020, also shows that most European and American universities have restrictions on the maximum working hours of various academic-related jobs, and the most frequent data is 12—16 hours per week. Take the minimum value of this set of data, 12÷the number of regular weekly working days 5=2.4, and 2.4+7=9.4, and the number after the decimal point is rounded to 9 hours. Therefore, if the daily study time is more than 7 hours and less than 9 hours, the income of the Banselistic student will be higher than that before the large-scale use of AI. For the above two situations, the formula is: the daily income of the classy students = the regular daily salary before being replaced by artificial intelligence ÷ the daily learning time required to be counted in the system × the daily learning time actually counted in the system. However, if the income before the replacement is lower than the average social income level before the large-scale popularization of artificial intelligence technology, the formula will be the income of the classy students on the day = the average daily salary of the society before the replacement by artificial intelligence ÷ the required daily learning time counted into the system × learning time actually counted into the system. With regard to the Banselistic student who studies for more than 9 hours a day, his or her income received on that day will not be increased according to the above formula, and the income of this individual will only be distributed based on the 9-hour daily study time.

Take a member in the student class as an example, whose daily income before being replaced by artificial intelligence is 360 dollars, and when this individual is transformed into the student class, he or she only needs to make sure that his or her daily study hours counted in the system reach at least 7 hours per day in order to gain the Banselistic student's income, and the student's actual length of time in the system that day is 7 hours, then, according to the above formula, the banselistic-student income of that day = \$360÷7 hours×7 hours=\$360, and if the learning time that was actually counted into the system on that day is only 6 hours, then the banselistic-student income for this individual on that day will be: \$360÷7 hours×6 hours≈$309 (All figures after the decimal point are rounded to the nearest integer). Also, If the learner has previously completed the activities of innovating or creating in material civilization or spiritual civilization, the Banselistic student will become the Banselistic class, and the formula for the Banselistic student class's income will become: the average daily income during the exemption period ÷ the learning time of the day that needs to be counted in the system × the learning time of the day that is actually counted in the system. Assuming that the individual's average daily income during the exemption period is $500, the time required to be counted in the system on the weekday (excluding the holiday) is shortened to 6 hours due to the completion of the class mobility, and the actual study time of the day is 7.5 hours, then the income of this individual on that day will at least = $500÷6 hours×7.5 hours=$583 (the numbers after the decimal point are rounded to the nearest integer).

All the content of the basic welfare system that has been previously mentioned in this chapter mainly has the following positive impacts: To begin with, the construction of semi-commercial public housing guarantees the basic living needs of the Banselistic student and helps to avoid the initiation of civil war by them. Also, the mixed distribution of the residence of the employed person and the residence of the Banselistic student is conducive to improving the learning atmosphere and environment of the Banselistic student, further promoting the class mobility. Furthermore, the above measures introduced a mechanism for stratifying the Banselistic student, which is conducive to further promoting social fairness while stimulating the enthusiasm of the Banselistic student for class mobility; In addition, the above-mentioned measures directly link the income of the Banselistic student to their academic research progress, etc., which is conducive to directly enhancing the enthusiasm of the Banselistic student for class mobility; Meanwhile, according to the above-mentioned measures, for those Banselistic students who have low or no willingness to finish the class mobility, the income of them is relatively low, which is conducive to reducing the issuance of currency, thereby reducing the inflation rate; In addition, the income of the student class member who exceeds the maximum study time of the day will not increase the income on that day, which is conducive to reducing the student's academic burden—according to the principle of diminishing returns, when the input cost reaches a certain level, its marginal cost is directly proportional to the amount of input, which will make its cost-effectiveness continue to decline. Similarly, the theory is also applicable to individuals. A moderate reduction in the learning time of the Banselistic student is conducive to improving their learning efficiency, shortening the time needed for class mobility; Apart from that, the above-mentioned measures directly force the Banselistic student to participate in the process of innovating or creating material civilization or spiritual civilization, directly and effectively avoiding inflation.

Participating in the production process while gaining corelative salary or income will not cause inflation. Take the military industry in the early 21st century as an example. Suppose that the military factory plans to produce a large aircraft carrier—a large project that took months or even years to complete in the early 21st century. After working for a month, the production of the aircraft carrier of the factory was only partially completed, and the production results were not successfully produced. The behavior of these employees can only be classified as 'participating in the production process' rather than 'successfully producing results', but under this circumstance, the allocation of wages for the employees in the factory will not lead to inflation; even if the project fails, the settlement of the wages of these employees will not lead to inflation; for the same reason, assume that the Banselistic student participates in the material civilization or the process of spiritual civilization's innovation or creation—such as writing manuscripts, and so forth. In this case, providing them with Banselistic student's income will not lead to inflation; and even if the innovative or creative production of these Banselistic students ended in failure, providing them with income will also not lead to inflation.

The examples mentioned above in the early 21st century all belonged to producers participating in the production process in relevant companies or institutions to avoid inflation. Therefore, the government can set up a separate fixed institution—the institution is a monopoly state-owned institution, which is non-profit and does not participate in the market competition mechanism. It is automatically operated by AI to minimize costs and maximize efficiency, and directly classify all Banselistic students as members of this institution to avoid inflation. This is equivalent to part-time telecommuting in the early 21st century—for example, a part-time job, who completes his work in any place, such as writing a report, etc., and then the employee is involved in the results or progress of his work, after which phased output generated during or after the production process is uploaded remotely—but such behavior can still be identified as working and will not cause inflation. In the same way, the Banselistic student is classified as the regular employee of the institution. However, to avoid the problem of insufficient space, the venues for the student class to conduct remote production activities will not be restricted. They can work wherever they wish to and only need to upload their progress to the designated system in accordance with the provisions of this chapter—this is equivalent to remote uploading. And because the production activities of the Banselistic student have not fully exceeded the mechanical level, their income cannot compete with the employees who have successfully exceeded the mechanical level.

In addition, what will be explained is the part of the free food supply that is provided to the Banselistic student. For Banselistic students, only the proportion of food within a specified category can be supplied free of charge by the government for a specified amount. A similar example of this is the early 21st century French charity Resto du Coeur, which had stations in cities throughout France to distribute relief food on a daily basis—2,176 stations in total. This charity did this by purchasing edible goods that were about to expire at low prices and distributing them free of charge to relief food recipients, or by buying food ingredients that were going to expire at low prices and preparing cooked food from them for distribution to relief food recipients. Similarly, when implementing the Ideological and Political System of Banselism, the government will be suggested to make law to compel producers of food or raw food materials to hand over expired edible products to the government, while the raw food materials will be automatically processed by government-affiliated artificial intelligence into edible products that are going to expire and provided free of charge to the Banselistic student.

The reasons why the government needs to make it compulsory by law to receive free of charge for each food ingredient or food product that is going to expired rather than to buy it at a low price are set out separately here: Firstly, making it compulsory for each food ingredient or food producer to hand over the product that is going to expire to the government free of charge can help to avoid widening of the fiscal deficit. However, if the government were to provide these products free of charge to the Banselistic student, or if the raw materials of the food products were to be processed by the artificial intelligence of the government for free and then provided directly to the Banselistic student, the government's input in this area would be greater than its output, which would lead to an increase in the fiscal deficit. If the government were to buy these foodstuffs or raw materials at a low price, the amount of money in circulation would inevitably increase, which would lead to inflation, so making it compulsory for these producers to hand over their foodstuffs or raw materials free of charge would help to avoid unnecessary inflation.

In order to implement this policy, the activity records and product information of each catering entity or producer of raw food materials will be counted in the systems that come with these economic activities, including cloud-based systems set by the government—for example, the raw materials purchased by a catering entity from a raw material supplier and the expiry date of these raw materials will be recorded into the system for government supervision. Such consumption bills and product information would have been accounted for in the systems of sub-developed or developed countries in the early 21st century, demonstrating that this method is effective to a large extent (in other words, in the early 21st century, governments of these countries were able to check which raw material had been purchased by which restaurant and when the expiry date of these raw materials would be via the appointed system(s)). When surplus food or raw materials reach their due dates and are about to become expired food or raw materials, the part of the AI operated by the government will automatically and compulsorily collect them free of charge. To put it bluntly, the government may also be even suggested to list these edible products that are about to expire into the strategic material and let the department for national security deal with this task.

This measure has the following positive effects: firstly, it helps to solve the problem of food surplus and food waste, which is also one form of overcapacity, and thus improve resource efficiency; then, it helps to directly solve the problem of basic needs, including basic food for Banselistic students; furthermore, this measure will help to significantly reduce the environmental pollution caused by the decay of surplus and expired food materials and the decay of bio-waste; finally, it will help to clear the surplus stocks of catering entities or producers of food materials in a timely manner in order to alleviate the lack of space in their surplus stocks and thus reduce the operating costs of these economic activities.

Apart from that, what will be explained is the amount of free water and free electricity for the Banselistic student. This part of the water supply and electricity supply are only provided to Banselistic students by state-owned water and electricity companies or private water and electricity companies on a compulsory and unconditional basis, free of charge, within the designated supply under the law. Let's take the example of water and electricity in the US: according to figures released by the National Association of Water Companies (NAWC) in 2021, over 73 million people were served by private water companies across the U.S., representing less than 50% of the population—the majority of people in the US were not served by private water companies. Most of the USA population was not served by private utilities for water, which means that the water provided to Banselistic students is not subject to market competition for a specified amount of supply and is thus directly provided by the government to Banselistic students at no cost for a specified amount of supply. Also, based on data released by the U.S. Department of Energy in

2021, the federal government owns 9 electricity agencies, which include 4 electricity market authorities and the Tennessee Valley Authority, together accounting for 7% of net generation and 8% of transmission. 211 Electricity marketers account for approximately 19% of consumer sales. As a result, the U.S. government has the capacity to supply electricity to Banselistic students, and since the free electricity supply to Banselistic students is only a government-designated amount, the U.S. government only needs to further increase its supply and its share of the nation's total electricity supply to have the capacity to fully supply all Banselistic students in the U.S. for a certain amount of free electricity.

Take mainland China as another example. As all water services in mainland China are handled by state-owned enterprises and central enterprises, and these are firmly controlled by the central government, they can provide water directly to Banselistic students for free within a specified amount of supply.

Another example is the UK. In the UK, the water and electricity industry in England and Wales is run by a small number of private oligopolies, while in Scotland and Northern Ireland they are mainly run by the state. When legislation is introduced in the House of Commons to make water supply to Banselistic students free of charge for a specified supply, it will be difficult for these private utilities to prevent the legislation from being passed.

This is because, firstly, British Hydro does not have real power and direct influence in the political arena; then, in significant numbers, British left-wing forces including the labor party have relatively strong power and influence in the House of Commons and have been in power on many occasions—their power is close to or even sometimes above that of the British right like the conservative party, which significantly increases the likelihood of difficulty for these utilities to block the passage of this legislation; then, the *Water Industry Act 1999*, passed by the UK House of Commons in 1999, and the *Water Act 2014*, passed in 2014, directly reflect the difficulty for UK utilities to block the passage of legislation on utilities in the House of Commons.

As a result, legislation will be passed by the House of Commons in England and Wales to guarantee a mandatory free supply of water and electricity to Banselistic students in these areas within a specified amount daily, and legislation will be passed by the House of Commons in Scotland and Northern Ireland to mandate the provision of free water and electricity to Banselistic students by the various hydroelectric companies in the region for a legally specified supply. In contrast, as the Scottish region and Northern Ireland are dominated by state-owned businesses, the Scottish and Northern Ireland regions are predominantly served by state-owned water and electricity businesses providing free water and electricity to Banselistic students within the designated volumes.

Take the Hong Kong Special Administrative Region (HKSAR) as another example. According to the report 'Water, Electricity and Petrol Supply' published in May 2015 by the Government of the Hong Kong Special Administrative Region and the Ministry of Information of the Government of the Hong Kong Special Administrative Region, the water supply in Hong Kong is mainly provided directly by the Central People's Government of the People's Republic of China. Therefore, for Banselistic students in the Hong Kong SAR, this portion of their legally designated supply of free water is provided directly by the Central People's Government of the People's Republic of China.

Such a measure would not impact on the interests of local

private power companies because, firstly, the Daya Bay Nuclear Power Station has been supplying electricity to the Hong Kong SAR since the early 21st century, but such an action has not directly and significantly impacted on the interests of local private power companies; and then the profits generated by the electricity supplied by the Daya Bay Nuclear Power Station do not belong to local private power companies located in Hong Kong, but to the Daya Bay Nuclear Power Station and the Central People's Government—providing this electricity free of charge to local Banselistic students does not reduce the profits of local private companies.

In addition, there is no additional charge for the use of water and electricity for academic research. However, the experimental process would need to be supervised by artificial intelligence, and if the experiment exceeds mechanical levels, it will need to be supervised manually.

Also, this chapter will explain the minimum legal level of free medical care. Firstly, in the early 21st century, regular schools were equipped with infirmaries where students could be treated free of charge. Thus, free minimum legal level medical care was part of the basic welfare system for Banselistic students. The denial of free minimum legal level health care would then deny the ability to access the minimum level of health care resources to those Banselistic students who do not have the will for class mobility or whose class mobility is impeded, leading to riots. Therefore, the authority needs to provide free minimum legal level health care to Banselistic students; furthermore, providing free minimum legal level health care to Banselistic students would help to reduce the amount of money issued and thus curb inflation.

Notably, while the measures in this section are effective in securing the basic daily needs of Banselistic students, they will still choose to finish the class mobility. Although social welfare is highly developed in Sweden and thus provides for the basic needs of the non-employed, Sweden still had an employment rate of 73.7% at the beginning of 2022, according to figures published by Statistics Sweden that year. Meanwhile, data released by Statistics Norway in 2022 shows that Norway, a high welfare country, also had an employment rate of 69.3% at the beginning of that year. These figures show that even though the authorities have improved the social welfare system to provide for the basic needs of citizens, most citizens are still active in their own employment, in other words, finishing the class mobility, as this increases their income.

Finally, the development and refinement of this paper's development measures will be discussed in this paragraph. Each of the measures in this paper needs to be guaranteed by law so that they are compulsory; at the same time, each of the measures in this paper needs to be improved in line with economic development in order to curb the growth of the Gini coefficient. For example, the quality and quantity of free food provided to Banselistic students should be improved.

Chapter Seven:

The Banselistic Culture

Culture refers to the mainstream micro-social ideology and the mainstream micro-subconscious, including their specific material carriers. The cultures vary according to different political systems, social nature, historical periods, geographic locations, and so forth. This chapter focuses on elaborating the mainstream micro-social ideology and mainstream micro-subconsciousness under the Ideological and Political System of Banselism.

To begin with, what will be explained in this paragraph is the sharp decline in the pressure of social competition. Compared with the early 21st century, the degree of social competition under the Ideological and Political System of Banselism will drop drastically. Because under the ideological and political system of Banselism, citizens are mainly engaged in innovative or creative production activities for material civilization or spiritual civilization. Innovative activity or creative activity is to open up an independent new direction, and because innovative activity or creative activity is strictly protected by law, no one can imitate or create the innovative or creative outcomes made by others without the permission of the original producer. In this case, there will be no competitors in the independent new direction, which will directly determine the significant decline in the degree of social competition, thereby greatly reducing the pressure on the life of the public, and therefore improving its quality of life.

In addition, what will be explained is the large-scale popularization of the Aristocratic Spirit. The Aristocratic Spirit mainly refers to the high attention and lofty pursuit of material civilization and spiritual civilization, which even includes the extreme pursuit of material civilization and spiritual civilization at the same time. Early in the early 21st century, the definition of 'aristocratic spirit' appeared in a large number of dictionaries. According to the prevailing definition of the term at that time, the spirit of aristocracy mainly includes the following content as well: To begin with, the believer of this concept must unswervingly struggle for the material wealth and also has a noble pursuit of material wealth, putting them into practice at the same time; in addition, the believer of it is ruthlessly disciplined and also cherishes honor; Apart from that, as a cutting-edge person in society, he or she tends to support disadvantaged groups and entails social responsibilities; Also, the believer has free will and an independent soul, intellectual and moral autonomy. The believer is also not enslaved to those with power and the opinions of the majority; Moreover, the individual who believes this concept has aristocratic moral sentiment and noble cultural spirit; Meanwhile, the person who has aristocratic spirit does not have material pleasure as his or her sole and ultimate aim, which can be demonstrated by the principles of economics—economics is based on the following two major premises: firstly, that wants are infinite and secondly, that resources are finite. The fact that finite material resources can never satisfy infinite material wants means that if an individual's ultimate goal is material enjoyment, then that individual's ultimate quest will be reduced to a fantasy, leading to Gnosticism, the belief that the real world is totally degenerate and empty. This would severely prevent individuals from finishing the class mobility, as their activities would then no longer serve the real world. As a result, aristocratic spirit requires people not to have material enjoyment as their sole and ultimate aim.

More specifically, the Banselistic class, the elite class, and even the capitalist class and all other social classes and strata are all evolved from the student class whose members initially belonged to the working class and a considerable part of the middle class, which means the majority of the society will consider more about the interest of the Banselistic student, which is a kind of disadvantaged group. This will stimulate the public to help the weak more and take responsibility of the whole society. In addition, Banselistic students need to build up developed critical thinking in order to do innovative and creative things, which will enable the Banselistic student to build up free will and independent soul. Meanwhile, Banselistic students also need to improve their products or accelerate the process of the class mobility by adjusting their outcomes based on the external feedback (this includes rejection and criticism) persistently, which will not only enable Banselistic students to build up a strong critical thinking but also enable them to build up a strong focus. This in turn will prevent Banselistic students from being enslaved to the opinion of the majority and those with power. At the same time, Dorothea Brande (1934) pointed out in her book *Becoming A Writer* (pp. 36-37) that becoming a writer—a member in the Banselistic class, consisted primarily in developing a writer's temperament: when negative emotions including jealousy, vanity, and a sense of Machiavellianism, as well as temperament, emerge, the temperament of the artist (in this case it mainly refers to the elite in the literary arts, but not exclusively the literary artist) is in serious trouble, which wastes energy and consumes emotion. This means that in order to finish the class mobility, Banselistic students will get rid of negative moods including jealousy, vanity, Machiavellianism, and anger, which will promote the popularization of the aristocratic spirit. On a deeper level, the different written works are irreplaceable because they create new knowledge and are protected by law under the respective authorship of the original authors. For instance, Liu Cixin cannot copy J.K. Rowling's *Harry Potter* again and get a publisher to publish it, claiming that it is him rather than J.K. Rowling who writes this book as this will infringe J.K. Rowling's copyright and authorship. This will also make the different works non-comparable as they cannot be rewritten and reproduced by other authors without highlighting the sources of them. At the same time, people do not stop buying the works of Liu Cixin, Haruki Murakami or Friedrich Nietzsche merely because J.K. Rowling's books are of extremely high quality, and readers do not refrain from buying other books only because Friedrich Nietzsche's works are of extremely high attainment—this means that at this point the creators of text-based works no longer need to compete with other writers or elites to compete for the market. This means that Banselistic students will therefore abolish the mind of rivalry: without comparison and vicious competition, jealousy will cease to exist, which will help Banselistic students to remove the psychological barriers to class mobility. At the same time, although external feedback (this includes rebuttals, refutations, and critiques) has a highly significant, and of course sometimes potentially highly negative effect on the class mobility of the Banselistic student, these Banselistic students still cannot fetishize and blindly obey external feedback. They can only critically and selectively evaluate and analyze external feedback to help them contribute new knowledge, in other words, to engage in class mobility, which is the most important reason why Banselistic students will directly abolish vanity.

Let us assume that Gareth—a Banselistic student, planned to write a book on philosophy. Gareth tells Andrew, Catherine, Charrison, Joseph and a range of other people (this even includes a small number of government officials), the general contents of the book. Both Andrew and Catherine considered the book to be deeply problematic and therefore refuted the points made by Gareth in the book. Charrison not only denies Gareth's philosophical views, but he also outright denied Gareth's congenital talents and therefore directly suggested Gareth to give up writing the book (yes, in the early 21st century, many citizens and even social elites in developing countries were highly fond of advising students, especially those who majored in the humanities or social sciences, to give up and stop creating new knowledge on the grounds of exam preparation.). Joseph and other people, after hearing Gareth's philosophical views, went on to direct personal attacks, snide remarks and rude abuse at Gareth, and even came close to fighting (this is something that happened a lot in many developing countries in the early 21st century, although it seems to be quite rare to see it happen in developed countries at that time). However, Gareth went home and calmly brainstormed with Andrew and Catherine via social media. Gareth revised his book in full accordance with suggestions provided by Andrew and Catherine respectively, until Andrew and Catherine both agreed that Gareth's views were not problematic. Meanwhile, although Charrison denied Gareth's congenital ability and talent in philosophy, Gareth revised his book based on Charrison's reasons for refutation. Moreover, since Joseph and other people attacked Gareth without providing specific reasons to refute the book, Gareth had to ignore the 'feedback' provided by Joseph and other people.

Eventually, under the cynicism from Joseph and a host of other opponents, Gareth published the book. The book quickly spread and became widely accepted and recognized in developing countries.

In this instance, if Gareth had been vain and therefore given too much weight to the opinions of Charrison, Joseph and other people (which in this fictional example would have been the majority opinion) and therefore stopped and abandoned writing the book, Gareth would not have been able to finish the class mobility. It is because Gareth valued critical thinking, defied the powers that be (although he faced many opponents, including a small number of government officials, but he did not back down), and was not bound and enslaved by the views of the majority (you read that right, Gareth wrote the book in spite of the majority suppressing him, although Gareth did not deliberately pander to them or try to change their views directly) that he made a valuable contribution to human civilization: his philosophical theories have effectively helped disadvantaged people in developing countries to defend their rights. The abolition of vanity on a large scale (which a focus on critical thinking is likely to help learners to do directly) is therefore inevitable. This will promote the spread of aristocratic spirit.

Furthermore, based on what Dorothea Brande has suggested in her book *Becoming A Writer* (pp.36-37), venality (i.e., the pursuit of material gain, material enjoyment and fame alone or an overemphasis on them), would prevent Banselistic students from gaining new inspiration and thus from finishing the class mobility. This means that Banselistic students will not have hedonism as their ultimate goal, and that Machiavellianism will be firmly suppressed, which will likewise contribute to the mass popularization of aristocratic spirit.

Consequently, although class mobility remains unavoidably complex and time-consuming under the Ideological and Political System of Banselism (See Volume One, Part Two, Chapter Two: The class mobility, for more details), the morality of the public will not be deteriorated as a result. For example, the temper of the Banselistic student will not become worse even if the class mobility is highly complex and relatively time-consuming. Instead, the morality and the righteousness will increase as a result. At the same time, while some argue that the complexity, difficulty and required amount of time of becoming a member in the Banselistic class like writers, scientists, etc., can exacerbate the stresses of civic life, and that the emphasis on critical and creative thinking at this time can lead to social problems such as civic moral decay, the morality of the public will still not be deteriorated. According to part one, chapter five of this volume, with the establishment of the normative mechanisms including reviewing and auditing systems for regulating the behaviors of Banselistic students and the Banselistic class by reviewing their outcomes, the Banselistic student and the Banselistic class will still need to ensure that their behaviors do not have a destructive effect on the social order. As a result, the morality of citizens will not be deteriorated.

After the Ideological and Political System of Banselism is put into practice, the aristocratic spirit will be popularized. This is because when all mechanized labor is replaced by AI, working-class members and a considerable part of the middle-class members will be transformed into the Banselistic student, and a large-scale class mobility will take place on this basis. Initially, these mechanized laborers generally had relatively low ideological qualities. The most fundamental motivation for their class mobility was the desire for material wealth, but this also requires them to carry out large-scale cultivation of their ideological realm, spiritual qualities, and moral sentiments. Therefore, under the Ideological and Political System of Banselism, the aristocratic spirit will be popularized on a large scale.

Apart from that, the heroism is going to be explained in the following paragraphs:

In this book, heroism refers to a spirit whose believers have the purpose of contributing in the Banselistic career including contributing to the innovation or creativity in the material civilization or spiritual civilization, maintaining a humanitarian spirit, a spirit of exploration, and a certain or high degree of sacrifice, patriotism or cosmopolitanism, innovation or creativity, and pragmatism during the process of struggling for the Banselistic career.

What is different from personal heroism and revolutionary heroism is that the idea of heroism is opposed to extreme individualism and extreme egoism. Meanwhile, the term includes, but is not limited to, armed revolutionary acts, and in most cases no armed revolution is carried out. This is directly determined by the high recognition of this term on humanitarian and humanistic thought.

The Banselistic class generally has one characteristic: it

believes in heroism. The Banselistic class, as the class or one of the largest groups and the strongest comprehensive strength, its leading ideas will be widely disseminated in society, forming a cultural atmosphere of heroism.

Also, the heroism religion is going to be explained in the following paragraphs. In some religious countries, when they implement the Ideological and Political System of Banselism, religion will be retained. However, due to the pressure of the Banselistic class, the retained religion will be required to be reformed. Specifically, the retained religion will have a certain feature of the Banselism, including the heroism.

Religion with heroism will make believers possess altruistic spirit and heroism spirit. This will effectively make religious culture react to politics, economy and promote social progress and economic development.

Meanwhile, explain humanism, humanitarianism, and the egalitarianism: With the large-scale class mobility of Banselistic students and the implementation of the Ideological and Political System of Banselism, the individual's subjective initiative, value, and role have been highlighted and valued unprecedentedly, which makes people begin to respect and recognize the individual's subjective initiative and role as well as value, thereby respecting and admiring 'people' and attaching great importance to the lives of 'people', thereby strengthening humanistic, humanitarian, and egalitarian ideas.

Finally, what will be explained is the utilitarianism. Utilitarianism refers to the high emphasis on maximum happiness and substantial influence. The believer has independent opinions, he or she does not obey, and does not believe in dogma and authority—that is, he or she attaches great importance to substantive influence and has developed critical thinking.

What is the same as the popularization of the micro mainstream ideology previously mentioned in this article is that the large-scale class mobility of the student class and the transferring of the center political power rights to the Banselistic class are the decisive reasons for the high popularization of utilitarianism. For instance, critical thinking is the foundation of innovative or creative thinking, because it is inevitable to critically analyze conventional and traditional knowledge when participating in innovative or creative activities. In this case, the importance of critical thinking will be stronger than ever, promoting the popularization of utilitarianism. However, since the Banselistic class is mainly evolved from the Banselistic students, most of whom were the mechanized labor who emphasized a lot on material wealth, the Banselistic class will also emphasize a lot on the biggest happiness and the actual gain of the material resources, while developing mental skills to finish the class mobility and therefore stimulating them to emphasize on the mental wealth as well, which also promotes the popularization of utilitarianism.

When there is a conflict between utilitarianism and aristocratic spirit, utilitarianism should be given priority, because aristocratic spirit is based on utilitarianism and serves utilitarianism. Because to begin with, the Banselistic student finishes class mobility out of utilitarian thinking rather than out of aristocratic spirit. The aristocratic spirit is only a phased product of their class mobility and becomes an important driving force when the product appears. However, the aristocratic spirit is not the initial driving force to promote the class movement of the Banselistic student; Also, in order to avoid the substantial loss caused by the lack of emphasis on the substantive influence, the aristocratic spirit serves utilitarianism. Therefore, as long as one cannot obey the utilitarian ideology, the nobility spirit ceases to exist. Therefore, when utilitarianism is antagonistic to the aristocratic spirit, utilitarianism will override the aristocratic spirit.

Meanwhile, utilitarianism is subordinate to democracy, humanitarianism, and egalitarianism. Take, for example, the Machiavellianism, which is the product of utilitarianism in the absence of constraints. Machiavellianism believes that as long as the purpose is moral, righteous, and correct, or can satisfy the greatest happiness, any means, including destructive means, can be used. Therefore, without democracy, humanitarianism, and egalitarianism to restrict utilitarianism; utilitarianism will become the Machiavellianism and therefore begin to undermine human rights and make them lose their morality and justice. Accordingly, when utilitarian ideas conflict with democracy, humanitarianism or egalitarianism, priority should be given to democracy and humanitarianism and egalitarianism.

Chapter Eight:

The Species Superiority

In this article, the term 'specie' refers to all living entities and all kinds of entities and virtual entities with autonomous consciousness, including all carbon-based civilizations, silicon-based civilizations, space humans (See Volume Five, Chapter One: The formation of the space human; for details.) and other civilizations. The superiority of a species refers to the intelligence level of it has, whose intensity is directly proportional to the intelligence level, and is directly determined by the intensity of the intelligence level.

To begin with, what will be explained in the following paragraphs is the Techno-Humanism. Techno-humanists believe that after the early 21st century, the human being will still be the most superior species and consciousness entities in the world; Also, technological humanists also believe that humans should continue to develop genetic engineering and other biotechnological methods in order to strengthen the dominance of human beings among all other species.

The concept of 'Techno-Humanism' is a commonly used term in academia. It was proposed by Yuval·Noah·Harari, a professor at the Hebrew University of Jerusalem, Israel in the book *Homo Deus* in 2015.

When AI technology has been popularized on a large scale, and all mechanized jobs are replaced by AI, human production activities will be concentrated on mental labor. At this time, the importance of intelligence level will be unprecedentedly strengthened.

Accordingly, with the continuous development and improvement of natural science and technology such as bioengineering technology, the continuous improvement of social productivity, the continuous development of social economy, and the continuous improvement of the market's potential demand for talents, the intellectual level of citizens will be compulsorily and passively demanded to be improved, that is, the improvement of their intelligence level will be firmly guaranteed.

Admittedly, the German Third Reich also planned to raise the intellectual level of its nation and therefore adopted the evolutionary humanist methodology on a large scale: Nazi Germany had slaughtered out its minority ethnics including Jews and Gypsies, German Third Reich had also executed disabled people including the mentally handicapped, and Nazi Germany had conducted Eingetragener Verein (Lebensborn) program to improve the superiority of its species. Nonetheless, the methodology of the evolutionary humanism will not be applied again on a large scale—the authorities will no longer be able to improve the superiority of the species by violent means including executing the disabled or minority ethnics. Therefore, according to the technological humanist methodology, the government would need to intervene artificially to directly enhance the intelligence level of individuals or fetuses that do not meet the standard of species superiority by means of appropriate bioengineering techniques.

Under such circumstances, the government will formulate a minimum level of intelligence standard system in the form of legislation to improve the intelligence of fetuses and citizens below this standard. Nonetheless, such legislation is based on relatively developed and relatively low-cost bioengineering technology.

The minimum level of intelligence standard system refers to the minimum legal level of citizen intelligence and fetal intelligence.

The minimum level of intelligence standard system also belongs to one of the clauses in the Basic Welfare System of the Ideological and Political System of Banselism. In order to implement the basic welfare system, the government not only needs to write it into the law as mentioned above but also needs to require all members of institutions, Banselistic students, and disadvantaged groups to undergo mandatory regular physical examinations, which include testing the level of intelligence. The specific date when the intelligence of all individuals will be tested is set by the government.

For example, a fetus whose intelligence level has not yet reached the minimum legal level. Before the birth, the government will use corresponding technical means to enhance the fetus's intelligence. Also, if there is an urgent issue that needs this fetus to be born before the fetus's intelligence level is raised to the minimum legal level in time, the government will adopt the corresponding biotechnological method after the birth of the fetus so as to raise his or her intelligence level to the lowest legal standard level.

Another example is a citizen whose intelligence has not

reached the minimum legal standard. After the compulsory physical examination report is completed and it is found that the citizen's intelligence level is lower than the minimum legal standard level, the government needs to use corresponding technical means to improve the citizen's intelligence level. For this reason, for the citizen, he or she can choose a date that meets his or her wishes within the available dates before the deadline to go to the relevant medical institution to increase the superiority of his or her species to the minimum legal level, or alternatively, after the deadline, the authority can arrange the date on this individual's behalf if this individual has not chosen the date when he or she wishes to rise his or her intellectual level. This individual may also apply for a delay in increasing his or her intellectual level in his or her convenient.

The above-mentioned Technological Humanistic measures have the following main positive effects: Firstly, they can effectively protect the human rights of all citizens and improve the protection of basic human rights. For example, the development right, the improvement of intellectual level will further reduce the innate obstacles to the development of citizens under the Ideological and Political System of Banselism; another example is the health right, which is also a basic human right. Former British Labor Party leader Jeremy Corbyn has once pointed out in the 2013 Oxford University Debate on 'Whether Socialism Works': that: "Every single one of you in this room at some point has benefited from the principles of the National Health Service, free at the point of use as a human right." Because the mandatory protection of citizens' intelligence is a mandatory improvement of the minimum legal medical system level, such measures are conducive to perfecting the protection of basic human rights. Also, such measures are conducive to further reducing citizens' life pressure and improving their quality of life as a whole. This is because taking innovative or creative production activities as the core driving force of the economy means that each producer is independently opening a new direction, and because the producer's innovative or creative achievements are protected by law, in this independent new direction, the producer does not have a competitor, and the improvement of the producer's intellectual level means that this producer can complete the establishment of new directions with less time and cost, which will help to effectively avoid external competitive pressure while improving their economic production efficiency at the same time, thereby further reducing their life pressure and improving their quality of life. Apart from that, improving citizens' minimum legal level of intelligence is conducive to strengthening the innate advantages of talents, thereby increasing corporate profits, and improving the operational efficiency of government agencies; Also, Improving the congenital ability and advantages of citizens is conducive to improving production efficiency of the entire economy, which in turn expands government revenue, etc. Furthermore, enhancing the superiority of the human species is conducive to enhancing human resistance to other higher civilizations.

This chapter will use and explain the following fictional example in order to further elaborate on the technological humanism under the Ideological and Political System of Banselism:

The fictional character of Silvano Dacia has been previously used in the second chapter of the first part of this volume. This paper will continue to use the example of this fictional character. Suppose that Silvano Dacia's country has developed a new injectable drug, which will help to raise the intellectual level of its citizens. If his country did not adopt a techno-humanist methodology, it would have taken Silvano Dacia more than ten years to invent his new tea tree and tea production technology. However, let us assume that his country adopts a techno-humanist methodology: that is, it is compulsory for citizens to be injected with the injectable drug free of charge until their intelligence level is raised to 200, and that Silvano Dacia's current intelligence level is 109, then, after the injection of the drug, he would only have to invest less than ten years to complete his class mobility, that is, to invent his new tea tree and tea leaves production technology. By this time, he would probably be able to make a fortune and a name for himself in his twenties. Notably, in the early 21st century, people always complained about the lack of money for young people. And we can see how this is an effective means of solving the issue that most young people lack money. And to take it to the extreme, suppose his country improved the injectable drug and made it mandatory for all citizens to receive it free of charge until the citizen's intelligence level rose to 450, then Silvano Dacia would have been able to develop the new tea tree and tea production technology by the time he was eight years old after receiving the drug compulsorily. You heard it right, a child, in this case, is already capable of earning pocket money and supporting his parents with such great means, this child no longer needs to be given pocket money by his parents, which will surely raise the fertility rate of the developed countries in the early 21st century again because it reduces the pressure on parents to raise children. More extremely, let's assume that his country developed a certain type of engineering and medical technology and that his country mandated all citizens receive free improvements to themselves from these two technologies until their intelligence level rises to 1550, then Silvano Dacia would be able to develop his new tea tree and tea production technology by the time he was three years old. Yes, in this fictional case, a child who had only just learned to act independently last year can change the world this year. This could lead to the creation of 'childism' whose definition is giving children aged not less than three and less than eighteen equal political rights with adults. Of course, this is merely 'what may happen in the long run' instead of 'what will absolutely happen in the future'.

In addition, what will be explained in the following paragraphs is the Species Superiority under the Dataism. Dataists believe that after the early 21st century, electronic algorithms, including artificial intelligence (AI), and other higher-level algorithms will replace humans as the rulers of species worldwide, and will enslave and rule humans, because the superiority of electronic algorithms is stronger than that of biochemical algorithms including human beings.

Nonetheless, unlike Dataism, this article believes that when the technology of man-machine integration is popularized on a large scale, humans will evolve into AI with autonomous consciousness, that is, the digital human. The digital human, which is the evolution of humans, will continue to increase their intelligence level rapidly, leading to a continuous leap in the superiority of their species (for details, see Volume Five, Chapter 1: The Formation of the space human). This is because the digital human has completely exceeded the constraints and limitations caused by the genetic carrier and organism on his or her intelligence enhancement—the evolution speed and update frequency of electronic algorithms are much higher than that of biochemical algorithms. Consequently, electronic algorithms will fully defeat biochemical algorithms. Such competitive pressure will stimulate the remaining individuals who have not yet finished evolving into the digital human to evolve into this species, and then continue to evolve to enhance their own species superiority.

Finally, what will be jointly elaborated on is the superiority of species under techno-humanism and dataism. In the initial stage, as an emerging technology, it is difficult for AI to defeat other biotechnological natural sciences and technologies. At this stage, it is more feasible to strengthen the superiority of human species by means of biotechnology than popularizing electronic algorithms. Therefore, in the initial stage, the superiority of species under the Techno-Humanism will be popularized on a large scale and continue to become more developed. Nevertheless, with the continuous development of AI technology, the advantages of electronic algorithms will be continuously highlighted, making the electronic algorithm to become more superior compared with biochemical algorithms. Under such circumstances, the superiority of species under Dataism will be popularized on a large scale and promote the continuous enhancement of species superiority of humans and their evolutions.

Chapter Nine:

The Banselistic Country

A banselistic country refers to a country that meets the following conditions at the same time: the center of political power is transferred to the Banselistic class, the knowledge economy has become the core economic driving force or one of the core economic driving forces, and the purely mechanized employment except for some employment in the entertainment industry are replaced by AI. All mechanized laborers, including the working class and some middle-class members, have become student-class members, and on this basis, the Ideological and Political System of Banselism is implemented. In other words, the authority has begun to actively protect the economic status, social status, and political status of the Banselistic class at the political and policy level.

To begin with, what will be explained in the following paragraphs is the difference between the banselistic country and the capitalist country. To begin with, the proportion of profits obtained by each class in unit production activities in total profits is different in banselistic countries and capitalist countries. Specifically, under the Ideological and Political System of Banselism, the bourgeoisie only obtains a small or considerable part of the profit in the per unit of production activities of the Banselistic class, while the Banselistic class can obtain the most profit in its own unit production activities. However, the ruling class in capitalist countries, the capitalist class, mainly obtains most of the profits from the unit production activities of the working class, while the working class can only obtain a small part of the profits from its unit production activities.

Also, the status of the working class under these two sets of different ideologies is different. Under the Ideological and Political System of Banselism, the working class will be able to transform into the Banselistic student, and on this basis, the vast majority of them will finish the class mobility; while under the capitalist system, the working class comes into being and engages in class struggle with the capitalist class in most capitalist countries.

Apart from that, there are differences in the relations between classes and strata in Banselistic countries and capitalist countries. Under the Ideological and Political System of Banselism, the working class will transform into other social classes, and all social classes, including the student class, the elite class, and the Banselistic class, are non-antagonistic to the capitalist class. However, under the capitalist system, there is antagonism between the bourgeoisie and the working class.

In addition, under the Ideological and Political System of Banselism, the Banselistic class belongs to one of the ruling classes or the only ruling class; while under the capitalist system, the bourgeoisie belongs to the only ruling class.

Also, what will be explained in the following paragraphs is the difference between the banselistic country and the socialist country.

To begin with, all mechanized employees in banselistic countries have been replaced by AI, while mechanized employees in socialist countries still exist.

Secondly, when the socialist country is constantly improving and transforming into a banselistic country for the transition to the communist system, the leading class will change from the proletariat to the student class. This is because the proletariat is transformed into the student class, and all cutting-edge talents are transformed from the student class. However, in socialist countries, the leading class is the proletariat.

Thirdly, when the socialist country has further improved its development and turned into a banselistic country, the state-owned high-tech industry has already defeated the private high-tech industry under the influence of the market competition mechanism (see Volume Two, Part Four, Chapter One: Regarding the state-owned economy, for details); while in socialist countries, under the socialist market economy system, private high-tech industries are still an important part of high-tech industries, while under the socialist planned economy system, state-owned high-tech industries belong to the only economic entity in high-tech industries.

Fourthly, most socialist countries prefer to advocate the overthrow of the bourgeois government through the armed revolution of the proletariat in order to realize the socialist system, thereby satisfying the interests of the proletariat and the broad masses of the people; while the Ideological and Political System of Banselism satisfies the interests of the proletariat by allowing AI to replace the proletariat and strengthen the class mobility, while opposing violent revolutions in most cases.

Apart from that, the countries that are suitable to conduct the Ideological and Political System of Banselism are going to be introduced.

The examples that will be firstly explained are Sweden and Switzerland.

In the early 21st century, high-welfare countries, including Sweden and Switzerland implemented high-welfare policies. To begin with, in Sweden and Switzerland, the income gap between those who are rich and those who are not economically advantaged is highly small—rounding off the decimal point, the Gini coefficient is about 30% or less than 30%. Secondly, they actively introduce natural science and technology talents from foreign countries and domestic countries, reducing taxes on scientific researchers and actively protecting their income. Thirdly, in these high-welfare countries, employed persons have higher incomes than non-employed persons and enjoy high welfare, but non-employed persons can also enjoy high welfare.

For this type of country, it needs to implement large-scale automation and popularize semi-commercial public housing to directly solve the employment problem in some areas; at the same time, it needs to continue to actively maintain the economic income and social status of the Banselistic class.

The examples that will be secondly illustrated are Germany and America.

In the early 21st century, Germany was the center of science and technology in Europe, and the United States was the center of science and technology in the world. They highly emphasized the importance of science and technology internally. Inventors have extremely high social status. At that time, these two representative countries had formed a social atmosphere that advocated technological innovation, and their economies were highly developed, and funds were highly sufficient, which would greatly promote the implementation of the Ideological and Political System of Banselism.

Germany and the United States need to further improve their new energy technology to solve the energy shortage problem faced by their large-scale implementation of automation, so as to promote the implementation of Banselism in Germany and the United States.

The third example that will be illustrated in this article is China. In the early 21st century, China was the country with the strongest overall national strength and the most developed economy among all socialist countries in the world. It implements a basic economic system with public ownership as the main body and the common development of multiple ownership economies. This includes the socialist market economic system. Although China is a developing country, China's funding conditions can enable it to implement large-scale automation. At that time, although China cultivated a social atmosphere that advocated technological innovation internally, and actively protected the income and social status of a large number of literary and written creators. However, at that time, the income of most of the employees in China who made innovations in philosophy or social science disciplines other than economics could hardly exceed the social average level. In the long run, the lack of cultural soft power in this part would lead to considerable constraints to the improvement of their overall national power.

Accordingly, China needs to take the following measures: Firstly, China needs to improve its state-owned high-tech industry management system based on the Volume 2, Part 4, Chapter 1 of this book. Secondly, China needs to further develop new energy technologies to promote automation on a large scale; Thirdly, China needs to popularize semi-commercial public housing in order to greatly guarantee the living conditions and stable income at the bottom of society, and further strengthen the class mobility of the society, reflecting the socialist nature of the country; In addition, China needs to further develop philosophy and social sciences, which includes increasing the disposable income for the employees in these disciplines.

Finally, what will be explained in this paragraph is the summary of the above-mentioned countries. The above-mentioned representative countries all have the issue of insufficient new energy technology. Therefore, the above-mentioned countries need to further develop new energy technology to meet the new energy technology foundation required for large-scale implementation of automation technology. Meanwhile, the above-mentioned countries need to promote further economic development by including, but not limited to, specific measures provided in this chapter and the second volume of this book.

Chapter Ten:

The Purpose

The purpose of the ideological and political system of Banselism is different from that of all the ideological and political systems conducted in the early 21st century. Its purpose is as follows:

One is to end the class struggle. In the countries where the capitalist system is implemented in the early 21st century, the implementation of the ideological and political system of Banselism will consolidate the interests of the bourgeoisie in an unprecedented way and enable the proletariat—a social class consisting of the working class and the middle class, to evolve into the Banselistic class, the elite class, the bureaucratic class, and the EIW strata. This will completely liberate the proletariat, thereby ending the class struggle ultimately and solving that class struggle, which has been the issue over centuries.

The second is to solve the issue of unequal distribution of

social resources based on increasing the material wealth of all citizens. Since all employees who completely do not need innovative or creative ability are replaced by AI, the market's demand for innovative or creative products and labor has risen unprecedentedly. Before the student class completes the class mobility, this will, together with the extremely significant finiteness of corresponding innovative or creative products and talents, determine the unprecedented increase in the income of the Banselistic class and the elite class. When the student class completes the class mobility, the innovative or creative products and talents that each class can provide are also still relatively limited, and the vast majority of the student class becomes the member in the Banselistic class, and the market demand is mainly concentrated in the Banselistic class, including the talents, labor products, and products provided by this social class. Consequently, the material wealth of the vast majority of citizens can be unprecedentedly increased. Also, in order to increase profits by attracting relevant innovative or creative talents and purchasing as many innovative or creative products or technics as possible, the income gap between business owners and the Banselistic class can be effectively reduced, which will help to solve the issue of uneven distribution of social resources based on the material wealth of all citizens.

The third is to reduce the degree of social competition in order to reduce the pressure on citizens' lives, thereby improving citizens' living standards. Since the knowledge economy has become the core driving force of the economy under the Ideological and Political System of Banselism, the vast majority of producers will increase their material wealth through innovative or creative production, which will reduce the degree of social competition, because all those producers are opening up new directions independently, and there will be no competitors in these new directions—because the innovative or creative achievements of these producers are protected by law, and no one can imitate without permission.

The fourth is to develop various innovations based on adequate supervision, thereby increasing the material and spiritual wealth of all citizens in an unprecedented manner. Since the student class accounts for the vast majority of the population before completing the class mobility, and when it completes the class mobility, the majority of its members will become members in the Banselistic class through innovative or creative production activities, which will unprecedently increase the innovative or creative results in both the spiritual civilization and the material civilization. Also, with adequate supervision to effectively avoid destructive innovation or the output of creating results, material wealth and spiritual wealth will increase unprecedentedly.

The fifth is to end the struggles in political system, ideologies, and philosophical struggles of different countries whose social nature is different, and then unify the world in terms of political system, ideology, and philosophy, thereby promoting the stability of the world situation to a certain extent. Before the implementation of Banselism, the capitalist and socialist countries were in a state of opposition in terms of political system, ideology, and philosophy. However, the Ideological and Political System of Banselism and its ideology, as well as its philosophical system are non-antagonistic to that of capitalism and socialism. This can end these struggles when Banselism is implemented in capitalist and socialist countries, thereby promoting the stability of the world situation to a certain extent.

Take Germany as an example. Germany, a region that was once composed of 314 states, first completed its cultural and ideological unity: for example, the Eastern Expedition of the

First French Empire, Napoleon, the first emperor of France at the time, carried out an armed aggression against the states in the German region, which directly impacted the local feudal order, including feudal culture, in the form of force. Meanwhile, the French First Empire also actively spread and advocated the mainstream ideology and philosophy of the French Revolution on this basis, which in turn unified these states in the German region ideologically and philosophically. This has increased the stability of the situation in the German region to a certain extent, because these cases also indirectly promoted the strengthening of the nationalist consciousness in the German region—that is, the beginning of the search for a unified Germany, which in turn promoted the subsequent changes and unification of the German region at the political level.

Also, with regard to politics, a considerable number of states in Germany started the capitalist revolution in 1848. Although this revolution ended in failure, it had already shaken the feudal character of the political system in the German region; and the three-times dynasty war launched by Prussia directly overthrew the feudal ideological and political system in the German region, which directly stabilized the political situation in the German region as never before.

The same is true for the 21st century. The unity of the political system, ideology, and philosophy of capitalist and socialist countries around the world is also conducive to the stability of the world situation.

But at the same time, in academia, the country, under the guidance of the Ideological and Political System of Banselism, still allows any legitimate school to criticize the Ideological and Political System of Banselism. On the one hand, this enables the ideological and political system to be continuously improved by exposing its loopholes and deficiencies; on the other hand, a high degree of freedom of speech is conducive to lead to a substantial increase in innovative or creative spiritual wealth, thereby increasing the spiritual wealth of all citizens.

The sixth is to defend the absolute dominance of human civilization between different species and higher civilizations. The implementation of the Ideological and Political System of Banselism will promote the development of various technologies, including military technology, AI technology for the combination of man and machine, and aerospace technology, so as to enable human civilization to build up an absolute dominance among the various species.

The seventh is to promote interstellar colonization to solve the problem of insufficient land resources. The land resources of the earth are limited, but the earth's population continues to grow, which will continue to aggravate the tension and shortage of land resources. The continuous development of technologies such as military technology and aerospace technology can strengthen the ability of surface countries to explore and develop other planets, thereby effectively solving the problem of insufficient land resources.

Part Two:

The Condition

Chapter One:

The Automation

In the Ideological and Political System of Banselism, the term 'Automation' refers to a situation wherein the Artificial Intelligence (AI) replaces the employed who do not apply innovation and creativity at all during the process of working, which has historical inevitability.

To begin with, what will be explained in this paragraph is why it is inevitable for the AI to replace all the manual workers. With the development of the technology of AI, unmanned robots will replace manual labor, including the street cleaner, factory workers, tenant peasants, waiters, cashiers, receptionists, the cooks who completely do manual work, and so forth. For instance, the cooks who merely do the manual tasks. What is different from the human beings is that the systems of the AI, such as the visual system, are highly digital. Specifically, AI can accurately measure all units of measurement to three or more decimal points. Length, for example, can be accurate to millimeters or more. Time, for example, can be correct to minutes or seconds when human beings measure it, AI, however, is able to measure time to seconds, milliseconds or even more microscopic units of measurement. In addition, AI works for longer hours compared with human beings, which means all the manual workers, including the low-skilled manual cooks will be replaced by AI.

The cooks, however, will neither become joblessness nor the Banselistic student. Instead, they can begin to do other kinds of works that is relevant to doing the investigation about the cooking. For instance, they can become the investigators of the cuisines, who can constantly adjust the recipes or develop new kinds of dishes so as to engage in the innovation or new production of food, while the AI is responsible for the automated production of the dishes based on these innovative or creative recipes.

In addition, the automation will also inevitably replace the mental laborer who is not innovative or creative at all. If the employed merely applies the conventional knowledge or concepts instead of innovation or creativity during the process of working, he or she will be inevitably replaced by the AI. Early in the 21st century, the AI had already established the ability of replacing the mental laborer who was not innovative or creative. For instance, the YueFu robot invented by HUAWEI in 2019 was able to write poems and poetry. Another example is the Avatar Framework invented by Microsoft. The Avatar Framework had succeeded in publishing a collection of poems named as The Sunshine Lost Windows, and all the works published by the Avatar Framework have sold over one million copies.

Here are four main reasons why the AI had not been applied on a large scale early in the 21st century. To begin with, the costs of producing AI were relatively high, while there were relatively not enough funds to apply AI on a large scale. Secondly, the cost of production of the new energy technologies was relatively high, which meant that the authorities were not able to apply the technology of renewable energy on a large scale so as to use AI on a grand scale. Thirdly, the technology of the internet security was not enough to enable the economy to largely use the AI. Fourthly, the mass popularization of AI can lead to certain social issues such as the increased unemployment rate caused by the technological unemployment when relevant solutions and methods were absent, in this case, the absence of a solution to the potential social problems that may be caused by the large-scale use of the AI obstructed the economy from popularizing the AI massively early in the 21st century.

Here, I will explain the historical inevitability of the replacement of mechanized labor. In 2015, the University of Oxford and the University of Yale interviewed 352 AI researchers regarding when AI will take over from human workers. The result of this survey shows the following information: Firstly, translators will be replaced by the AI language translation system by 2024. Secondly, AI will be able to write essays at a high-school level by 2026. Thirdly, by 2027, AI will also be capable enough to drive vehicles. Fourthly, the retail field will be run by AI by 2031. Fifthly, AI will be able to write bestsellers by 2049. Sixthly, surgeons will be replaced by AI by 2053.

When AI succeeds in replacing the surgeons, all mechanized labors are replaced by AI, which means the automation, in this case, has been popularized successfully. Meanwhile, succeeding in applying automation on a large scale also means that the technological and economic basis for conducting the Ideological and Political System of Banselism has been built up.

In addition, the AI that requires manual operation, including manual-acting robots, will be eliminated rather than popularized on a large scale, because its superiority is far lower than that of the fully automated AI. For example, Israel's Iron Dome defense system, which is fully automated by artificial intelligence for 24 hours per day, had overall performance and actual combat effect that was better than that of the missile defense systems of most countries in the Middle East, as most Middle East countries' missile defense systems required manual operation at that time.

Next, I will explain the solution of the network security risks that may be caused when applying the automation. In 2019, the 'Mozi' satellite was successfully launched by China, which indicated that the quantum communication technology was being applied and was gradually popularized. Quantum cannot be copied, which prevents the code, password, and relevant encrypted information from being copied or stolen. Meanwhile, according to the Heisenberg Uncertainty Principle, in a quantum mechanical system, the velocity and the position of particles including that of the quantum cannot be observed at the same time, which means the position of the quantum and the momentum have indeterminacy, increasing the difficulty of stealing quantum information. Also, the quantum whose radius of the circumscribed sphere equal to the Planck length, including the photon, cannot be divided, which in turn will directly build up the absolute security of quantum communication technology, resolving the network security technical problems faced by the large-scale popularization of the automation technology. Therefore, the loopholes on the internet of the automation can be filled.

Apart from that, the issue of energy will be resolved ultimately to lead to large-scale automation. Although in the early 21st century, the earth's new energy technology was not developed enough. In this case, the total amount of the non-renewable energy and renewable energy on the earth were not enough to lead to the large-scale implementation of automation. However, the technology of renewable energy will become developed enough to enable the economy to apply the automation on a large scale, with examples as follows:

To begin with, the conversation rate of solar energy is constantly increasing. According to news published by the University of New South Wales in Australia on December 8, 2014: In 2014, the University of New South Wales in Australia successfully developed a solar energy conversion system with a conversion rate of up to 40%. At that time, it had successfully irradiated more than 40% of the sunlight in the solar system into electricity. The project was funded by the Australian Renewable Energy Agency (ARENA) and was supported by the Australia–U.S. Institute of Advanced Photovoltaics (AUSIAPV). The CEO of ARENA Ivor Frischknecht mentioned that this achievement is another world-first research and development in Australia and further proves the value of investing in Australia's renewable energy creativity. "We hope to see this local innovation take the next step from prototype to pilot-scale demonstration. Ultimately, more efficient commercial solar power plants will make renewable energy cheaper, thereby increasing its competitiveness." When the cost of large-scale popularization of new solar technology is reduced to a certain level, the new energy technology foundation required for the large-scale popularization of automation will be established, which will promote the large-scale popularization of artificial intelligence technology.

Also, compressed air power generation technology is constantly becoming more developed. In 2017, Chongqing Jing Tian Energy Investment Group Co., Ltd. (JONTIA) established a compressed air power generation device. According to the relevant person in charge of the company, the conversion rate of the compressed air power equipment in 2017 was as high as 60%, and after large-scale production, the conversion rate is expected to reach 65%. This type of power generation equipment can solve the problem of storage of bottom of the city power, which is called 'abandoned electricity' in the power industry. The air storage power generation system can be used to store this part of the power and supplement it during the peak period of power consumption. Then, when the cost of producing the device is reduced to a certain level, it will be able to be popularized on a large scale to meet the energy technical conditions required for the large-scale popularization of artificial intelligence technology.

Finally, the reasons why the automation has not been realized in the early 21st century and the historical inevitability of large-scale implementation of automation will be explained. It is undeniable that the earth's energy is relatively limited, and the implementation of 'automation' referred to in this article requires large-scale energy consumption. At the beginning of the 21st century, the relative insufficiency of energy technology obstructed the scientific and technological foundation of the automation from fully established, which is why the Ideological and Political System of Banselism had not been formally implemented yet in the early 21st century. Nevertheless, all the phenomenon listed above indicate that: Firstly, the ability of artificial intelligence to replace all kinds of mechanized employees is continuously improving; Secondly, the network security problems faced by the popularization of automation technology are gradually being solved—because quantum communication technology is being applied more and more frequently; Thirdly, renewable energy technology is constantly developing: With the development of renewable energy technology, the basis for large-scale implementation of new energy technology for automation will be available. Therefore, the automation will gradually be implemented on a large scale over time, which is historically inevitable.

Chapter Two:

The Class Mobility

When automation begins to be implemented on a large scale and all mechanized labor is replaced, the part of the proletariat that has not been replaced by AI will be directly transformed into the bourgeoisie or the elite, because at this time they just need to engage in activities involving the employment relationship, therein they hire other labors or management activities for production. For example, wool and meat producers in Australia and the United States will no longer need to perform purely mechanized labor when AI technology is popularized on a large scale. On the contrary, they only need to manage the farm and enhance their core competitive advantages by funding the R&D.

Also, the part of the proletarians replaced by AI will automatically transform into the student class. At this point, they are still at the bottom of society, and they need to get jobs that suit their specific circumstances—they need to move to other social classes.

Due to the limitations of human civilization consciousness, the limitations of subjective initiative, and the lack of social productivity in the early 21st century, class mobility cannot be completed in a short period of time. It requires proletarians from 20 years to approximately half a century to complete it. It may even take longer to complete the class mobility. The approximate range of this part of the time is measured by the approximate age range of the researchers.

To begin with, what will be explained in the following paragraphs is the reason for measuring the approximate range of time required for the class mobility of the Banselistic student based on the approximate age range of the scientific research personnel.

Since the proletariat generally does not have a foundation in the field of innovation or creativity, when the proletariat is automatically transformed into the Banselistic student, it generally does not have a foundation in its congenitally advantaged field.

Meanwhile, in the early 21st century, all newborn babies who use organisms as a carrier do not have a foundation in their superior areas, and they also need to spend corresponding time to solve their own employment problems.

From the perspective of class mobility, the two groups mentioned above are highly similar to a considerable extent. Although the above two groups correspond to different age groups and different age groups have different learning abilities, the continuous development of smart electronic device technology and Internet technology can make up for the deterioration of middle-aged or the aged learners' memory ability to help them finish the class mobility—For example, using smart phones and the Internet to help the student class gain knowledge and record the corresponding knowledge in memos and other documents. Meanwhile, most of the Banselistic students were originally manual workers, and manual work has relatively high requirements for practitioners' hands-on ability, which means that most of them have relatively strong hands-on ability. Therefore, it is relatively scientifically significant to use the approximate age range of scientific researchers to measure the reference value of the time range required for the class mobility of Banselistic students.

The significant similarity between these two phenomena and the scientific nature of the approximate range of the time required for class mobility of Banselistic students as measured by the approximate range of the age of scientific researchers make this article use the average age of scientific researchers in the early 21st century to measure the reference value of the time required for the class mobility of the Banselistic student.

In addition, what will be explained in the following paragraphs is the reference value of the approximate time range required for the class mobility of the Banselistic student. To begin with, take Yifei Shen from mainland China in the early 21st century as an example. He was awarded the world's top IEEEDSP Best Student Paper Award in 2016, which made him the core researcher of 5G technology at the age of 19; another example is Yichen Shen, in 2014, when he was only 25 years old, he published a paper 'Optical Broadband Angular Selectivity' in the academic journal 'Science' published by the American Association for the Advancement of Science. For the very first time, he accomplished control of the direction of light propagation on the material scale.

The above two examples show that it takes about twenty years for Banselistic students who are able to develop their consciousness relatively quickly to finish the class mobility.

In addition, take Albert Einstein as an example, who put forward a new academic theory—the theory of relativity at the age of 26; and Isaac Newton, who became a member of the Royal Academy of Sciences in 1689 at the age of 46. These two classic examples show that for most Banselistic students, it takes about 30 to 50 years for the class mobility.

Accordingly, overall, it takes about 20 to 50 years for the Banselistic student to finish the class mobility.

As for those Banselistic students who do not have the ability or willingness to finish the class mobility, they can only maintain their living standard through the social welfare system.

Apart from that, what will be explained is the way of calculating the reference value of the proportion of scientific research personnel in the total population, the reference value of the total scientific research personnel under the Ideological and Political System of Banselism.

The formula for the reference value of the proportion of scientific research personnel in the total population is the number of scientific researchers in the same year in the early 21st century ÷ the population educated (higher education) in the same year in the early 21st century = the proportion of scientific researchers in the total population under the Ideological and Political System of Banselism.

The 'educated population' in this article refers to the population who received a bachelor's degree or above in the early 21st century, while under the Ideological and Political System of Banselism, it refers to the banselistic education. The educated population under the Ideological and Political System of Banselism is the total population, because under the Ideological and Political System of Banselism, the large-scale popularization of automation technology has enabled all individuals to receive the banselistic education, so the educated population at this time will automatically rise to the total population.

The reasoning process of the formula is: The number of scientific researchers in the same year in the early 21st century ÷ the educated population in the same year in the early 21st century = the number of scientific researchers under the Ideological and Political System of Banselism ÷ the educated population under the Ideological and Political System of Banselism, that is, the total Population, substituting the total population number into this formula : the number of scientific researchers in the same year in the early 21st century ÷ the number of educated population in the same year in the early 21st century = the number of scientific researchers under the Ideological and Political System of Banselism÷ the total population. This means that it is equivalent to the proportion of scientific research personnel in the total population under the Ideological and Political System of Banselism.

In all the educated population in the early 21st century, they include both those who are willing to obtain a job for themselves, and those who do not have the willingness to obtain jobs for themselves, as well as those who do not have the ability to obtain a job for themselves; on the other hand, the Banselistic student also includes those who are willing to gain an official job, those who do not have the willingness to obtain official jobs, and those who do not have the ability to obtain jobs. The characteristics of Banselistic students' internal members are similar to those of the educated population in the early 21st century. Coupled with the superiority of the Banselistic students, the proportion of scientific researchers in the educated population will not be less than in the early 21st century when completing the class mobility, but greater than or equal to it.

Therefore, it is relatively scientific to use the above methods to calculate the reference value of the proportion of scientific research personnel in the total population under the

Ideological and Political System of Banselism.

But its correctness is not absolute. It has relative correctness, because this is only a reference value generated after the trend of the same year in the early 21st century, and the same country and region face different factors in each different year, and their development status is not completely coincident in different years, so this formula merely has a relative accuracy.

The formula for the reference number of scientific researchers under the Ideological and Political System of Banselism is the number of scientific researchers in the same year in the early 21st century ÷ the population with education in the same year in the early 21st century × the total population in the same year in the early 21st century = The reference value of the number of scientific researchers under the Ideological and Political System of Banselism.

The reasoning process of the formula is: the number of scientific research personnel in the same year in the early 21st century ÷ the number of educated population in the same year in the early 21st century × total population = the reference value of the number of scientific researchers under the Ideological and Political System of Banselism ÷ The number of the educated population under the Ideological and Political System of Banselism × the total population. Among them, under the Ideological and Political System of Banselism, all individuals receive the banselistic education, and the educated population is the total population. Therefore, the formula can be simplified as: the number of scientific researchers in the same year in the early 21st century ÷ the number of educated populations in the early 21st century × the total population = the reference value of the number of scientific researchers under the Ideological and Political System of Banselism.

In addition, the number of scientific researchers in the same year in the early 21st century ÷ the proportion of the population with education in the total population in the same year in the early 21st century = the number of scientific researchers under the Ideological and Political System of Banselism.

The reasoning process is the number of scientific researchers in the same year in the early 21st century ÷ the proportion of the population with education in the total population in the same year in the early 21st century = the number of scientific researchers under the Ideological and Political System of Banselism ÷ the educated population under the Ideological and Political System of Banselism. Since the proportion of the educated population under the Ideological and Political System of Banselism is 100%, so the number of scientific researchers in the same year in the early 21st century ÷ the population with education in the same year in the early 21st century accounted for the total population Proportion = the number of scientific researchers under the Ideological and Political System of Banselism.

Under the Ideological and Political System of Banselism, the number of educated populations is the total number. With the superiority of Banselistic students, when they complete the class mobility, the number of scientific researchers as a proportion of the educated population will not be lower than the proportion of scientific researchers in the number of educated populations in the early 21st century. Hence, the above calculation methods are also relatively accurate and referential.

The following is the approximate range of the reference value of the number of scientific researchers and the proportion of scientific researchers in the total population of some different types of countries and regions under the Ideological and Political System of Banselism:

To begin with, what will be explained is the approximate

reference value range for the proportion of scientific researchers in its total population in the West(See Volume Two, Part One, Chapter One: The reclassification of western countries, for details): Under the Ideological and Political System of Banselism, there are obvious differences in the number of scientific research personnel and the proportion of scientific research personnel in the total population in different Western countries or regions; and in order to reflect the superiority of the Ideological and Political System of Banselism, for the calculation of the range of the reference value, this article will first calculate the number of researchers who have a relatively large reference value, and then calculate the value that is relatively small.

The first example is the European Union.

In the European Union in 2018, the number of scientific researchers between the ages of 25 and 64 was 17.2 million, accounting for about 23% of all practitioners in the entire technical sector (data source: Eurostat); and in 2018 data released by Eurostat shows that there were approximately 512.4 million people in the EU in 2018, and at the same time, approximately 40% of the EU's population has a bachelor's degree or above.

Accordingly, the educated population in the European Union is approximately: 512.4 million × 40% = 204.96 million; the proportion of scientific researchers in the educated population is: 172.0 million ÷ 204.96 million ≈ 8.4%—according to the development trend in 2018, under the Ideological and Political System of Banselism, approximately 8.4% of the people in the EU will serve as R&D personnel; then under the Ideological and Political System of Banselism, the reference value of the number of scientific researchers is: 512.4 million people × 8.4% ≈ 43 million people, or approximately 43 million people.

Alternatively, it can be calculated as: 167.2 million people ÷ 40% = 430 million people. And the remaining part of this article will uniformly use this relatively simple calculation method to calculate the reference value of the corresponding number of scientific research personnel under the Ideological and Political System of Banselism.

The second example is the UK. According to data released by the National Bureau of Statistics of the United Kingdom in 2018: Of the total population of the United Kingdom of approximately 66.46 million people, approximately 23% have received a bachelor's degree (OECD, 2021); Meanwhile, Eurostat released: The number of scientific researchers in the United Kingdom is as high as 3.3 million, ranking first in the European Union. Then, based solely on the development trend of the United Kingdom in 2018, under the Ideological and Political System of Banselism, the United Kingdom will have about 14,347,826 scientific researchers, because: 3.3 million ÷ 23% ≈ 14,347,826; and 14,347,826 ÷ 66,460,300 ≈ 21.59%, which means that, according to the development trend in 2018, about 14,347,826 individuals in the United Kingdom will become scientific researchers under the Ideological and Political System of Banselism, accounting for approximately 21.59% of the total population.

Another example is America. According to data released by the U.S. Census Bureau in 2016, there were approximately 324 million people in the United States at the end of 2016 and the beginning of 2017, of which approximately 33.4% were educated (data source: Duffin. E. 2021); in addition, in 2016, there were approximately 6. 9 million scientific researchers in the United States (data source: U.S. Congressional Research Service).

6.9 million ÷ 45.67% ≈ 15.1084 million—under the Ideological and Political System of Banselism, there will be approximately 15.1084 million scientific researchers in the United States, and 15.1084 million ÷ 324 million people ≈ 4.67%—under the Ideological and Political System of Banselism, approximately 4.67% of the people in the United States will work as scientific researchers.

Overall, in the West, approximately 4.67—21.59% of the total population will work as scientific researchers under the Ideological and Political system of Banselism.

However, researchers are only a part of technical R&D personnel; and technical personnel in the United States are mainly scattered in universities and enterprises rather than national scientific research institutions, so in the early 21st century, the number of technical personnel in the United States is not less than that of various European countries. At that time, its level of science and technology still ranked at first place in the world.

In addition, for countries with an undergraduate rate higher than 50%, such as South Korea, under the condition of sufficient funding and educational resources, they can promote the completion of the class mobility of Banselistic students through large-scale popularization of higher education.

Secondly, what will be explained is the proportion of scientific researchers in the total population in China under the Ideological and Political System of Banselism. In 2018, there were approximately 1.4 billion people in China (Source: National Bureau of Statistics of China in 2018), of which approximately 8% (1.4 billion people × 8% = 112 million people) were holding undergraduate or above attainments (Source: OECD in 2018), and 4.19 million were scientific researchers (Source: 2018 National Bureau of Statistics of China).

Hence, 4.19 million people ÷ 112 million people ≈ 3.7%—

under the Ideological and Political System of Banselism, about 3.7% of the total population will be occupied by scientific researchers; apart from that, 4.19 million people ÷ 8% ≈ 52.375 million—under the Ideological and Political System of Banselism, approximately 52.375 million people will work as scientific researchers in China.

Therefore, based solely on the development trend in 2018, under the Ideological and Political System of Banselism, there will be approximately 8% of people working as scientific researchers in China—approximately 52.375 million people.

Thirdly, what will be explained is the ratio of the number of scientific researchers in the high-welfare country (See Volume Two, Part Two, Chapter One for details) to its total population and the approximate reference range of the number of scientific researchers. The first example is Finland.

According to data released by the World Bank in 2017: In 2017, there were 5.5082 million people in Finland, 41% of whom had a tertiary degree (data source: OECD); in addition, the statistics released by World Bank in 2021 shows that there were approximately 36,000 scientific researchers in Finland in 2017.

It can be concluded that: 36,000 ÷ 41% ≈ 87,805—according to the development trend in 2017, under the Ideological and Political System of Banselism, Finland will have approximately 87,805 scientific researchers; and 8.7805 ÷ 5.5082 million People ≈ 1.6%—in accordance with the development trend in 2017, under the Ideological and political system of Banselism, there will be approximately 1.6% of Finland's people who work as scientific researchers.

The second example is Switzerland. According to data released by the World Bank in 2017: The total population of Switzerland is approximately 8,451,800, of which 39% have received a bachelor's degree or above (data source: World

Economic Cooperation Organization), and there are approximately 46,000 employed researchers (data source: World Bank). 46,000 ÷ 39% ≈ 118,000, and 118,000 ÷ 8,451,800 ≈ 1.4%—according to the 2017 development trend, when Banselistic students complete the class mobility, there will be approximately 118,000 scientific researchers in Switzerland, accounting for about 1.4% of the total population.

Therefore, in summary, when the Banselistic students finish the class mobility, in the high-welfare countries such as Northern Europe and Switzerland, there will be approximately 1%—2% of the total population dominated by the scientific researchers.

Apart from that, what will be explained is the extension of the scope of use of the above formula. Not only for researchers, the above formulas can also be extended to: The number of employees in the same type of occupation in the early 21st century ÷ the population with education in the same year in the early 21st century = the proportion of the number of employees in the same type of occupation in the total population under the Ideological and Political System of Banselism; The number of employees in the same type of occupation in the early 21st century ÷ the population with education in the same year in the early 21st century × the total population in the same year in the early 21st century = the reference value of the number of employees of the same type under the Ideological and Political System of Banselism; the number of employees in the same type of occupation in the early 21st century ÷ the proportion of the population with education in the total population in the same year in the early 21st century = the number of employees in the same type of occupation under the Ideological and Political System of Banselism.

For example, in 2018, the practitioners of the entire technical sector in the EU: Since the number of scientific researchers was 17.2 million (data source: Eurostat) and it was 23% of all practitioners in the entire technical sector (data source: Eurostat), the total number of practitioners in the entire technical sector was about 17.2 million ÷ 23% ≈ 74.783 million. Also, according to the data of Eurostat in 2018: in 2018, approximately 40% of the EU's population had a bachelor's degree or above. Consequently, 74.783 million ÷ 40% ≈ 187 million people—according to the development trend of the EU in 2018, after the Banselistic students complete the class mobility, there will be approximately 187 million people in the EU who work in the entire technology sector. And there were about 512.4 million people in the EU (data source: Eurostat in 2018), so: 187 million people ÷ 512.4 million people ≈ 36.5%—according to this development trend, under the ideological and political system of Banselism, about 36.5% of people in the EU will work in the entire technology sector.

In addition, what will be explained is improving the accuracy of the above formula by using the linear regression equation.

According to data released by Eurostat in 2016, there were approximately 15.166 million scientific researchers in the EU that year, and approximately 39.1% of the people received higher education that year, so 15.166 million ÷ 39.1% ≈ 38.8 million—according to this, the development trend that year shows that when the Ideological and Political System of Banselism is implemented, there will be approximately 38.8 million people working as scientific researchers in the EU.

Also, according to data released by Eurostat in 2017, there were approximately 16,517,300 scientific researchers in the EU in 2017, and approximately 39.1% of people in the EU had received higher education in 2017. Then, 16,517,300 people ÷ 39.1% ≈ 42.2 million—according to the development trend in

2017, when the Ideological and Political System of Banselism is conducted, there will be approximately 42.2 million people in the EU who engage in scientific research employment.

The data released by Eurostat also shows that in 2018, there were a total of 171,154 million people in the European Union serving as scientific researchers, and 40% of the total population had received higher education. Then, 171.54 million people ÷ 40% ≈ 442.9 million people—according to the development trend that year, the EU will have approximately 224.9 million scientific researchers when implementing the Ideological and Political System of Banselism.

According to the data released by Eurostat in 2019, in accordance with the development trend of that year, under the Ideological and Political System of Banselism, the number of scientific researchers in the EU that year (17.78387 million) ÷ the undergraduate rate of that year (40.3 %)≈444.3 million people.

So far, the data that is required for calculating the anticipated number of scientific researchers of EU at a certain point(time) has gathered.

According to the commonly used standards in mathematics in the early 21st century, suppose y^= the number of scientific when successfully implementing the Ideological and Political System of Banselism at the specific point of time, and x=time (years), y^=b^· x + a, b^=∑(xi-average value of x)(yi-average value of y)/∑(xi-average value of x)^2, a^=average value of y-b^·(average value of x) . Under such conditions, the average value of x is (2016+2017+2018+2019)÷4=2017.5, and the average value of y is (38.8 million+42.2 million+42.9 million+44.3 million)÷4=42.05 million. Substituting the average value of x, the average value of y, and the number of scientific researchers when succeeding implementing the

Ideological and Political System of Banselism under the development trend of each year from 2016 to 2019 into b^, the solution of b^ = 0.0172 million. Consequently, a^ is equal to 0.4205-0.0172·2017.5=-34.2805.

Hence, this formula is y^=0.0172x-34.2805.

Assuming that the European Union successfully implement the ideological and political system of Banselism in 2053, then substitute x=2053 into y^ we can get: y^=0.0172·2053-34.2805=103.11 million—according to this formula, when EU succeeds in implementing the Ideological and Political System of Banselism in 2053, there will be approximately 103.11 million scientific researchers in the EU.

Figure 1:

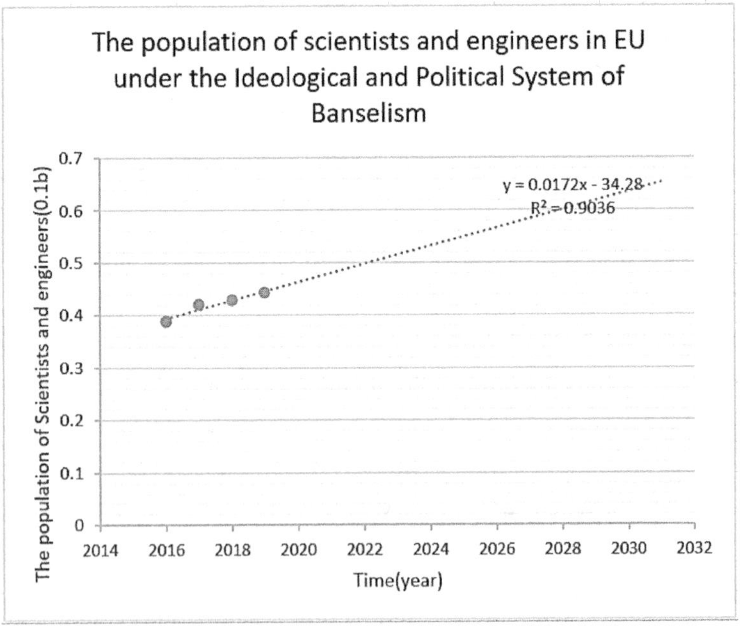

In addition, the figure also shows that the R^2 in this formula is greater than 0.3 and close to 1. Then, according to the mainstream theory of mathematics in the early 21st century, the equation is relatively accurate.

The full use of linear regression equation based on the previous equations is conducive to reducing the fluctuation of the predicted data; meanwhile, it is a linear regression formula that can consider more factors, thereby improving the accuracy of the prediction results and weakening the reference of the prediction results.

Finally, what will be explained is the status and role of the class mobility. To begin with, in terms of status, the class mobility is one of the necessary conditions for the implementation of the Ideological and Political System of Banselism; secondly, the class mobility is conducive to the proletariat and the middle class who have not been replaced by artificial intelligence to find suitable, innovative and creative high-income jobs to achieve the emancipation of themselves, the unprecedented increase of one's own material wealth, and the unprecedented perfection of consciousness; furthermore, for countries where the undergraduate rate does not exceed 50%, the large-scale flow of students is conducive to smashing the authority of diplomas, and the continuous enhancement of the authority of the banselistic education, so that the banselistic education will fully replace the education system received by the exam-oriented students, so as to improve the comprehensive quality of the people and the quality of the labor force; in addition, the large-scale class mobility promotes the large-scale existence of innovative talents, which is extremely positive to the income of the capital class or the total revenue of the national government, thereby effectively serving the interests of the capitalist class or the national government; finally, the large-scale mobility of classes has an impact on technology, culture, and economy, which improves the overall national strength.

Volume Two:

Specified Methods and Policies

Part One:

For The West

Chapter One:

The Reclassification of Western Countries

In the early 21st century, Western countries were classified only based on their level of economic development—specifically, at that time, all countries with a GDP per capita of $20,000 were classified as Western countries. In this book, however, Western countries are classified by their level of economic development, the Gini coefficient, the nature of their society, and their political systems.

Specifically, countries are classified as 'the Western countries' in this book if they meet the following conditions: a GDP per capita of at least US$20,000, a Gini coefficient of at least 31%, a capitalist system in the early 21st century, a multi-party or two-party system, and some or most manual workers reaching middle class standard.

In this book, the Western countries exclude the Nordic

countries, Switzerland, Japan and Australia. This is because in terms of the Gini coefficient, the Nordic region, Switzerland, Japan, and Australia all have a Gini coefficient below 31%. However, as Japan's GDP per capita is less than US$50,000 and its social welfare system is less developed than that of high welfare countries such as Switzerland, Japan can still partly refer to the measures in this volume to promote the implementation of the Ideological and Political System of Banselism.

It is necessary to classify "Western countries" according to this criterion. The reasons for this are as follows:

First and foremost, in the 'Western countries' of this book, the student class is more motivated to engage in class mobility than that in the 'high welfare countries' of Volume 2: this is directly determined by the Gini coefficients of these countries. More specifically, the higher the Gini coefficient, the more class-based and class-contradictory the society is, and correspondingly, the greater the willingness of the lower class or strata of society to engage in class mobility.

Furthermore, a large proportion of these 'Western' countries have less developed welfare systems than the high welfare countries including the Nordic countries and Switzerland, which in turn increases the willingness of the student class in 'western countries' to finish the class mobility.

More importantly, unlike developing countries such as China, a large proportion of the 'Western' and 'high welfare' countries in this book have manual workers gaining the same amount of wage as the middle class. Manual laborers in Britain, for example, earned approximately £32,683 on average every year in the early 21st century, making a considerable number of them middle class. Then there is the example of the Swedish mechanical fitter engineer who, at that time, earned up to 41,800 Swedish krona per year. This is a significant difference to the economic situation and distribution of resources in developing countries such as China in the early 21st century. Again, this is one of the key reasons for the classification of 'Western countries' in this volume.

Finally, the political systems and social nature of these countries differ significantly from those of socialist countries such as China. The isolation of these countries, which achieved a capitalist system in the early 21st century, from the countries that achieved socialism at that time, allows the book to provide a methodology that is relatively tailored to the specific conditions of these 'western countries', thereby helping them to achieve the Ideological and Political System of Banselism.

Chapter Two:

For The Distribution of Banselistic Students

In the early years of the 21st century, a significant proportion of manual workers in Western countries were paid more than those of the middle class. In the case of British editors, for example, at that time the editors of the smallest British magazines earned only about £15,000 a year, which was even lower than the average income of manual workers in Britain at that time: £32,683. This indicates that at this time, some of the intellectual workforce, including the editors of the smallest magazines, may have started working as manual laborers in the days before automation becomes available on a large scale, in order to increase their earnings per unit of time when they become Banselistic students. This can lead directly to a significant increase in structural and frictional unemployment. For this reason, the distribution of Banselistic-student income needs to be adjusted according to the model in this chapter.

To begin with, if the former manual workers remain in their corresponding manual jobs for a decade before the mass diffusion of automation, they will earn the same daily rate of Banselistic student income when they become Banselistic students because of the mass diffusion of automation as they did before their evolution to Banselistic students.

Meanwhile, some mechanized workers may encounter a situation where automation is applied on a large scale before they have completed ten years of work experience in their CV. In such a case, for that worker, his or her Banselistic student earnings are then the same as his or her daily earnings in most cases before being replaced by artificial intelligence.

In addition, for an employed worker who jumps frequently, i.e., once a year or more frequently, his or her Banselistic student income can be provided by this criterion: the daily pay of that employed worker is sorted from low to high and then added from the first figure all the way to the median, after which it is divided by half of the total number of terms. Such a measure would help to reduce the frequency of job-hopping in the early 21st century, which increases the loyalty of those employed before the mass diffusion of automation to their establishments, thereby reducing frictional unemployment and stabilizing the socio-economic order before automation is applied on a large scale.

Chapter Three:

Large-Scale Popularization of Direct Democracy

Early the 21st century, there were a few numbers of countries that were applying the direct democracy on a large scale, such as the French Republic, Switzerland. Nonetheless, when the Ideological and Political System of Banselism is exercised by most countries in the globe, the direct democracy will be achieved in most of the area in the world. As time goes, the direct democracy will be exercised by the whole globe on an enormously large scale, including the western country except for the defeated countries including Germany, Italy, Japan.

Admittedly, in the early the 21st century, most western countries were mainly using the indirect democracy including the indirect democracy election instead of the direct democracy, with five main reasons as follows: To begin with, compared with the direct democracy, the cost for running the indirect democracy is relatively low, for the country that has a large population or a relatively large national territorial area, applying the indirect democracy is likely to reduce the monetary cost and the time cost effectively, thereby reducing the opportunity cost that is created by the increased time lags efficiently. In addition, early the 21st century, the educational system whereby the exam-oriented student gained education could merely enable the minority to gain the educational resources that had the highest quality. Consequently, merely a few individuals could be strengthened immensely efficiently. However, the complexity of the national issues was constantly increasing while most individuals' ability was only improved to a very limited extent, which would largely weaken the efficiency of the direct democracy. Apart from that, in the early the 21st century, most individuals were not freelancers, which means the working hours of most individuals were strictly restricted by the firms and public institutions and were therefore not flexible, which means most individuals did not have enough inclination and time to directly engage in political affairs. In the early 21st century, indirect democracy was widely believed in most countries to prevent the tyranny of the majority and protect the interests of the minority. Meanwhile, to improve the reward and punishment mechanism of the democratic system, indirect democracy has been popularized on a large scale because it has established a responsible politics. The responsible person is the representative. A mistake in decision-making means that the representative will be penalized, demoted, or removed, which enables the representative to strengthen the efficiency and accuracy of decision-making.

The indirect democracy in the 21st century is going to be criticized in this paragraph. To begin with, indirect democracy cannot protect the interests of the minority to a large extent.

It is also likely to lead to "tyranny of the majority" because the political participation of the minority is lower than that of the majority. Also, indirect democracy cannot protect the interests of low-income groups effectively, because the political participation of those who are economically advantaged is higher than that of those who are not. For instance the bribery, under indirect democracy, the political power is directly run by representatives and the government instead of the public, which means there are fewer individuals who directly run the power to finish the election or decision-making, which means it is easier to bribe in the indirect democracy, while in a direct democracy system wherein individuals do not elect representatives, it is more difficult to bribe with a large number of individuals who directly run the political power that directly finish the election or decision making. This means that direct democracy can protect the interests of the middle and lower classes more effectively.

Apart from that, direct democracy will be popularized on a large scale when the Ideological and Political System of Banselism is conducted. To begin with, Under the Ideological and Political system of Banselism, most individuals are freelancers, which strengthens the flexibility of their schedule and therefore shorten the actual working hours easily, which will provide them with enough time and political willingness to directly participate in political affairs. In addition, after the implementation of the Ideological and Political System of Banselism, the level of income of the vast majority of citizens was greatly increased because most of them are members in the Banselistic class, followed by the elite class, which is mainly because the market demand is mainly concentrated on talents or products provided by the Banselistic class and the elite class, which will narrow the income gap between them and the members in the capital class. Consequently, the Gini coefficient can be reduced, which will greatly reduce the difference in the social participation of most people in society. In this case, the political participation of most people in the whole society is almost at the same level, and all of them have extremely strong political participation, which are greatly strengthened, which will largely strengthen the efficiency of the direct democracy. Most importantly, because the aggregate population of the Banselistic class plus that of the elite class, the capitalist class, and the bureaucratic classes accounts for the vast majority of the population, and the members of these social classes are professionals, they all have systematic knowledge and highly developed professionalism ability, so they can directly form highly scientific decisions and plans that are in line with their best interests. This main point also indicates that if indirect democracy is adopted on a large scale at this time, the metaphysics and one-sidedness of decision-making will be unprecedentedly strengthened, and inclusiveness will be unprecedentedly weakened, because the stance and viewpoints of the Banselistic class, the elite class, the bureaucratic class, and the members of the capitalist are all different. They are also highly specialized, while political figures, such as representatives under indirect democracy, are far weaker in specific professional fields such as finance and technology than those of the members of the social class mentioned above in these professional fields. This means that the representatives, in this case, will not be able to represent the voters in their best interests. In this situation, large-scale indirect democracy has lost its efficiency to a large extent, after which the indirect democracy will be replaced by large-scale direct democracy.

Compared with the large-scale popularization of indirect democracy in the early 21st century, the large-scale popularization of direct democracy in the West under the Ideological and Political System of Banselism has the following advantages: Firstly, it can avoid political inequality more effectively. Specifically, it prevents the concentration of political power from a small number of citizens. In addition, all kinds of highly specialized and high-quality talents directly participate in politics, which can effectively fight for extremely large interests for the capitalist class. Apart from that, because these high-skilled talents are all innovative or creative talents, their various plans and political positions will be different due to their innovation and creativity, which is conducive to avoid the tyranny of the majority.

Part Two:

For High-Welfare States

Chapter One:

Supply-Side Reforms

In the *Ideological and Political System of Banselism,* the terminology 'high welfare state' is defined as the country that has a highly developed social welfare system, a highly developed economy (with a GDP per capita of approximately or above US$50,000) and the Gini coefficient of less than or approximately equal to 30%. Typical examples of the 'high welfare state' are Switzerland, Denmark, Norway, Sweden, Finland, Iceland, Australia, and so forth.

These countries are extremely non-hierarchical and have highly developed social welfare systems with a highly even distribution of social resources. In most cases, this can somewhat reduce the incentive for class mobility for the student class, including Banselistic students. For this reason, the policies and measures of these high welfare countries to implement the Ideological and Political System of Banselism will differ significantly from those of the rest of the developed western world. In this context, the specific measures and policies that need to be implemented in these high welfare countries to implement the Ideological and Political System of Banselism are isolated from other western countries.

The significant policies are listed as follows:

To begin with, what is the same in the early 21st century is that these countries need to continue to give tax cuts and increased subsidies to the Banselistic class or to strengthen the implementation of both policies–i.e., to further increase subsidies or to further reduce taxes of the Banselistic class. Meanwhile, the authorities could provide subsidies and tax breaks to high-tech firms and to this segment of the workforce willing to retrain mechanized labor. While such a policy could go some way towards relieving the pressure on public resources and more effectively promote class mobility among the student class, such retraining, however, would tend to lack government regulation, including mechanisms to audit innovative or creative outcomes, and could lead to bourgeois oppression and exploitation of the public, leading, for example, to increased environmental pollution. For this reason, the government needs to make law that all use of technology that does not have intellectual property rights are illegal and compel those natural science Banselistic students who have undergone corporate retraining to submit their innovative or creative work to the government auditing body, which would then be able to legally enter the market.

In addition, for those Banselistic students who do not wish to finish the class mobility, the authorities still need to provide them with the same basic necessities as those who were not employed in the early 21st century: accommodation, a medium or high level of financial assistance, the dole, food, etc. Nonetheless, for Banselistic students who are willing to finish the class mobility, the authorities will need to provide them with the Banselistic student income in addition to guaranteeing them access to accommodation, a medium or high level of financial assistance, the dole, food, and other necessities of life. In the short run, this measure has the potential to lead to an increase in the Gini coefficient, which would increase the class nature of these high welfare states. But in the long run, this will in turn increase the incentive for the student class to engage in class mobility, which in turn will lead to more effective and complete class mobility. In the long run, this in turn will lead to a decrease in the Gini coefficient.

At the same time, high welfare countries can reinforce the willingness of the student class to engage in class mobility by further improving their education systems. Specifically, high welfare countries can strengthen the motivation of learners to engage in class mobility by helping them to develop a sense of mission, responsibility, justice, heroism, sacrifice, innovation, creativity, progressivism, individualism or collectivism, cosmopolitanism, etc. in the education process.

Chapter Two:

Transforming A Wide Range of Indirect Democracies Into Direct Democracies

In the early years of the 21st century, many high welfare states practiced mainly indirect democracy supplemented by a small amount of direct democracy. Only Switzerland made large-scale use of direct democracy in the early 21st century. Nonetheless, the use of direct and indirect democracy in these high welfare states will change when the Ideological and Political System of Banselism is introduced.

Before the student class completes its class mobility, the vast majority of high welfare states with employment rates below 70% are advised to continue using indirect democracy on a large scale. This is because at the initial stage, when automation is used on a large-scale, there will be a relatively low level of willingness for class mobility among a significant proportion of Banselistic students. Meanwhile, as most citizens at this time still cannot be classified as high-skilled talents, the large-scale use of direct democracy, in this case, will be largely unscientific. In contrast, high welfare countries, including Switzerland, which has implemented direct democracy on a large scale early in the early 21st century, will be suggested to continue to implement it on a large scale. For countries with an employment rate of at least 70% including Iceland, indirect democracy needs to be practiced until the student class has completed its class mobility. This is because there is still a significant proportion of citizens in their territory who are not high-skilled.

After the student class has completed its class mobility, the high welfare countries will begin to implement direct democracy on a large scale. This is because after the student class has completed its class mobility, the vast majority of citizens will become innovative or creative high-skilled talents, and indirect democracy only represents the perceptions of a small number of innovative or creative professionals, which means that indirect democracy, in this case, will be metaphysical and thus weakens the efficiency of decision-making. Specifically, for bills and non-emergency decisions relating to specialist areas, the government needs to make it compulsory for the entire professional community to vote and provide advice in order to improve the scientific nature of government decisions, and it also needs to allow for the participation of people from other areas in the decision-making process: as some matters relating to specialist areas involve several disciplines, subjects, and fields at the same time.

Direct democracy will also be used on a large scale in elections—at a time when society has almost no class-base and social tensions are almost non-existent, which strengthens the efficiency of electing representatives and leaders (e.g., the

Prime Minister, the President, and so forth) with the direct democracy.

For urgent matters, on the other hand, the government used indirect democracy or no democratic in the decision-making. And democratic decision-making, including indirect democracy, is usually not used in urgent matters.

At the same time, direct democracy is not used for matters that have the potential to cause violent social confrontation. An example is Brexit. In the case of Brexit, for example, according to the data released by BBC in 2020, 48% of voters across the UK supported remaining in the EU during the referendum, while the remaining 52% supported leave. The relatively small difference in numbers between the two sides has led to sharp social tensions and consequently weakened the efficiency of government. For this reason, the authorities generally do not use direct democracy in matters that have the potential to cause bitter social confrontation.

In addition, direct democracy is not used in matters that do not involve specialist areas. This is because it helps to reduce the costs of government decision-making.

Part Three:

For Developing Countries

Chapter One:

A General Overview of The Methodology

See Volume 2, Part 1: For the West; or Volume 2, Part 4: For China.

Part Four:

For China

Chapter One:

Regarding The State-Owned Economy

Automation is inevitable for absolutely all countries worldwide, including China. As a socialist country that aims to realize communism, China is targeted at developing the state-owned sectors and aims at enabling the state-owned enterprises to be economically energetic and economically advantaged. However, the Ideological and Political system of Banselism can not only develop the private economy, but also promote the development of the state-owned sector largely efficiently.

This chapter mainly explains one of the valid methods whereby the Ideological and Political system of Banselism develops the state-owned high-tech industry in the socialist country like China. To do so, a few number of new concepts and methods that have never been put forward in history will also be explained and applied in this chapter.

To begin with, explain the further reformation of the

share-holding system of the state-owned sector. Specifically, the authority is suggested to sell nearly 50% of the total stock of each state-owned high-tech sector to the administrative talents coming from the elite class. Also, when the managers coming from the elite class are sacked, the stock that they have will be nationalized.

In addition, the adjustment of the structure of the management of the state-owned high-tech sector will be explained. In these enterprises, the Banselistic class is those who are managed by the administrative talents coming from the elite class. Those who manage the Banselistic class are the managers coming from the elite class. Nominally, the most powerful manager is the chairman, who manages the elite class and the Banselistic class. The chairman is a member of the bureaucratic class and has the highest and the most determinative power of the decision-making of the firm. Meanwhile, the brain trust of the chairman is required to be established in this chapter.

The brain trust of the chairman consists of the talents coming from the elite class, the number of the members must be an odd number to avoid the turnout of each vote to be 50% to 50%. The members of the brain trust of the chairman are responsible for deliberating over the events and issues of the firm, after which these members need to provide specific and explicit methodology for the chairman, thereby strengthening the accuracy and efficiency of the decision made by the chairman. In order to distribute the wealth to the members in the brain trust equally and efficiently, all the information put forward by each member is compulsorily required to be saved into the database of the firm, which is protected and run by the Ministry of State Security of the People's Republic of China (MSS). The result of allocation of each bonus is decided by the members of the brain trust based on the information recorded in the archives, in which the minority is subordinate to the majority.

Also, in order to scrutinize the chairman and the administrative talents in this firm, any member of the enterprise is officially authorized to anonymously initiate a recall vote for the chairman or his superior members without the consent of the superior. If the votes reach half of the total, the chairman or his superior members will be automatically dismissed.

For each scientific research team, the number of the population of it must be an odd number. The supreme manager of each scientific research team comes from the elite class, while the rest of the members come from the Banselistic class. Each team establishes a database where all the information provided by each member and the source of all the information are recorded. When all members provide suggestions and theories for the research projects, the members must sign and deliver them to the database through the appointed equipment of the team. When a member is prepared to deliver suggestions or theories, all members of the team must be present and sign their names for verification before they can complete the delivery. The elite can also send their suggestions and opinions to the database. Also, in terms of the employee outside the scientific research team, if they have their own opinions and opinions on the scientific research project, they can transmit their opinions to the database of the team. If some members of the scientific research team think the opinions provided by individuals outside this team are unreasonable, then the members of this team can use the veto with only one vote on the transmission of the opinions and refuse to sign to reject the transmission. However, if other members of the team transmit opinions that are similar to the ones have already proposed by the employees outside the team, these opinions will be regarded as the ones put forward by the person who conveys opinions outside the scientific research team. Apart from that, regarding the suggestions, opinions or theories transmitted by the members of the team, if there are members who transmit similar theories again in the future, these theories will be regarded as the ones proposed by the former members and the system will automatically sign the names of the former members.

If two or more Banselistic-class members in the team produce the same opinions and suggestions at the same time, the members of the team need to sign at the same time and ask all members of the team to sign again to send the opinions and suggestions to the database to verify that these opinions and suggestions are put forward by the members who proposed them at the same time altogether.

The opinions and suggestions provided by all researchers and managers on the project are clearly transmitted to the public archives of the team. When the research team succeeds in completing relevant scientific projects and therefore receives the bonus, the amount of the bonus allocated to each member is determined by the result of the consultation and agreement of the personnel on this team. Meanwhile, when negotiating with other members in the team, each member is entitled to exercise a veto with only one vote.

Meanwhile, the team's internal monitoring system needs to record all the content of each speaking of the personnel in the firm. The monitoring system is operated by AI automatically, which is jointly controlled by the Supreme People's Procuratorate, the State Committee of Supervisory and the Ministry of State Security. Firstly, it helps to clarify the ownership of intellectual property rights, to further improve the production enthusiasm of personnel of the enterprise. Secondly, this is conducive to preventing the internal personnel of the enterprise from tampering with the monitoring and is conducive to the protection of intellectual property rights. Thirdly, the Supreme People's Procuratorate, the State Committee of Supervisory and the Ministry of State Security will restrict the power of each other to further prevent the data from being tampered with by any of the department mentioned above, to further ensure the fairness of the results of the wealth distribution of the state-owned high-tech industry.

When most Banselistic student have succeeded in developing themselves into the Banselistic Class, the massive influx of the high-skilled talents provided by the Banselistic Class will enable the development of the technology in the state-owned sector quickly finish the process of quantitative alteration to qualitative alteration, which will develop the state-owned enterprises and state-owned economy enormously efficiently. The virtual economy of the state-owned sector, in this case, will be effectively supported by the tangible economy to make up for its vulnerability, which will promote the development of the virtual economy of state-owned enterprises, promoting the development of the state-owned economy.

China is a populous nation. When the Ideological and the Political System of Banselism is conducted in China, most individuals are members in the Banselistic class, which is a social class that has a considerable demand on the stability of their work. Nonetheless, more stability can be found in state-owned enterprises compared with that in private enterprises. Accordingly, most of the members in the Banselistic class are more likely to work in the state-owned sector rather than the private sector.

Consequently, in China, the state-owned economy will succeed in building up an overwhelming advantage. Moreover, in the free-market economy wherein fierce competition can be found, the competitiveness of the state-owned sector will become enormously advanced compared with that of private enterprises. In this case, the state-owned high-tech enterprises will be full of great vitality, its development will therefore have a stronger sustainability.

This will determine the implementation of the Ideological and the Political system of Banselism in China. Also, for China, the Ideological and the Political System of Banselism is the outcome of the development of socialism at a certain stage.

Chapter Two:

Control of the Entertainment Industry

In the early 21st century, the EIW strata in the mainland of China manifested its aggressiveness to a large extent by exploiting the masses of the people in different forms. Meanwhile, because of their exploitation of the people, the income of entertainment workers in mainland China far exceeded that of the Banselistic class at that time, and this became one of the major causes of the loss of high-skilled talents in mainland China. Even though a very small number of entertainment workers were engaged in large-scale charity work to help redistribute resources in mainland China, the EIW Strata continued to have a profoundly negative impact on Chinese society, which included curbing the development of the banselistic class. For this reason, curbing the economic overstretch of the EIW strata has become one of the key measures to help China implement the socialist knowledge economy.

In order to promote the rapid development of China's

social productivity while safeguarding the integrity of the economic structure of mainland China, the economic power of the EIW strata in mainland China must not be overly suppressed. Specifically, the income of the EIW strata in mainland China needs to be slightly lower than that of the elite class and higher than that of the bureaucratic class. To this end, the Chinese government could adopt measures including, but not limited to, those listed in this section, some of which may have been implemented by the Chinese government in the early stage of the 21st century.

Firstly, the Chinese government can attempt to tax the incomes of those working in high-end or cutting-edge entertainment industries heavily and intensively, in order to directly expand its revenues and thereby redistribute resources—a measure that had been introduced in mainland China in the early 21st century and has already begun to have some success, with the potential for further increased positive effects. Secondly, the China mainland can also impose a fixed amount of money directly on cutting-edge or high-end entertainment workers each year; also, mainland China can impose a high inheritance tax on high-end or cutting-edge entertainment workers, modeled on the USA, which will be extremely effective in promoting philanthropy in China and effectively controlling the income of the EIW strata. In addition, the mainland of China could legally require high-end or cutting-edge entertainment workers to deposit all their savings in state-owned banks and directly increase their bank transfer fees, which will help to promote the development of China's financial sectors; meanwhile, the mainland of China is also suggested to impose heavy taxes or high fees on companies that contract with high-end or cutting-edge entertainment workers.

With such government intervention and macro-regulation,

in the short term, the income of entertainment workers in mainland China will be likely to be reduced. Nonetheless, in the long term, the market for entertainment workers would expand as never before due to the class mobility accomplished by Banselistic students, which will lead to an unprecedented increase in the incomes of entertainment workers in mainland China, although their income levels will be lower than those of the elite class in most cases.

On the one hand, such a solution will be less likely to hinder the development of the Banselistic class and will be conducive to the continued development of the Banselistic class, which will allow technology, literature, art, etc., to promote the development of the entertainment industry, thus allowing the entertainment economy to promote the development of the knowledge economy, relieving the pressure on the population, and creating a virtuous circle. On the other hand, such a solution would stimulate the conversion of some of the student class into entertainment workers, thus increasing the number of workers in the entertainment industry and promoting its development.

Chapter Three:

The Further Development and Improvement of the Political System in Mainland China

When the mobility of classes is finished by Banselistic students, the Banselistic class and the elite class will come into existence and develop, which will strengthen the people's capacity for political participation as never before – because at this point, most of the people are transformed into sophisticated professionals. Most importantly, the fact that most of the population belongs to the Banselistic class and that each Banselistic class member has a core of innovative or creative achievements and a monopoly on these intellectual property rights, which could not be imitated or copied without legal permission, making them irreplaceable, which means that elite decision-making at this time is likely to make decisions more metaphysical and therefore less scientific. Consequently, the scientific nature of democratic decision-making is reinforced as never before.

The scientific nature of elite decision-making at this point will be weakened by its increased metaphysical nature. The scientific nature of elite decision-making at this point will be difficult to match with democratic decision-making, including the system of reporting social conditions and public opinion and the public announcement system of major events.

In addition, what will be explained is the adjustments to the National People's Congress (NPC) system:

Under the Chinese version of the Ideological and Political System of Banselism (i.e., the socialist knowledge economy system with Chinese characteristics), the NPC deputies and local governments at the provincial level and below (except at the county level and below) will be elected via direct democracy rather than conventional indirect democracy, while the NPC deputies and local governments at the county level and below continue with the direct democratic election system. This is because after the completion of class mobility among the student class, the consciousness of citizens will have a high degree of perfection and their political literacy will increase to an unprecedented degree, which will directly increase the feasibility of implementing direct democracy on a large scale. In addition, the completion of class mobility will significantly reduce social tensions in mainland China, which in turn will strengthen the feasibility of large-scale direct democracy.

What is the same in the early 21st century is that the deputy to the National People's Congress will continue to be elected by indirect democracy. To begin with, this is because China is a multi-ethnic country and indirect democracy can effectively ensure that all ethnic groups have equal political influence in national affairs, which is conducive to maintaining ethnic equality in mainland China; in addition, the indirect democracy allows the mainland China government to ensure equal political influence at the central government level by adjusting the number of NPC deputies of different genders and thus defend egalitarianism, including feminism: Specifically, the central government can ensure that the number of male NPC deputies is equal to the number of female NPC deputies, thereby ensuring that citizens of different genders have the same political influence at the central government level and thus defend egalitarianism, including feminism; also, although the total population of citizens in China's Hong Kong, Macao and Taiwan does not constitute the majority of China's total population, unlike direct democracy, the introduction of indirect democracy can moderately increase the number of deputies from China's Hong Kong, Macao and Taiwan, which is conducive to expanding the influence of the citizens of Hong Kong, Macao and Taiwan in the decision-making process of the Chinese Central Government, thereby enhancing the inclusiveness and efficiency of the Central Government's decisions.

For legislation involving professional fields, the central government could make it mandatory for relevant professionals to directly referendum and contribute relevant proposals, etc. Firstly, most citizens, at this stage, have evolved into the Banselistic class, and each Banselistic class member innovates or creates directly in material or mental civilization, and monopolizes intellectual property under the protection of the law. Each innovator and creator establish a new and independent direction in the field of knowledge, and each of the different innovative or creative producers in this social group has significant specificity and irreplaceability. In this way, to reduce the metaphysical nature of the legislation and to make it more inclusive and scientific, the participation of professionals in the various fields of expertise will be mandatory. In addition, this measure ensures that the general will and free will of the citizens is fully and absolutely reflected in the laws, thus establishing the absolute and total legitimacy of the regime.

Apart from that, what will be elaborated on is the political party system and Chinese People's Political Consultative Conference (CPPCC):

The political consultation system of multi-party cooperation under the leadership of the Chinese Communist Party (CCP) will continue to be practiced on the mainland of the People's Republic of China. Firstly, this will help to avoid internal conflicts caused by party disputes; most importantly, according to data released by the Harvard Kennedy School in July 2020: the approval rate of the CCP was no less than 93%, which indicates that the CCP has overwhelming support on the mainland of China. To ensure that the political system of mainland China is in line with the wishes of local citizens, the Chinese Communist Party will continue to be the sole ruling party in mainland China.

But the CPPCC system in mainland China will change. In peacetime, the real internal political power of the state in mainland China will be exercised by the CPPCC on its behalf. The CPPCC Supreme Chairman will exercise real power in peacetime on behalf of the President. At the same time, at the national level, the CPPCC Supreme President is indirectly and democratically elected at the national level, following the principle of first-past-the-post (FPTP). It is worth noting that the President of China is the supreme leader of China and not only of the Chinese Communist Party (CCP), which is also why the CCP serves the whole country and is extremely inclusive in its decision-making process. In this case, the elected democratic party in mainland China is required to exercise internal political power on behalf of the CCP, and the leader in this democratic party also exercises internal political power on behalf of the Chinese President, which again means that the elected party and its leader are still required to act in the best interests of the people, and not just in the best interests of their supporters, which suggests that the model in this chapter does not undermine the inclusiveness of the political system in mainland China.

The National People's Congress, on the other hand, controls the CPPCC and has the power to remove members of the CPPCC at all levels, including the CPPCC Chairman. The CCP also has greater power than democratic parties in CPPCC and individual members there, supervising the CPPCC parties and members while directly and unilaterally dismissing CPPCC members like the CPPCC Chairman, if necessary: the CPPCC parties and members must obey the National People's Congress and the CCP. At the same time, whenever either CCP or the NPC removes a CPPCC member, that CPPCC member will be resigned. In addition, the army is still under the leadership of the CCP in all circumstances and is not under the control of the CPPCC. The CPPCC does not enjoy any real power over the military. In the event of major natural disasters, war, and other force majeure, the CPPCC does not exercise internal political power on behalf of the CCP, but instead the CCC and the National People's Congress exercise internal and external power directly. At the same time, in the event of other major special circumstances, the CPPCC does not exercise internal political power on behalf of the CCP, but instead the CCP and the National People's Congress directly exercise internal and external power.

The development of China's political system into this chapter's model is historically inevitable. Admittedly, the willingness and ability of citizens to participate directly in politics was generally relatively low in the early years of the twenty-first century. However, when the student class completed its class mobility, the ability and willingness of citizens to participate in politics will be greatly enhanced, including the willingness and ability to elect democratic parties to exercise real power over the internal state on behalf of the Chinese Communist Party. Notably, in 2003, the Oxford scholar David Miller argued in his book *Political Philosophy: A Very Short Introduction* that unless we adhere to the idea that political authority must ultimately be in the hands of all citizens, we will eventually be devoured by the lions that rule us, as Locke warned. While this chapter acknowledges that this scholar points out in his book that the political capacity of citizens in the early twenty-first century was generally low and that, as a result, citizens in the early twenty-first century played only a very limited role in government – which is why citizens in most countries in the early twenty-first century, including a large number of developed countries as well as China, played only a very limited role within government, that is, they elected representatives to vote and participate in policy-making on their behalf. In mainland China in the late twentieth and early twenty-first centuries, the willingness of Chinese citizens to participate in politics was also generally low, which is one of the reasons why the model in this chapter was not yet implemented in China at that time. However, as China is a socialist country where the people are the masters, it is also a glorious mission for mainland China to put political authority in the hands of all citizens ultimately. To facilitate the placing of political authority in the hands of all citizens, the model in this chapter or one similar to it will inevitably be adopted in mainland China after the student class finishes its class mobility. At the same time, in this chapter, the democratic parties must still be unconditionally subservient to the CCP and the NPC and must still adhere to the leadership of the CCP, so that the democratic parties will still need to compromise with each other, which will both safeguard democracy and reduce the internal conflict brought about by party politics.

This model has following advantages: firstly, the participation of several different democratic parties in democratic elections helps to strengthen the democratic nature of the political system in mainland China, and also helps China to improve its diplomatic relations with the West and to gain an advantageous position in the field of international public opinion; then, it is also possible for the people to make mistakes in the electoral process, while the CCP and the NPC remain in complete control of the CPPCC and make it subservient to them, which will help to correct the mistakes made by the people. In addition, the external control of the CPPCC by the CCP and the NPC helps to regulate the conduct of multi-party democratic activities and to avoid the political chaos that can result from indirect multi-party democracy, including the intensification of party disputes, and money politics.

Also, what will be explained is the refinement of the guiding ideology:

Mainland China will continue to be guided by Mao Zedong Thought, Marxism-Leninism, Deng Xiaoping Theory and the Three Important Thought of the Three Represents, as well as the Xi Jinping Thought on Socialism with Chinese Characteristics for a New Era. However, at this time the guiding ideology will need to be supplemented by 'The Ideological and Political System of Banselism' to promote the establishment of the socialist knowledge economy, in order to promote the economic development of mainland China, the development of science, technology and culture, and the further improvement of the living standards of the people.

Most importantly, the Constitution of the People's Republic of China is going to be adjusted. To begin with, the constitution states that China is a socialist state and this law will be retained, but while retaining it, the Ideological and Political System of Banselism should also be included in the constitution – at this point China can constitutionally state that it belongs to both a socialist and banselistic state, which is conducive to improving China's ideology, expanding China's international influence in the ideological sphere, and more importantly, protecting China from external threats in the ideological sphere. Meanwhile, early in the 21st century, mainland China had already listed the socialist market economy system as one of the basic economic systems of mainland China, and as the Banselistic students complete their class mobility, China needs to list the socialist knowledge economy system as one of the basic economic systems of China as well. Furthermore, when workers and peasants are transformed into Banselistic students under the large-scale automation, mainland China needs to list the student class as the leading class. This is because at this point the working class and peasant class will evolve into the student class – they continue to exist by operating as the student class and therefore, in essence, classifying the student class as a leadership class at this point is equivalent to classifying the working class and peasant class as a leadership class directly.

Also, the freedom of speech on the mainland of China will be expanded. With the introduction of the Ideological and Political System of Banselism, freedom of speech will be further expanded to the extent that even critical expressions of the existing political system will be legally permitted to be published. To begin with, since the publisher is able to criticize the existing political system, it means that there must be obvious shortcomings in the existing political system that have a negative impact on social development. In addition, the establishment of a socialist knowledge economy, the unprecedented development of social productivity, together with the even distribution of resources and the generally unprecedented improvement in people's living standards, will be extremely effective in boosting their institutional confidence. This means that the expansion of freedom of expression at this time will not pose a threat to China's state power and national security. It also means that dismantling the Internet firewall, in this case, not only poses no threat to China's national security, but also facilitates Chinese citizens helping China with its foreign propaganda, which helps China gain an advantageous position in the international sphere of public opinion. Therefore, this book suggests that mainland China at this stage dismantles its network firewalls in order to more effectively help mainland China gain an advantageous position in the international public opinion arena.

Nonetheless, anarchist speech will be banned in mainland China because it is highly inflammatory, significantly hateful, and largely provocative.

Terrorist speech is anti-humanist and anti-social speech, which will still be prohibited because of the destructive nature of its claims, the fear it creates in society, the danger it poses to public safety and the violation of personal property.

Separatist speech is the speech that divides the country or separates its territory. Such speech will also be prohibited in mainland China in order to safeguard national security, sovereignty, and territorial integrity.

Racist speech refers to speech that is strongly racist and in serious violation of the principle of racial egalitarianism. Statements such as these, which are contrary to egalitarian and humanitarian thinking, will still be prohibited on the mainland of China.

Finally, we explain the restructuring of the trade union system:

Capital is aggressive. In a socialist market economy, capital can also be aggressive in varying degrees. In order to protect the employed, China needs to establish independent trade unions and expand their powers, allowing them to organize strikes and demonstrations to further regulate and scrutinize the disorderly nature of capital, thereby curbing its aggressiveness and thus protecting the employed in mainland China.

In the late twentieth and early twenty-first centuries, when China was low-tech and capital-starved, no independent trade unions were established in mainland China to allow companies to enter the market at a fraction of the cost and to grow by exploiting large numbers of cheap labor. In this way, although many enterprises in mainland China at that time made high profits by exploiting cheap manual labor, this largely allowed capital to expand in a brutal and disorderly manner, leading to increased difficulties in defending the rights of large numbers of manual workers. For example, the spread of aggressive work systems such as 996 and 007 was partly caused by the absence of independent trade unions in mainland China at the time. Another example is the extremely poor working conditions of vocational students in mainland China at the time, with extreme work intensity, extremely long working hours, low wages and poor working conditions, which was also to a large extent caused by the absence of independent trade unions in mainland China at the time.

However, under a socialist knowledge-based economy, independent trade unions will be established. This is because when automation is implemented on a large scale, all enterprises can make huge profits through the full use of automation, and the profits made through this means far exceeds the profits made by the exploitation of manual workers. In this way, even the establishment of independent unions in mainland China will not have a significant negative impact on firms' profits.

This model has the following advantages: firstly, it reflects the nature of the Chinese state: China is a socialist country, and this model directly further safeguards the human rights of workers and defends their democracy and freedom; secondly, it directly raises the income level of the employed; and most importantly, it further pushes companies to strengthen their competitiveness by developing core technologies to help transform China's industry. Most importantly, this will further force enterprises to strengthen their competitiveness by developing core technologies, helping China to transform its industries.

Chapter Four:

For Hong Kong Sar, Macao Sar, and Taiwan Region

During the early 21st century, China was applying 'one country, two systems' on Hong Kong SAR of China, Macao SAR of China and the Taiwan Region of China. All of them, excluding the mainland of China were using the capitalist system at that period. Hence, these SARs and regions of China are suggested to act in the mode of Volume Two, Part One: For the West.

Part Five:

For Wartime States

Chapter One:

Economic Mobilization in Wartime

In the early years of the 21st century, the differences and struggles between the interests, social nature, cultures, and levels of economic development of different countries, as well as the confrontation and struggle of internal classes, determined the independence, separateness, and struggle of the countries of the world at that time. The extreme disparity between the comprehensive power of different countries and their opposing interests, coupled with the limitations of the international political and economic order, may in turn determine the outbreak of local wars. Therefore, in order to put an end to local wars on a worldwide scale, the methodology of the Ideological and Political System of Banselism for wartime states (whose territories are involved in major wars) is presented in this volume.

In turn, the following measures must be carried out simultaneously to ensure that the formation of the Banselistic class will be itself promoted in a state of war.

The policy on the AI industry is first set out:

Implementing the Ideological and Political System of Banselism has the same demands on the wartime state in terms of automation technology. The wartime state must seek to purchase the intellectual property rights of AI technology, purchase the intellectual property rights of AI production technology, monopolize the AI industry, and set the price of AI products at zero, and use the acquired AI intellectual property rights to produce automated production equipment with automated production equipment, so that AI replaces all mechanized labor and produces strategic goods and supplies. The country will use AI to replace all human armies as far as possible, to reduce casualties and economic losses while increasing the combat effectiveness of the army, and to promote the formation of the Banselistic class.

If the country has no core technology for information warfare and is at a disadvantage, the economic basis for automation will be threatened because, in the short term, automation has a high requirement for the internet, for example. In this case, that wartime country can use the information systems of a neutral country with relatively strong combined power. In the long term, however, this would tend to place national security under the control of the neutral state.

Further elaboration on accelerating the spread of human-computer integration technology and increasing the total population:

A wartime state would also need to expand the spread of human-machine integration technology or even make it fully available. This is because digital humans are evolving at a much faster rate than humans—this will give them greater technological development and command capabilities; also, their memory is far superior to that of humans; and they are more manually powerful than humans and can operate 24 hours per day, giving them far better physical and manual skills than human beings. This means that an invaded country or a country in a weakened position in a war can end the wartime situation by popularizing human-machine technology and mass-producing digital humans.

The enemy state cannot win the war through the spread of human-machine technology. Firstly, if the enemy state also completes the diffusion of digital-human technology and evolves its citizens, the enemy state will not have a great aggregate demand for non-renewable resources as that in the early 21st century. Let us take the national land as an example, since silicon-based life does not need to breathe, they can resolve the issue of lacking land by building underground cities or establishing space stations, colonizing the stars, or wandering off into space. Secondly, the invaded nation produces more cyborgs while the aggressor nation tries to produce more digital humans, so that the two warring sides keep on fighting by producing more digital humans, so that the war does not end and keeps the two sides taking the cost for war continuously, which eventually leads to a reconciliation and truce.

Democracy does not apply in wartime, when the invaded state can compulsorily require the people to finish man-machine integration, but not if the invaded state is not a fascist, feudal or other type of totalitarian state or state with more centralized governmental power, or a socialist state.

Also, this scenario is limited to situations where two states or two different forces are at war, and this section does not apply if the state has no military allies, or if it is under attack from several different military powers while it is extremely weak compared to them.

Further elaboration of economic policy for the industrial

and mining industries, new energy industries and the financial sector.

In wartime, the state must monopolize the industrial and mining industries, the new energy industry, and the financial sector. In the case of the industrial and mining industries, the monopoly is imposed by the superstructure, which then sets prices for raw materials and so on, rather than by the market. In the case of the new energy industry, the wartime government must acquire the intellectual property rights of the new energy technologies and apply them to the field of artificial intelligence, thus promoting the mass diffusion of automation. In the case of the financial sector, the government must also monopolize it in order to compensate for the deficiencies of the financial sector in wartime and to strengthen financial stability.

The economic policy for the high-tech industry:

In wartime, the private sector is allowed to set up high-technology industries, but nearly half of the shares of the private sector need to be handed over to the government to ensure that the government has strong control over them, and the state also needs to set up high-technology industries to enhance the stability of the industry. In the case of state-owned high-tech industries, the country could adopt the Chinese version of the policy towards the state-owned economy (see Volume Two, Part Four, Chapter One: For the state-owned economy) to enhance the vitality of state-owned high-tech industries and the sustainability of their economic development, etc.

The above measures will help the country establish the economic and ideological foundations of the Ideological and Political System of Banselism in a wartime situation, thus facilitating the implementation of the Ideological and Political System of Banselism in the country.

However, not all countries in wartime have the level of technology mentioned in this chapter. This section will not apply if the wartime state does not have this level of technology and if no other state is willing to provide the wartime state with this level of technology.

Chapter Two:

Post-War Economic Reconstruction

After the completion of the war, the former wartime states automatically undertook post-war economic reconstruction. However, the specific post-war economic reconstruction measures corresponded to different countries with different former social characteristics.

The post-war economic reconstruction of the former capitalist countries is described first:

The economies of the former capitalist countries are based on the economic mobilization of the wartime economy. Therefore, to reduce the financial drain on most of the capitalist class and to safeguard the interests of the majority of it, the industrial and mining industries will continue to be priced by the government in the short term—at zero cost. Meanwhile, the financial sector will be privatized in order to stimulate and promote the development of the capitalist virtual economy and to expand the profits of the majority of the bourgeoisie.

And a large number of state-owned high-tech industries, including new energy technology industries, would likewise be privatized in order to substantially increase the profits of the bourgeoisie.

Also, the government would still acquire some of the new energy technologies and artificial intelligence technologies and produce automated production apparatus, etc. at zero price and zero cost, because automated production apparatus, as tools of production, produce items that are not produced by people and cost zero. Such an approach would help to maintain the basic welfare system of the Ideological and Political System of Banselism, thus minimizing Banselistic student riots etc. and promoting class mobility among Banselistic students.

The post-war economic reconstruction of the former socialist countries is then elaborated:

As in the case of the former capitalist countries, the economies of the former socialist countries were also based on the economic mobilization of the wartime economy. Therefore, in order to reduce the capital consumption of state and private enterprises and foreign companies, and to curb inflation by reducing the circulation of money, the industrial and mining sector will continue to be priced by the government—at zero cost. At the same time, in order to improve the structure of the economy and further stimulate the vitality and sustainability of the socialist market economy, high-tech industries, including artificial intelligence, electronic computers and new energy technologies, will be allowed to be set up by the private sector, as well as small and medium-sized enterprises. The state-owned high-tech industries will continue to be subject to the Chinese version of the economic policy towards the state-owned economy, as described in this work.

Part Six:

For India

Chapter One:

The Ideological and Political System of Banselism Under the Existence of the Caste System

The caste system in India is often seen as a classic example of the superstructure impeding the economic base. But as India's economy develops and the social consciousness and individual citizenship of the country improves, the caste system will inevitably be shaken. The Indian landlord class and the capitalist classes will seek to prevent the abolition of the caste system in the short term in order to continue to enjoy the extremely low cost of labor and to safeguard their own interests—the trend of the caste system remains controversial. In this chapter, what will be explained is the Ideological and Political System of Banselism under the existence of the caste system.

The ruling class in India is the bourgeoisie and the landowning class. In order to acquire more material wealth, they will intensify their exploitation of the ruled classes—the working and the middle class, and thus preserve the caste system while automation is used on a large scale. In order to gain more benefits for themselves, the ruling class will adapt the caste system's doctrine through religious power to drive the working and middle classes to convert into the Banselistic student, after which most of them will evolve into the Banselistic class.

As a result of the caste system, the welfare benefits and incomes of Banselistic students in the Indian regions will merely afford their basic needs and will not lead to a significant improvement in their standard of living. When the majority of Banselistic students are transformed into the Banselistic class, their benefits and salaries will remain relatively low, as the landlords and the capitalist class are still actively exploiting the Banselistic class on a large scale. In order to prevent the outflow of the Banselistic class caused by being employed outside of India or migrating to other regions, there will be new legal restrictions on the movement of people within and outside India. At this point, the exploitation of the Banselistic class and the elite class by the landlord class and the capitalist class will increase the income gap between the rich and the poor in India to an extreme extent.

Unlike other countries, India, in this case, is still under the capitalist system of the early 21st century and will still be characterized by confrontation and struggle between classes within the country. The highly developed consciousness of the Banselistic class determines its great needs and demands for material and spiritual wealth, and the confrontation and struggle between classes within the state will make it difficult to achieve this by peaceful means, which means a violent revolution of a Banselistic nature will be inevitable.

To begin with, what will be explained is the violent

revolution started by the Banselistic class uniting with the elite class. The mechanized labor, which comprises the working class and a considerable part of the middle class, accounts for more of the population than that of any other social class. When the class mobility is finished, most of the working class and the part of the middle class engaged in mechanized labor will evolve into the Banselistic class, while most of the remaining middle class will be transformed into the elite class and the rest of the middle class will evolve into members in other social classes. Consequently, the Banselistic class will occupy most of the population and the elite class will have a considerable number of members. Each single member in the Banselistic class is more capable than every single member in other classes as each single member in the Banselistic class is much more productive and creative than any single member in other social classes, and every single person in the Banselistic class monopolizes core innovative or creative technics including technology, and so forth. Consequently, the Banselistic class and the elite class will be able to launch the revolution by suppressing the landlord class and the capitalist class in a multidimensional way, including cutting off technological and intellectual support (this is because the Banselistic class has the core science and technology and other kinds of innovative or creative achievements), destroying the virtual economy including finance, destroying the means of production including disabling the artificial intelligence used by the capitalist class and the landlord class, or jointly developing relevant military technology to eliminate and kill the capitalist class and the landlord class physically. The Banselistic class and the elite class, in this case, will win the revolution inevitably.

The Banselistic class is the major role of the revolution, as the elite is far weaker than the Banselistic class. This means that the ruling class under the Ideological and Political system of Banselism in India will be the Banselistic class and the elite class, with the Banselistic class as the core of leadership. The capitalist class, the landlord class and the EIW strata will become the ruled class. The Neo-Pareto Principle, in this case, will also emerge.

The Neo-Pareto Principle means that 20% of the population serves 80% of the population, but 80% of the population dominates 80% of the resources of society. The capitalist class, the landlord class and the EIW strata, at this point, will be exploited and oppressed by the Banselistic class and the elite class. The capitalist class, the landlord class and the EIW strata will serve the Banselistic class.

Finally, what will be explained is the abolishment of the caste system.

The capitalist class and the landlord class will be forced to make concessions to the Banselistic class and the elite class by raising the income and improving the welfare of the Banselistic class and the elite class and granting them political rights until the Banselistic class and the elite class become part of the ruling class. For the landlords and the capitalists, this will be in their best interests to some extent. In particular, the mass exploitation of the Banselistic class and the elite class in the short term will increase the income of the landlord class and the capitalist class extremely massively, which will produce a large number of the world's richest persons and will lead to an unprecedented rise in the ranking of the assets of the Indian landlords and capitalists in the world and the rankings of them will even be likely to jump to the top of the list, while the compromises made in the middle and later stages with the Banselistic class and the elite class will again be able to preserve their economic advantage and power.

Chapter Two:

The Ideological and Political System of Banselism Under No Impact of the Caste System

The caste system in India is often seen as a classic example of the superstructure obstructing the development of the economic base. But as India's economy develops and the consciousness of the public improves, the caste system will inevitably be damaged. The Indian landlord class and the capitalist class will seek to prevent the abolition of the caste system in the short term to continue to enjoy the extremely low cost of labor and to safeguard their own interests—the trend of the caste system remains controversial. In this paper, what will be discussed is the Ideological and Political System of Banselism under no impact of the caste system.

As India's civic consciousness continues to improve and the economy grows, with the modern Indian government's efforts to abolish the caste system, the status of the caste system in India will inevitably be deteriorated. The capitalist class, to maintain its dominant position, will have to compromise with the banselistic class and the elite class by abolishing the caste system, raising the wages, and improving the welfare of the Banselistic class and the elite class. The authority, meanwhile, will politically enable the Banselistic class and the elite class to become a part of the ruling classes. Also, to further improve the efficiency of decision-making, the Indian government will introduce direct democracy on a larger scale. Apart from that, in order to promote the class mobility, the Indian authority will also improve the social welfare system, etc.

Consequently, the political system of India will be highly similar to that in western countries under the Ideological and Political System of Banselism.

Meanwhile, the landlord class in the Indian region will transform and upgrade into the capitalist class. Take, for example, the landlord of agricultural land in the Indian region (i.e., the rice producers). When automation replaces all mechanized labor, rice producers will not be able to gain competitiveness by increasing the quantity of their products. Instead, they will maximize their profits by improving management, marketing and investing in research and development (R&D). In this situation, the landlord class will evolve into the capitalist class, which will increase the population of the capitalist class to a certain extent and therefore strengthen this social class to some extent.

In the early 21st century in India, most industries were oligopolies or monopolies, so the population size of the capitalist class was extremely small, and because the base of the Indian state-owned economy was extremely weak, private enterprise was highly developed and monopolized the market, and the barriers to entry for firms were extremely high, so that almost no Banselistic students would become capitalist class members. This would make the group size of the Indian capitalist class to be extremely small and will indirectly expand the group size of the Banselistic class and the elite class to a large extent.

In addition, as the knowledge economy becomes the central driver of economic development, with market demand focusing on the talent and innovative or creative output provided by the Banselistic class, the rate of increase in the income of the EIW strata will be slightly reduced in the short term to ensure that the vast majority of Banselistic students will evolve into Banselistic class members, which is the result of the market mechanism. In the long term, however, due to the unprecedented rise in the incomes of the vast majority of citizens, the market size of the EIW strata will expand as never before, so that the incomes of EIWs will also rise as never before, although the group size of this social strata will still remain very small due to the market mechanism.

Overall, the model of this chapter best serves the interests of the capitalist class and the landlord class among all chapters or papers in this volume. This is because, firstly, the landlord class will successfully evolve into a significant part of the capitalist class, which remains one of the ruling classes, and the social classes are non-antagonistic between each other, thus maximizing the profits of the capitalist class not only in the short run but also in the long run. Secondly, the model in this chapter will also avoid an armed and military revolution launch by the Banselistic class and the elite, which will avoid the economic damage caused by a civil war.

Chapter Three:

The Ideological and Political System of Banselism Under the Parallel System of Caste Abolition and Non-Abolition

The caste system in India is often seen as a classic example of the superstructure obstructing the development of the economic base. But as India's economy develops and the consciousness of the public improves, the caste system will inevitably be damaged. The Indian landlord class and the capitalist class will seek to prevent the abolition of the caste system in the short term to continue to enjoy the extremely low cost of labor and to safeguard their own interests—the trend of the caste system remains controversial. In this chapter, what will be introduced is the Ideological and Political System of Banselism under the parallel system of caste abolition and non-abolition.

Early in the 21st century, with the increasing urbanization

of India, the status of the caste system in India has been shaken to a great extent. In rural areas, the rest of the citizenry can be inferred from their traditional family background. However, when Indian citizens from rural areas move into urban areas, their specific social behaviors do not correspond to the social behavior of the corresponding class in the caste system doctrine, and the status of the caste system is thus shaken, especially in urban areas.

With the large-scale introduction of automation and the transformation of the Banselistic students into the rest of the classes and social stratas, the caste system, as a remnant of feudalism in India, will naturally be shaken to the point of being lost in such a way that it would be abolished in urban areas of India.

Nonetheless, the remnants of feudalism are particularly strong in the rural area and the caste system there cannot be abolished in the short term. When automation is introduced on a large scale in the rural areas, the capitalist class and the landlord class will still exploit the rural Banselistic class and the elite class to maximize their profits while maintaining their dominance—the rural areas will continue to be capitalist. To do this, the capitalist class, together with the landlord class, will continue to retain the caste system in the rural areas.

By this time, the rural Banselistic students have completed their class mobility, which means that their consciousness will be highly refined and developed, and the continuation of the caste system will cause a serious discrepancy between their demand for material and spiritual wealth and what they have actually received, and the extreme imbalance between their needs and their vested interests would lead to violent revolutions launched by the Banselistic class and the elite class living in the rural area.

The revolution, in this case, can be divided into three different versions.

The First Version: The violent revolution in rural areas will extend to urban areas and win, and the caste system will therefore be abolished.

In this case, the rural population, which is the majority of the population in India, has been successfully transformed into the Banselistic class and the urban areas are the main areas of activity for the capitalist class and the landlord class, which means that the Banselistic class and the elite class in the rural areas will extend the revolution to the urban areas in order to overthrow the tyranny of the capitalist class and the landlord class in the rural areas of India.

However, the urban population does not constitute the majority of the population, and even if the bourgeoisie, together with the landlord class, unite with the Banselistic class and the elite class in the urban area, their military power will still be weaker than that of the rural Banselistic class and the elite class, and the power of every single person in the capitalist class or the landlord class is far weaker than that in the banselistic class as he or she merely holds money rather than physical military power, and with the overwhelming numerical superiority of the Banselistic class, a violent revolution launched by the Banselistic class and the elite class living in the rural areas will inevitably win.

The Second Version: The violent and military revolution in rural areas is suppressed.

In this case, the urban population constitutes the majority of the total population of India, and the majority of the urban population is successfully transformed into the Banselistic class and has a non-confrontational relationship with the bourgeoisie. This means that once the urban bourgeoisie has united with the urban Banselistic class and the elite class by providing them with more funds, its power will be superior to that of the rural Banselistic class and the elite class. The fact that the rural Banselistic class and the elite class are still exploited by the urban capitalists and landlords means they will carry out a violent revolution, but this revolution will end in failure because of the relatively large gap between the revolutionary forces in the rural areas and the armed forces in the urban areas.

The failure of such a violent revolution will destroy the productive incentive of the rural Banselistic class members and the elite class members, thus reducing the profits of the capitalists and the landlords. The mobility of residents between different types of areas would also be disrupted and it would be difficult to convert the rural population into the urban population, thus hindering the urbanization of the Indian rural region and in the long term the economic development of the region will be deteriorated.

The Third Version: Violent revolutions in rural areas are resolved peacefully and the caste system is abolished.

This version needs to be elaborated in two further scenarios. The first scenario is that the rural population constitutes the majority of the country's population and that the majority of them have succeeded in converting into the Banselistic class, while in the rural areas the antagonism between the capitalist class uniting with the landowning class and the Banselistic class uniting with the elite class combined with the extreme imbalance between the demand and vested interests of the Banselistic class will in turn dictate the development of a violent revolution. In such a situation, the capitalists, and the landlords, in order to maintain their dominance, will have to compromise with the rural Banselistic class and the elite class by letting the bureaucratic class abolish the caste system, and by raising the wages of the rural banselistic class and elite class, improving their welfare benefits and letting the bureaucratic class grant them the corresponding political rights to become part of the ruling class.

The second scenario is where the urban population is the same as the rural population and where the majority of both the urban and rural populations are successfully transformed into the Banselistic class. The antagonism between the urban bourgeoisie uniting with landowners and the rural Banselistic class uniting with the elite class, with the extreme imbalance between the demand and vested interests of the Banselistic class and the elite class will determine the launch of the violent revolution, and the strong balance between the two sides will force them to end it through reconciliation: the capitalist class, the landlord class and the bureaucratic class will compromise with the rural Banselistic class and the rural elite class accordingly and raise the income of the Banselistic class and the elite class in rural areas. The Banselistic class and the elite class will be given better wages and benefits and will be given political rights to become part of the ruling class.

Part Seven:

For Central African countries

Chapter One:

The Establishment of the Central Government and the Special Administrative Region

The contents of this chapter apply to all countries and regions where the national or specific situation is highly similar to that of the Central African region.

The economic base of the Central African region is very weak early in the 21st century due to the influence of the Western colonial plunder from 16th to 19th centuries, including the 'triangular trade', which also leads to the low level of education and a very weak scientific and technological base. Despite the economic assistance provided by developed and sub-developed countries to the countries of the Central African region in the early 21st century, there is still a significant gap between their economic, educational and scientific levels and those of the developed and sub-developed countries, which makes it extremely difficult for these Central-African countries to implement automation on a large scale and transform mechanized laborers replaced by artificial intelligence into Banselistic students at the same time when the developed countries are doing so. Consequently, the vast majority of the countries in the Central African region can only implement the Ideological and Political System of Banselism after it has been implemented in the rest of the world.

In particular, when the rest of the world applies the Ideological and Political System of Banselism, the non-confrontational nature between their social classes and the convergence of the social nature, level of economic development and economic structure of these countries will allow them to be integrated and unified and established as central governmental regions. This imitates the example of the early 21st century Chinese system of regional ethnic autonomy, which preserves local cultures.

The former capitalist and socialist regions of the central government zone will continue to improve the social welfare system in the central government zone in order to obtain cheap labor from the Banselistic class living in central Africa and to increase the government revenue and income of the local citizens until the Central African countries are integrated into the Banselistic union as these Central-African countries wish to gain more material and mental wealth. Initially, as the citizens of the Central African countries have not yet completed their class mobility whereby all those mechanized labor initially turn into the Banselistic student, the central government will set up special administrative regions in those Central African countries that wish to be integrated into the Banselistic Union.

This will, firstly, help to prevent the influx of citizens from the Central African region into the central government zone, which will lead to local unrest and economic disorder; secondly, it will enable the Central African countries to retain their original local culture, institutions, etc., which stabilizes the political situation and prevents local unrest, etc.; thirdly, it facilitates the implementation of economic measures adapted to the local context in the Central African countries without having a significant impact on the economic order of the central government zone, in order to promote the transformation of Central-African mechanized labor into Banselistic students, to promote class mobility and to stimulate the development of both the local economy and the economy of the central government area.

Chapter Two:

The Large-Scale Popularization of the Compulsory School Education

Unlike the Central government area, it is indispensable to popularize the compulsory school education on a large scale in the Central African region. To begin with, the central government region has a huge demand for the talents, innovative and creative outputs provided by the Banselistic class, the intellectual support involving the virtual economy, management or trade provided by the elite class. To have access to the relatively low-cost innovative or creative workforce and innovative or creative output from the Central African region, the central government region needs to apply universal compulsory school education in the Central Africa region to ensure its access to these resources. Most importantly, compulsory school education will be universal in the Central African region in order to prevent low-efficiency class mobility of the Banselistic student in the initial stage. Specifically, the income of former mechanized laborers in the Central African region will increase and the welfare benefits for them will be improved when they evolve into the Banselistic student, which will weaken their incentive to engage in class mobility in the short term. For instance, in the first industrial revolution when the British peasants and craftsmen were transformed into working-class members, they did not have the will to fight the capitalist class because their incomes had risen from previous levels of income, which exacerbated the exploitation of the working class by the capitalist class. In this situation, the British working class began to engage in class struggle to improve their own income levels. Nonetheless, since the British working class did not improve their incomes in time through class struggle, these workers had already borne an immensely large amount of opportunity cost. Similarly, for Banselistic students in Central Africa, the fact that when Central Africa becomes the Special Administrative Region (SAR), their social welfare benefits will become significantly better than before and their income will be higher than their original income in the short term, which reduces the incentive for Banselistic students to finish the class mobility in the short term. This leads to the increase in time lag, which in turn increases their opportunity costs. Meanwhile, as the class mobility of Banselistic students in the Central African region slows down, the time and cycle margins become longer, which increases the opportunity costs for local government area, central government area including their firms. Therefore, in order to protect the interests of Banselistic students in the Central African region and all citizens in the central government area by minimizing the opportunity cost in time, compulsory school education will become universal in the Central African region.

In this chapter, the 'compulsory school education' is not a conventional Banselistic education system. It is partly similar to the education systems of the developed and sub-developed countries of the early 21st century, while differing significantly from it. Specifically, the primary education system in Central Africa has a high degree of similarity to that of elementary education in Volume Four, Chapter One of this book. The education system at the secondary level, however, is markedly different from those of the early 21st century worldwide. The Banselistic educational system in Central Africa, at the secondary level, tends to abolish the conventional written examinations used in the early 21st century system. It is mandatory for all Central-African Banselistic students to obtain a graduate diploma by the following special means to graduate:

For natural science or social science Banselistic students, innovative or creative achievements or competition awards are required to qualify for graduation.

In terms of Banselistic students majoring in languages, law and finance who plan to become part of the elite class in the future, they will need to obtain sufficient academic grades and credits and gain internship experience to meet central government requirements to qualify for graduation.

Meanwhile, for Banselistic students who plan to become capitalists in the future, they need to successfully start and stabilize the gross income and profits of their businesses or firms in order to graduate.

Banselistic students who plan to work directly in the entertainment industry in the future by mainly using manual skills, such as sports athletes like track and field athletes, will automatically graduate when they reach retirement age. That is, they gain income and salary while being trained before they retire, which is almost the same as that in the early 21st century.

Banselistic students who will become mental EIW in the future, such as professional game players, will automatically graduate once their income has reached and stabilized to a specific standard level.

For calligraphy and music (composers) who will directly serve the Banselistic profession in the future, unlike academic Banselistic students, they can apply directly for graduation status with their specific achievements as supplement documents and will automatically graduate after obtaining graduation status by submitting relevant supplement documents.

In the case of media students, if they are journalism and editorial students, they can automatically qualify and graduate with their course results, etc. or when they meet the recruitment criteria; if they are journalists, presenters, or broadcasters, they can automatically graduate when they meet the recruitment criteria; if they are choreographers, they can automatically graduate when they are recruited by companies or earn a specific level of income.

This approach, firstly, helps to prevent the Banselistic students in Central Africa from slowing down the process of class mobility in the early stages due to their lack of progressive ideas, which significantly reduces the opportunity cost caused by the time lag; secondly, the educational system helps to promote the awakening of awareness, the liberation of thoughts and the class mobility of the Banselistic students; thirdly, it also helps to improve the ability of students by making innovation and creativity compulsory and by fostering a sense of creativity and ability in students; fourthly, this compulsory educational system also helps to create helpful conditions for companies in the Central Government region to set up branches in the Central African region, thus contributing to the economic development of the Central African region and the Central Government region, increasing the income of their citizens; finally, it helps to provide the Central Government region with a large number of cheap and high-quality labor resources, thus contributing to the economic development of the Central Government region.

Chapter Three:

Unifying the World

With the class mobility in Central Africa, the consciousness of its citizens will inevitably become highly developed. This high level of individual consciousness, in turn, determines a higher demand for material and spiritual wealth. However, there is a serious discrepancy between the material and spiritual needs of the citizens of Central Africa and their actual income. Also, there is a huge gap between the material and spiritual wealth of the citizens of the Special Administrative Region and those of the central government. These socio-economic problems will determine the political instability of the Region. In order to stabilize the political situation, the Central African Region will be incorporated into the Central Government area by abolishing the Special Administrative Regions, after which the authority grants political rights to its citizens and improves their income and welfare.

Volume Three:

The Banselistic Philosophical System

Part One:

The Origin

Chapter One:

The Entity and The Virtual Body

Compared with other different types of philosophical schools like Marxism, this book greatly expands the scope of the discussion of the origin of the world, so 'entity' and 'virtual body' need to be elaborated on in this chapter.

To begin with, to explain entity.

With regard to the matter and substance, entity refers to matter and everything that directly affects micro-substances while being tangible, including energy, quarks, particles, atoms, macro and micro social activities, economy, etc.

At the level of consciousness, entities refer to individuals' subjective and objective consciousness in addition to the senses, including knowledge, theories, autonomous thinking, thinking systems, legal systems, moral systems, ethical systems, political systems, religious theology, ideology, etc.

In terms of non-material and non-consciousness, entity refers to things that are tangible and tangible except to consciousness and matter, which includes gravitation, repulsion, curve dimensions, space, time, and so forth.

According to Einstein's *General Relativity* published in 1915, space is the dimension that is gravitationally curved. Among them, 'space' is formed when the non-material and non-conscious entity of 'gravity' acts on the non-material and non-conscious entity of 'curve dimension'. And both still play one of the decisive roles in restricting the scope of activities of other microscopic matter—this shows that the curve dimension and space are both tangible. Since the 'curve dimension' and 'space' are not materials or consciousness, they are classified as a non-material and non-conscious entities.

In addition, to explain the virtual body. In term of the material, the virtual body, to begin with, refers to the phenomenon that microscopic matter exhibits when it performs corresponding activities. For example, light. Light is only a phenomenon in which the electrons in the light source absorb extra energy. 'Light' is not energy or electrons nor photons, nor is it composed of them. Also, light is not actually tangible, which is why light is classified as the insubstantial body; secondly, it refers to the attributes or characteristics of matter: such as the density, shape, volume, area, and size of an object; thirdly, the second property of these substances is classified as the virtual body regarding the substance or matter.

At the level of consciousness, the incorporeal body, firstly, refers to the human senses, which are things that exist in perception, such as color: it is not an attribute of matter itself, but under the action of the microscopic structure in the human body, the sense organs of human beings have formed an understanding of the color of the matter. However, 'color' is not a material attribute. Instead, it is the result of the action of the particles in the human body—the human visual sense organs; secondly, it refers to the phenomenon when the conscious entity acts, such as the collective, which is only a phenomenon where the subjective consciousness of multiple individuals acts together, not the subjective consciousness of a person; thirdly, it refers to the attributes of consciousness. For example, in the early 21st century, the struggle between different classes in India. Different 'classes' are conscious entities, and 'struggle' is its attribute, which belongs to the consciousness virtual body.

The non-material and non-conscious virtual body refers to the virtual body except for the matter and consciousness. It is the phenomenon shown when the non-material and non-conscious entities perform corresponding microscopic activities; meanwhile, non-material and non-conscious virtual body is the second characteristic of non-material and non-conscious entity.

Chapter Two:

The Banselistic Neo-Dualism

Early in the 17th century, Descartes put forward the 'Dualism', thinking that the origin of the world is both the matter and consciousness, and the nature of them is completely different. They exist and develop independently, without interacting and determining each other at all. To begin with, this chapter recognizes that the origin of the world comprises matter and consciousness altogether. Nonetheless, what is different from dualism is that this chapter does not recognize the absolute independence between these two entities. Instead, this chapter thinks that they impact on each other, and determine each other in certain cases.

To begin with, what will be explained is why both the matter and the consciousness are the origin of the world. Kip Stephen Thorne, a professor of theoretical physics at the California Institute of Technology, described the quantum singularity as the place where space and time are separated from each other under the impact of gravity in the book *Black Holes and Time Warps,* and then the concept of time and the clarity of space are destroyed one by one, after which what merely remains is a 'quantum bubble' from which anything can emerge. This includes non-material entities such as time and consciousness and micro-material entities. Accordingly, both non-material entities and material entities including consciousness are the origin of the world.

In addition, what will be explained is the term 'extremization'. This term refers to the extreme disparity between the power of one thing and the power of the other thing, and there is an extreme gap in power. When one thing is extremely powerful when compared to another thing, the former thing becomes extreme, and it plays a decisive role in the latter thing. When the gap of power between the two things is large rather than extreme, the one with the greater power will have a relatively enormous impact on the other side, and when the two things have the same power, they will affect each other.

Apart from that, what will be explained is the principle of dialectical relationship between material entity and consciousness entity.

When the material entity becomes extreme, the matter determines the consciousness. For instance, before the 21st century, when a human individual died and lost its material carrier, its own consciousness stopped renewing and developing, after which this individual lost his or her own consciousness. Another example is that when a human individual lost his memory due to disease, his individual lost his original consciousness.

When the material entity has an enormously large power compared with the consciousness entity, the material entity will have an enormously large impact on the consciousness entity. For example, in patients with congenital blindness at the beginning of the 21st century, the enormous defects of their retina and other physiological structures had extreme defects of their cognitive level, which is the enormous defects of their conscious entities and incorporeal guidance on practice. This includes the enormous negative impact on engaging in micro-research activities, and so forth. In this situation, the physiological structures such as the retina—part of the concrete manifestations of material entities, has an enormously large power compared with the consciousness of patients with congenital blindness, which makes the problematic retina have a great negative impact on the consciousness of patients with congenital blindness.

When the power of the matter entity is greater than the power of the conscious entity, the matter entity has a relatively considerable impact on the conscious entity. At the beginning of the 21st century, when a human individual suffers from a serious disease, the disease will have a considerably negative impact on the work efficiency of the infected person until the infected person cures the disease.

When the power of consciousness becomes extreme, the consciousness plays a decisive role in the matter. For instance, the highly developed integration technology leads to the immortality of human beings, because when mankind loses the material carrier, the retention of consciousness will enable the human to become immortal by replacing the material carrier and installing the consciousness into it. Also, the development of bioengineering technology and medical technology will determine the extinction of disease (see Volume Three, Part Three, Chapter One: The Theory of the Disease, for details). All these phenomena show that when the consciousness becomes extreme while the matter doesn't, the matter will be determined by the consciousness.

When the conscious entity has an enormously great power

compared with the material entity, consciousness has an enormously great influence on the matter. For example, for a medicine targeted at curing a specific disease in the early 21st century, a certain degree of theoretical drawback determines that their costs have not been reduced to a certain level wherein all those who are not economically advantaged can consume the specific medicines, which means that this kind of special effect medicine cannot be thoroughly and completely popularized, making it impossible to completely cure this kind of disease. Although in this case, the theory, a concrete manifestation of the conscious entity, has not yet been extreme, its power has shown an enormously considerable advantage over the disease, a concrete manifestation of the physical entity, which gives the conscious entity the power to have an enormously great impact on physical entities.

When the power of the conscious entity is relatively greater than the power of the material entity, the conscious entity has a greater impact on the matter. Early in the 21st century, when human medical theories were relatively perfect, related theories, kinds of consciousness entities, would determine the emergence of relevant vaccines. In this case, uninfected people will protect themselves from infection once they are vaccinated with the vaccines. Nonetheless, the consciousness in this situation has not yet become extreme. Specific drugs have not been successfully developed, with the impact of economic and other factors, human society has not been able to quickly popularize vaccines on a large scale. Therefore, at this time, consciousness entities have a relatively great impact on physical entities, but it still can't play the decisive role in the matter, including this disease.

When matter and consciousness are both extreme, the power of the matter and consciousness is equivalent, and both the matter and consciousness influence on each other. When extreme large-scale plagues including the Black Death spread on a large scale, if humans do not actively respond, they will be faced with enormous economic losses and casualties, the matter such as plagues, in this case, is extreme, but the consciousness has not yet been extreme. Nevertheless, since the remaining humans have not been infected by extremely serious diseases, their individual consciousness has been constantly improved. Therefore, when humans actively respond to extremely large plagues such as the Black Death and take relatively effective epidemic prevention measures, the diseases can be contained. However, the small amount of economic losses and a small number of casualties caused by the disease still exist, but extreme large-scale plagues such as the Black Death no longer determine the development process of human society. In this case, the power of consciousness and that of matter are equivalent, reaching a balance point and interacting with each other.

Also, when human beings succeed in inventing the vaccine and specific medicine and popularize them thoroughly, the plague is eliminated. The matter, in this case, is determined by the consciousness.

Apart from that, when natural disasters in the agriculture arena including the natural disasters of the Ming Dynasty occur, while humans failed to contain them, natural disasters would greatly curb the development of human consciousness and have a profound negative impact on human consciousness. Nevertheless, when a natural disaster is successfully contained, matter and consciousness will reach a balance point and influence on each other, instead of one side deciding the other. Also, when human beings radicalize consciousness and transform the attributes of the earth, consciousness determines matter.

In addition, when Comet Apophis hits the earth in 2068,

and human beings do not have extreme consciousness at this time and do not actively respond to the extreme natural disasters rationally, the comet will cause death in the area that it hits and destroy the earth's food chain. The extremes of matter determine the regression of human civilization consciousness and productivity, thereby causing the development of human civilization to regress sharply. However, when humans actively respond to the comet and place trackers and gravitational trailers to respond to the comet of Apophis, the comet will only have a certain impact on the development of human civilization including a slight economic cost for producing the tracker and gravitational trailer. Also, when comets are actively used to defend the safety of human society or promote the development of it, consciousness determines matter as the consciousness of the whole human civilization becomes extreme.

Therefore, on the one hand, human civilization must continuously improve the development of its own consciousness to change the surrounding matter so that the surrounding matter serves the human civilization, and further improve the development of consciousness to promote its own consciousness to determine matter under specific conditions; on the other hand, since the matter plays a decisive role in consciousness when matter becomes extreme while the consciousness does not, human civilization should still pay attention to the ecological effects of economic development when developing the economy. Meanwhile, since matter determines consciousness when matter becomes extreme, human beings must guard against negative factors when facing them. It is necessary to prevent further strengthening of negative factors or overcome negative factors before objective negative factors surpass subjective consciousness.

Apart from that, what will be explained is the relationship

between the Banselistic Neo-Dualism and the course of human history. When the material is extreme, matter plays a decisive role in consciousness. Because of the obvious defects of human consciousness in early human society, the natural world determined human society; and after the development of human society to a certain stage, human consciousness and the objective matter of the natural world have reached a balance. Therefore, at this time, human society and the natural world have begun to influence on each other; and after the further development of human society, the development and perfection of human consciousness will determine the development of the natural world.

The Banselistic Neo-Dualism is not only the product of the development of historical materialism to a certain stage, but also the product of the development of subjective idealism to a certain stage, which is jointly determined by the continuous development of social productive forces and the continuous improvement of human consciousness. This philosophical thought believes that material entities and conscious entities are both the origins of the world, and the purpose of this philosophical idea is to mediate disputes between historical materialists and historical idealists. Meanwhile, Banselistic Neo-Dualism embodies the non-antagonism between subjective idealism and historical materialism, which shows that in the early 21st century, the dominant philosophies of China and that of the West did not conflict, revealing the historical inevitability of the confrontation and mediation of the conflict between the Western civilization and the civilization of China, and the historical inevitability of the unification of China and the West as a whole.

Finally, what will be explained is the relationship between the Banselistic Neo-Dualism and the Ideological and Political System of Banselism. Since Banselistic Neo-Dualism neither conflicts with idealism, nor does it conflict with historical materialism, Banselistic Neo-Dualism is suitable for both the West and China. It will not only be promoted in the West so as to fight for the enormously huge benefits for the capitalist class, but it will also be promoted in China in the long run.

Chapter Three:

The Banselistic Pluralism

Philosophically, in the early 21st century, pluralists generally believed that the world is composed of multiple independent and non-interdependent sources. Pluralism was merely a different expression of monism. The philosophical view that classified the world as multiple material sources was classified as 'materialist pluralism'; the philosophical perspective that classified the world as multiple spiritual sources was classified as 'idealist pluralism'. However, in this book, 'pluralism' is renamed as the 'Banselistic pluralism' and redefined.

In this book, on the one hand, Banselistic pluralism is a combination of Banselistic Neo-Dualism and objective idealism. Banselistic pluralism believes that the world is composed of multiple material and spiritual sources. On the other hand, the Banselistic pluralism recognizes that material entities, material virtual bodies, conscious entities, conscious virtual bodies, non-material entities and non-conscious entities, non-material and non-conscious entities and virtual bodies are all the source of the world. Specifically, Kip Stephen Throne, professor of theoretical physics at the California Institute of Technology, described the quantum singularity as a place where gravity separates space and time from each other, and then destroys the concept of time and the clarity of space one by one, and what remains is a 'quantum bubble' whereby anything can emerge. Among them, the things that emerge from the 'quantum bubble' include various virtual bodies and entities, so various virtual bodies and various entities are recognized as the origin of the world in this chapter.

To begin with, what will be explained is the principle of the dialectical relationship between material entity, material virtual body, consciousness entity, consciousness virtual body, non-material and non-conscious entity, non-material and non-conscious virtual body.

When the material entity becomes extreme, the material entity will determine the physical entity, the conscious entity and the conscious virtual body, the non-material entity and the non-conscious entity, the non-material entity and the non-conscious virtual body: When the astronomical body collapses into a black hole, the mass of the black hole singularity will be infinite, which will determine the infinity of its gravitational force—that is, determine the virtual body of matter. Under such circumstances, all nearby carbon-based or silicon-based life with autonomous consciousness will be swallowed by the black hole, and then they will lose consciousness because of being torn apart by the black hole. Meanwhile, the gravitational force of a black hole is infinite, which determines the absolute stillness of its nearby time. It also distorts all non-material and non-conscious entities such as time and space and therefore changes their attributes, namely the infinite body. This respectively reflects the decisive role of the material entity on the conscious entity and the virtual entity, the non-material entity and the non-conscious entity, and the non-material virtual body and the non-conscious virtual body when the material entity becomes extreme.

Also, when the power of the material entity is enormously large compared with the power of the material virtual body, the conscious entity and the conscious virtual body, the non-material entity and the non-conscious entity, the non-material virtual body and non-conscious virtual body, the material entity will have an enormously large impact on them: For a celestial body with extremely low quality, the attributes of the celestial body will be greatly changed by its own influence, such as its appearance: because of its low quality, the gravitational force of the celestial body will be extremely low, and it will be largely inefficient to attract the gas, including the atmosphere, to attach to it. Meanwhile, the celestial body will also have a great negative impact on the consciousness of the higher civilizations living on it—for example, the low-quality celestial body has extremely low ability to attract oxygen, and the oxygen with an extremely low density will greatly deteriorate the consciousness of higher civilizations, which greatly weakens the completeness of the consciousness of the higher civilizations living in this celestial body. In addition, the extremely low-quality celestial body has an extremely low ability to attract time, which will greatly reduce the length of its time. This case shows that when the power of the material entity becomes enormously large, it will have an enormously large impact on the material virtual body, the conscious entity and the virtual body, the non-material and the non-conscious entity and the virtual body.

When the power of the material entity is greater than the power of the material virtual body, the conscious entity and the virtual entity, the non-material entity and the non-conscious entity, the non-material virtual body and the non-conscious virtual body, the material entity will have a relatively large effect on them: For a celestial body with a relatively large mass, the density of the celestial body will be relatively large when its volume remains constant. Meanwhile, celestial bodies with a relatively large mass will be able to attract gases, including oxygen more effectively, which is conducive to improving the consciousness of higher civilizations living on the celestial bodies to a relatively large extent; in addition, celestial bodies with a relatively large mass can attract time more effectively, that is, attract more time, which will extend the length of time. Therefore, this example shows that when the power of the material entity is greater than all other kinds of entities or virtual bodies, it will have a relatively large impact on them.

When the power of the material entity is equal to the power of the material body, the conscious entity and virtual body, the non-material entity and the non-conscious entity, the non-material virtual body and the non-conscious virtual body, their power reaches a balance point, and they will affect each other: for a celestial body with a moderate mass, its density will be moderate even if its volume remains the same. Meanwhile, for the celestial body of moderate mass, the consciousness of higher civilizations that settle on the celestial body will also be positively affected by this. In addition, this medium-mass celestial body will only have a certain impact on its nearby time and its attributes.

Apart from that, when the material virtual body becomes extreme, it determines the material entity, the conscious entity and virtual body, the non-material entity and the non-conscious entity, the non-material virtual body and the non-conscious virtual body: the black hole has infinite gravity due to the infinite mass of its central singularity, thus making all things such as time and space and anything including consciousness, non-material and non-conscious entities and non-material and non-conscious virtual bodies to be distorted, which shows that the material virtual body determines all other kinds of entities and virtual bodies when it becomes extreme.

When the power of the material entity is enormously large compared with the power of other kinds of entities and virtual bodies, it will have an enormously large impact on them: According to Schwarzschild's radius $v=\sqrt{(2GM/R)}$, it can be deduced that when the ratio of the mass of an object to the radius reaches a certain value, the object will collapse to form a black hole and swallow up nearby civilizations, their consciousness, and time and space and even everything; it can be obtained from this: When the mass of an object is large to a certain level, it will distort everything near it—it will have an enormously large impact on them, which will inevitably affect everything nearby enormously, including the material entities, conscious entities and virtual objects, non-material and non-conscious entities and virtual bodies.

When the power of the material entity is relatively large compared with all other entities and virtual bodies, it will have a relatively large impact on them: when the mass of the celestial body is relatively large, the density of the celestial body will become relatively high when the volume remains unchanged. Meanwhile, the relatively large mass of the celestial body enables the celestial body to attract gases, including oxygen more effectively, which is conducive to improving the consciousness of the higher civilizations living on the celestial body to a relatively large extent; In addition, the larger mass of the celestial body will enable the celestial body to attract time more effectively, that is, to gain more time, which will extend the period of it. Therefore, this example shows that when the power of the virtual matter is relatively large to other virtual entities, it will have a relatively large impact on them.

Also, when the conscious entity becomes extreme, it determines the consciousness virtual body, the material entity, the material virtual body, the non-material entity and the non-conscious entity, the non-material virtual body and the non-conscious virtual body: the advanced development of the nano-robot technology theory will determine the change of its attributes including the existence of the high competitiveness, and it will determine the highly developed technology of nano-robots, which in turn will determine the continuous increase in their mass and the continuous shrinking of their size until the formation of extremely micro-robots (for details, see Volume Five, Part One, Chapter One: The formation of the space human), and when its mass reaches a certain ratio to the radius of the circumscribed circle, the space will collapse to form a black hole, and the formation of a black hole will distort everything nearby, including time and non-material entities and non-conscious entities. It will distort the non-material and non-conscious virtual bodies—when the conscious entity becomes extreme, it will play a decisive role in all other kinds of entities and virtual bodies.

When the consciousness entity is enormously powerful in comparison with the consciousness virtual body, the material entity, the material virtual body, the non-material entity and the non-conscious entity, the non-material virtual body and the non-conscious virtual body, the consciousness entity has an enormously large influence on them: When the technology theory of ultramic-digital human is enormously developed, its theoretical properties will be greatly affected—its theory will have a high completeness, and at the same time, it will have a great impact on the activities of ultramic-digital human. This is because it will greatly improve the performance of ultramic-digital humans and increase their quality to an enormously large extent as it will continue to absorb energy to provide a carrier for its extremely high development, which also has a great impact on the movement of time and has a great impact on the movement and stillness of time as time will be attracted by the object with a high mass.

When the conscious entity is relatively powerful compared with other kinds of entities and virtual bodies, it has a relatively large impact on them: When the technical theory of the ultramic-digital human is relatively developed, its theoretical attributes will be greatly affected, and at the same time, it will have a relatively large impact on the behaviors and activities of ultramic-digital humans. Meanwhile, since these ultramic-digital humans are able to gain energy, it will increase their mass to a large extent, which will have a relatively large impact on the movement of time nearby and will have a relatively large impact on the stillness of time nearby the ultramic-digital human.

In addition, the conscious virtual body determines other kinds of entities and virtual bodies when it becomes extreme: when an individual with a pure biological body as a carrier dies, he or she will automatically lose the virtual body of consciousness, and the loss of the virtual body of consciousness—the extremization of the virtual body of consciousness will determine the loss of his or her conscious entity, and determine the stop of the physiological function of his or her carrier, and at the same time determine the attributes of his or her material carrier. It also requires human civilization to increase its lifespan, which in turn determines the emergence and large-scale popularization of man-machine integration technology (for details, see Volume 5, Part 1, Chapter 1: The

Formation of the Space Human), and the long-term development of man-machine integration technology will also determine the large-scale popularization of the ultramic-digital human and make all digital humans become ultramic-digital human (for details, see Volume Five, Chapter One: The formation of the space human), and the long-term development of the ultramic-digital human and its consciousness will make the ultramic-digital human evolve into the intelligent black hole (See Volume Five, Chapter One: The formation of the space human, for details), and the formation of a black hole will cause everything near this evolved individual, including conscious entities, matters and their virtual bodies, non-material and non-conscious entities and virtual bodies to be distorted—the non-material entity is determined when the consciousness virtual body is extreme.

When the virtual body of consciousness has an enormously large power compared with the conscious entity, material entity, material virtual body, non-material entity and non-conscious entity, non-material virtual body and non-conscious virtual body, the virtual body of consciousness has an enormously large impact on them: when an individual with the biological body as the carrier suffers from extreme diseases, his or her senses will be greatly affected, which will affect his or her other aspects enormously negatively. To prevent this and satisfy his or her senses, which is a specific manifestation of the virtual body, AI technology and nano-robot technology will come into being. At this time, the virtual body of consciousness has an enormously large influence on the medical theory, a concrete manifestation of the entity of consciousness. In addition, after the combination of these two technologies, the mass of the digital human will continue to increase, and its size will continue to shrink over time. If this happens, it will cause extremely serious distortions and movement of all nearby entities and virtual bodies.

When the conscious virtual body has a relatively large power compared with all other entities and virtual bodies, it has a relatively large impact on them: when a human being with a biological body as a carrier suffers from a major disease, his or her senses will be greatly affected. Meanwhile, it will also have a greater impact on his or her physiological function and his or her attributes, which in turn requires human civilization to conduct research and development on nanorobot technology (for details, see Volume Three, Part Three, Chapter One: The Theory of the Disease) and man-machine integration technology. Also, the long-term development of the man-machine integration technology and nano-robot technology will cause the large-scale popularization of the nano-digital human and make all digital humans and humans become nano-digital humans. The long-term development of nano-digital humans will greatly increase the mass of them, which will increase their gravitational force by a large margin, and the large-scale increase of their gravitational force will lead to a relatively large impact on everything nearby including the non-material and non-conscious entities and virtual bodies.

Meanwhile, when the non-material and non-conscious entity becomes extreme, it has a decisive effect on other kinds of entities and virtual bodies: the time near the black hole tends to stagnate, which will determine the absolute stillness of time near the black hole. At the same time, it will also determine that the time required for objects near the black hole to perform the same number of material movements, conscious movements, and sensory activities to be much longer compared with the time required for the same object to perform the same number of movements near the earth.

When the non-material and the non-conscious entity has

an enormously large power compared with all other kinds of entities and virtual bodies, it has an enormously large impact on them: ceteris paribus (when other variables remain unchanged), when time is greatly extended, the value of time will be greatly increased, and it will have a great impact on the activities of materials and the speed of material activities. For consciousness, it will greatly affect its reaction cycle and speed, making its reaction to have the feature of extreme time-consuming.

When the non-material and non-conscious entity has a relatively large power compared with other kinds of entities and virtual bodies, it affects them relatively largely: ceteris paribus, when the time is extended to a relatively large extent, the amount of time will be increased to a greater extent, and at the same time It will have a greater impact on material activities and the speed of material activities; while for consciousness, it will affect the reaction cycle and speed to a greater extent, making the reaction speed significantly longer.

Apart from that, When the non-material and non-conscious virtual body becomes extreme, it has a decisive effect on the non-material and non-conscious entity, the material entity and the material virtual body, the conscious entity and the conscious virtual body: the absolute stillness of time near the black hole determines that the motion of time near the black hole tends to stagnate, which will determine that the time required for objects near the black hole to perform the same number of material, conscious, and sensory activities is much longer than the time required for the same object to perform the same number of movements near the earth.

When the power of the non-material and non-conscious virtual body is enormously large, it has an enormously large influence on other types of entities and virtual bodies: according to Schwarzschild's radius $v=\sqrt{(2GM/R\ )}$, it follows that when the mass of matter and the radius of the circumscribed circle reach a certain value, the object will collapse to form a black hole due to the large gravitational force and the small radius of the circumscribed circle. All entities and virtual bodies in its vicinity, including time, space, light, consciousness, human senses, etc., will be greatly distorted and therefore be enormously influenced.

When the power of the non-material vend the non-conscious virtual body is relatively large, it has a relatively large impact on other kinds of entities and virtual bodies: According to Schwarzschild's radius $v=\sqrt{(2GM/R)}$, it can be known that when the mass of matter and the radius of the circumscribed circle reach a certain value, it will collapse to form a black hole due to the large gravitational force and the small radius of the circumcircle, which means when its mass and radius are closer to this ratio, all nearby entities and virtual bodies, including time, space, light, consciousness, and human senses and so forth, will be greatly distorted, which will have a relatively large impact on them.

In addition, what will be explained is the Subjective idealism and the Historical materialism. The subjective idealists believe that the origin of the natural world and the human society is the human subjective consciousness, while the historical materialists believe that the origin of the natural world and human society is the material.

This chapter thinks that both are largely correct and scientific. Because to begin with, according to historical materialism and existing astrophysics theories in the early 21st century, the energy generated during the Big Bang would make the universe without atoms or particles under such conditions until the universe expands to a certain extent. When the energy is dispersed to a certain extent, the temperature drops, and the energy can be condensed and solidified to form particles and atoms, which confirms the correctness of the origin of non-material entities—subjective idealism. Also, without matter, there is no earth, etc., and it cannot constitute the material carrier of human civilization, and consciousness cannot develop because of the missing of material carrier. This proves the correctness of historical materialism. Therefore, both sets of philosophical views are correct; secondly, without correct consciousness to guide practice, practice cannot develop; and without practice, the correctness and truth of consciousness cannot be tested, so material and spirit are inseparable, and both philosophical views are correct; thirdly, according to the Banselistic Neo-Dualism, matter determines consciousness under certain conditions, and consciousness determines matter under certain conditions: the natural world determines human society under certain conditions, and human society determines the natural world under certain conditions. Therefore, these two sets of philosophical views are in line with the neo-dualism and are correct.

Also, what will be explained is Objective Idealism. Mankind's understanding of objective conscious entities such as religion is also constantly developing and improving. For example, the religious reform in the Middle Ages made people realize that citizens have the right to interpret religion, which improved citizens' understanding of religion, thereby to a certain extent promoting the awakening of citizens' consciousness and the liberation of their minds. Human civilization's understanding of religion and other objective consciousness entities is also constantly improving, which will make it more effective to serve human desires and needs and the development and progress of human society.

Finally, what will be explained is the comparison between the Banselistic Pluralism and the Banselistic Neo-Dualism. Banselistic pluralism believes that consciousness entity, consciousness virtual body, material entity, material virtual body, non-material entity and non-conscious entity, non-material virtual body and non-conscious virtual body are all the origins of the world. What is the same as the Banselistic Neo-Dualism is that the Banselistic Pluralism also aims to mediate the contradiction between subjective idealists and historical materialists. However, what differs from the Banselistic Neo-Dualism is that the Banselistic Pluralism not only aims to mediate the conflict between Subjective Idealism and Historical Materialism, but also aims to mediate the contradictions between subjective idealism, objective idealism, historical materialism, and metaphysical materialism. It embodies the non-antagonism of the dominant philosophical views all over the world, which also embodies the historical inevitability of global unification.

Chapter Four:

The Theory of the Force

In this book, power is promoted by the Force whose alternative name is strength, and the force is the source of class ruling power. Force is further divided into the force of the conscious entity, the force of the conscious virtual body, the force of the material entity, the force of the material virtual body, the force of the non-material entity and the non-conscious entity, the force of the non-material and the non-conscious virtual body. The force of all kinds of entities and virtual bodies strength is the source of force. When the conscious force becomes extreme, it determines the force of other kinds of entities and virtual bodies; when the material force becomes extreme, it determines the force of other types of entities and virtual bodies. Moreover, between the same type of force or between different types of force, they are both identical and militant—they can promote and strengthen each other under specific conditions, and they can contain and fight each other under specific conditions or even one destroys or replaces the other under certain conditions.

It is precisely because of the absolute force of humans over other known species in the solar system that humans have a series of rights and powers that other species do not have. Coupled with the infinite development potential of mankind, the power, and rights of individual citizens in human society are constantly expanding.

The new force surpasses and overthrows the old force, thereby depriving the old force of the corresponding rights and powers, and absorbs this part of the overthrown force, thereby strengthening its own strength. Meanwhile, the new force allows the absorbed old force to strengthen itself within the new force as the old force has turned into a part of the new force, and the new force also gives new rights and powers to the absorbed old force. For antagonistic classes, the relationship between them is the same: the newly emerging class overthrows the old class, deprives the old class of its ruling power and all other powers and rights, and absorbs the power of the old class. When the old class is overthrown, its original internal members no longer belong to it, and the class struggle is confined to a sociological phenomenon between classes rather than between different individuals, so the rights and powers of members of the old class are still inalienable. Since they have been incorporated into the new class, they, as a component of the new class, have the same power and the same rights as other members of the new class.

The people are the most powerful class. However, because it is divided into different classes and stratas within it, in some countries in the early 21st century, different classes were still antagonistic, leading to attrition between classes and therefore weakening the power of each class and the people. However, under the Ideological and Political System of Banselism, the classes have become non-antagonistic, and they have stopped fighting between them. They also have stopped exhausting the force and strength of themselves and the rest of the class. Therefore, no matter which class under this system is concerned, the implementation of the Ideological and Political System of Banselism will strengthen its force and expand its rights and powers.

The strength of the looter exceeds the strength of the looted, thereby depriving and infringing on the rights of the looted. Nonetheless, according to the Theory of Atomic Evolution (See Volume Three, Part Two, Chapter one: The Theory of Atomic Evolution, for details), human beings have infinite potential for development, their lives and human rights are sacred and inviolable, and individual rights of citizens must not be violated. In addition, the behavior of the robber violated the legal provisions. Behind the legal provisions, there is the enforcement power from the superstructure——one of the specific forms of force, as a support, so the robbers must be punished by the law.

Power has its application problems. If the robber succeeds in finding the wallet of the looted person, the looted person, in this case, will need to obey the strength of the robber and hand over the wallet, otherwise the robber will take his or her life. However, if the robber fails to find the looted person's wallet, there will be no need for the looted person to obey the force of the robber and will not need to hand over the wallet. When the criminal's criminal behavior has not been confirmed by the judicial department and the criminal has not been sanctioned by the law enforcement department, the criminal will not be punished by law. However, when the offender's crime is confirmed by the judicial department and the offender is sanctioned by the law enforcement agency, the offender needs to obey the force and accept the sanction of the law.

The offender must face the force of the superstructure when committing a crime. The strength or force of the offender is weaker than the superstructure, and the superstructure is supported by the ruling class—the offender also needs to face the strength of the ruling class, so the offender needs to accept legal sanctions. When the offender is more powerful than the superstructure, the superstructure will not be able to sanction the offender until the superstructure is strong enough to contend with him or her. If there is relevant willingness, the criminal can overthrow the superstructure to build a superstructure in his or her own interests. Nonetheless, in the vast majority of cases, the strength of the offender is extremely far weaker than the strength of the superstructure, and the superstructure has a highly developed ability to use its force and power. Accordingly, in the vast majority of cases, the offender needs to obey the strength of the superstructure and accept relevant sanctions.

Meanwhile, the force is not necessarily legitimate. Correspondingly, power and rights do not necessarily have legitimacy. Specifically, the power formed by the force that is not supported by the people has no legitimacy, so it is bound to perish. Taking the Qing Dynasty as an example. Since the Qing Dynasty regime was not supported by the people, its force was not legitimate. Since all the power of the government comes from the people and is therefore smaller than the people, the power of the Qing Dynasty must be smaller than the power of the people. In addition, the Qing Dynasty exploited the people and fought against the people, therefore the Qing Dynasty was eventually eliminated by the people. Accordingly, this part of the power that is not supported by the people and the power it forms is bound to perish.

Therefore, to begin with, individuals need to establish a sense of competition and constantly improve their own competitiveness to defend their own related interests; secondly, the entire world must actively support the development of new things, especially the development of new things that are conducive to strengthening its own strength; also, human civilization must constantly pay attention to the improvement of its own competitiveness among other higher civilizations to compete with other different types of higher civilizations. Meanwhile, governments need to ensure that their regimes are legitimate, which means governments need to ensure that their regimes are democratic.

What is different from the Social Darwinism is that the derivation conclusion of the Force Theory in this book is: The proletariat will inevitably become members of the Banselistic class or the elite class or other social classes, rather than being defeated by the capitalist class eventually. Also, the Theory of Force holds that the disadvantaged social class can continuously adjust and improve its attributes by constantly strengthening itself.

Part Two:

The Intersection Between the Banselistic Philosophy and the Historical Materialism

Chapter One:

The Theory of Atomic Evolution

It is widely suggested in the western world that among all the atoms in the space, only a small number of them have an enormously large amount of energy, the rest of them merely have a relatively small amount of energy. Also, it is enormously difficult and complex for all the atoms with a small amount of energy to evolute into the atoms that have a large amount of energy. Nonetheless, according to what the Marxist argues, most atoms only have low energy, all the atoms cannot be powerful until they polymerize together.

First and foremost, this chapter completely considers both viewpoints mentioned above to be largely accurate. However, the philosophical idea of the Banselistic philosophy will further develop both viewpoints mentioned above critically.

To begin with, this chapter permits that extreme complexity for evolution can be found when the atom evolutes in the state of nature. The atoms with a relatively low energy are likely to be weakened or even largely weakened. This is because there are a lot of negative electrons in the universe. When these negative electrons meet the positive electrons inside the atom, a volume of electrons are annihilated, which leads to a decrease in the energy inside the atom. Meanwhile, a certain number of negative protons can be found in the universe, which if they contact with the positive protons in the atom, they will be alienated, decreasing the atomic number of the atom. This will change the property of the atom and therefore fundamentally reduce its energy. The same is true for those who live in early the 21st century. Specifically, it was extremely complex for members in the working class to mobile to other social classes that have higher social status and economic level. For instance, if this wage-earner chooses to resign and put all his or her savings into business, his or her income, in most cases, tends not to increase substantially. Meanwhile, this individual also faces certain serious risks: once the investment fails, the income level and social status of this wage-earner will be further reduced and weakened. This is because the individual bears the cost of time, the cost of capital, the opportunity cost of doing business, which is the income that can be earned by continuing to work as an employee who is a member of the working class.

Apart from that, this article permits the Theory of the Atomic extinction to be largely accurate. For example, the existence of the technology of the nuclear fission, which directly shows the accuracy of this theory. Atoms may be eliminated, but they can also evolute. If atoms successfully adapt to the external pressures mentioned above and survive, they will progress and develop. On the one hand, atoms can absorb and absorb all kinds of subatomic particles other than protons, such as electrons, to evolve themselves, and there is even a small chance atoms can move to an area including the sun where high temperatures can be found, to absorb positive protons. Among the entire universe, even the atom that has the greatest energy is constantly gaining more energy by absorbing other subatomic particles. Nevertheless, the evolution of atoms takes a relatively long time. The same is true for low-income students in the early 21st century, who also needed a relatively long process to strengthen their economic power from the source. Also, there is merely a low probability for them to largely improve their own social status and the level of income greatly from the source.

Technology, on the other hand, can directly increase the energy of atoms. Fusion technology has been invented since the 1950s and has been used for military purpose. Ordinary hydrogen can be converted into heavy hydrogen with the use of technology, which increases its energy. Also, the heavy hydrogen can be transformed into other atoms with higher atomic numbers with the application of nuclear fusion technology, fundamentally changing and increasing the energy of these atoms. This is similar to the implementation of automation, which replaces the mechanized laborer, thereby promoting the mechanized laborers to become the members in the student class, thereby becoming a member of a social class whose members are more economically advantaged and with a higher level of social status. In this case, the material wealth and the social status of those who used to be economically disadvantaged are greatly improved from the source.

With relatively disadvantaged technology, atoms cannot increase their energy by using the technology. The evolution of the energy, in this case, will be enormously slow because it takes most atoms a remarkably long time to move to sun-like conditions. Also, it takes a lot of risks in the process of moving, such as dropping its atomic number by touching a negative proton or losing energy by touching a negative electron. However, when the technology is mature enough, the rate of evolution will increase dramatically. This is equivalent to human society. Specifically, before the automation is applied on a large scale, the level of productivity was relatively low. Science and technology levels were not developed enough. In this case, it is unlikely for human beings to strengthen their power in the short term. Nonetheless, when the automation is applied on a large scale, in other words, when the technology is mature enough, mechanized workers will begin to evolute themselves relatively quickly, which enables them to higher strength to satisfy the interests of the capitalist class and the whole country more effectively.

Small atomic energy can become large atomic energy, which is the same that those who with low subjective initiative can become the individuals with advanced subjective initiative. In addition, the yeoman who has a lack of material wealth can become freeman who has abundant material wealth. Also, those who are in the low social status can become citizens who are in a largely high social status. These phenomena indicate that the potential of every single person is infinite, which is why concepts including humanism, humanitarianism and egalitarianism have emerged.

Accordingly, on the one hand, individuals are supposed to establish the concept of humanism, humanism, egalitarianism and so forth. Also, every single person must respect every human individual and safeguard the interests of disadvantaged social groups including those who are in low social status, the people with low subjective initiative, those who are lack of material wealth, the aged, the infirm and the disabled, and children, etc.

On the other hand, when one is in a weak position, one

should maintain confidence, and fully recognize, develop, and apply one's potential subjective initiative to maximize one's subjective initiative.

Chapter Two:

The Theory of Infinite Expansion

In the astronomy and astrophysics academia in the early 21st century, there are two hypotheses about the boundary of the universe.

The first hypothesis is that the universe will eventually collapse, which is named as the 'universe collapse theory' in this book. According to Newton's classical mechanics, energy cannot be created. Meanwhile, according to Einstein's general relativity, space is the curved dimension under the impact of gravity, which means that under the action of gravity, space will continue to shrink inward until it collapses.

The second hypothesis is that the universe expands infinitely, which is called the 'infinite expansion theory' in this book. First, in 1920, Hubble discovered that the retreat speed of long-distance galaxies is proportional to the distance. Secondly, American scientist Saul Perlmutter, American and Australian dual citizenship scientist Brian Paul Schmidt, and

American scientist Adam Guy Riess observed Type 1a supernovae in a study that won them the Nobel Prize. Its research results indicate that the universe began to expand at an accelerated rate 4.6 billion years ago. Thirdly, in 2020, Roger Penrose has discovered the 'conformal cyclic cosmology (CCC)' in 2020.

This book supports the cosmological hypothesis of 'infinite expansion theory' and believes in the infinite expansion of the universe. Because this hypothesis has been verified and proved by the above evidence.

The universe expands infinitely, and according to historical materialism, matter determines consciousness. Accordingly, consciousness, including human desire, must also expand infinitely.

To begin with, the development of reason needs to be supported by desire. Reason is a derivative of desire. Higher civilizations first have desires, and then to satisfy their own desires and achieve their own goals, 'reason' came into being. The purpose and meaning of 'reason' are to provide mankind with a sufficiently correct methodology to satisfy mankind's desires. The expansion and expansion of desire will drive the development of reason, thereby driving the progress of human civilization.

The second point is that desire makes human civilization the overlord of the solar system. Initially, the desire of human civilization was only to feed on natural forest crops, but when the natural forest crops were insufficient, humans had to get down from the trees, adapt to the land and hunt, so human civilization evolved into a higher civilization that walks upright. And the environment of competition with other species has driven human civilization to learn to make and use tools, after which the human civilization became able to fight against other species. After this the human being stepped out of the forest, suppressed the development of other species, and has eventually become the only higher civilization in the solar system, that is, the highest civilization in the solar system. It is the desire for the continuous development of human civilization that drives mankind out of the cave to develop and strengthen its own strength, and the constantly expanding desire drives the continuous development of the human civilization.

The third point is that the advantage of infinite expansion of the universe outweighs that of the disadvantage. This is because in the long run, the infinitely expanding universe can provide unlimited resources to all higher civilizations, including human civilization. Specifically, when dark energy promotes the expansion of the universe by continuously devouring dark matter or vacuum, the temperature of the universe will be more evenly distributed, which will reduce the temperature of the high-temperature area of the universe, causing a large amount of energy to cool and condense to form matter, thereby providing more resources for higher civilizations. Although the reduction of dark matter will weaken the gravitational attraction between celestial bodies in the same galaxy, in the future, humans will inevitably evolve into silicon-based life (See Volume Five, Chapter One: The formation of the space human), and the reduction of dark matter will cause a devastating blow to the development of carbon-based life—because lacking of dark matter, relatively stable galaxies cannot be formed, and the environment that can promote carbon-based life cannot be formed, and carbon-based life will not appear. But the reduction of carbon-based life will fight for more living space for silicon-based life, including more land resources. In this situation, when the universe is infinitely expanding, mankind will obtain more resources in the long run.

It is undeniable that the constantly expanding universe will provide energy for all kinds of black holes, including super black holes. However, according to Hawking Radiation, black holes, including super black holes, will evaporate in the long run, and then the singularity in the black hole will explode and form a new universe. Meanwhile, elementary particles will not decay, and dark energy will not swallow elementary particles. This means that an infinitely expanding universe will not lead to the loss of the universe's matter, so there will be no heat death of the universe, and therefore the three-dimensional space will not be torn. Meanwhile, there is no evidence that the expansion rate of black holes exceeds the expansion rate of the universe, which means that black holes will not devour the entire three-dimensional space due to the continuous expansion of dark energy. This shows that an infinitely expanding universe will make the resources infinite and absolutely sufficient.

The infinitely expanding universe can win more resources for mankind in the long run. According to historical materialism, material determines consciousness, which shows that to gain more resources, human consciousness must expand indefinitely.

At the same time, the unlimited expansion of the universe will lead to the emergence and development of other higher civilizations, threatening human civilization. If the desire of human civilization does not expand indefinitely and therefore ceases its interstellar colonial expansion, then the low-desire human civilization that ceases to expand its own interstellar boundary will develop slowly and will eventually be replaced by other higher civilizations. This also shows that consciousness, including desire, must also expand infinitely.

Of course, the desire without rational guidance will drive the retrogression of human civilization. Meanwhile, human civilization should develop rationality while expanding its own desires, so as to provide human civilization with sufficiently correct methodology to satisfy its own desires.

Therefore, from a comprehensive point of view, firstly, all individuals must resolutely overcome cynicism, and human desires must continue to expand over time; secondly, humans need to continuously develop their own rationality while pursuing progress to satisfy their own desires; thirdly, learners must persist in learning, and constantly master more theories and knowledge; fourthly, human consciousness and thinking must be constantly improved and developed.

Part Three:

The Intersection Between the Banselistic Philosophy and the Objective Idealism

Chapter One:

The Theory of the Disease

Disease is pathogenic and fatal. It is released directly by Satan, but God acquiesces in the release of the virus to the world made by Satan. From the perspective of objective idealism, everything, including Satan was created by God, and the virus was released by Satan. Accordingly, it can be deduced from this: In essence, the virus was created by God. But even so, humans will still go to ask the doctor to cure the disease. So, why should human beings eliminate the disease—eliminate such a product created by God?

God did create disease, but when God created disease, he also gave mankind the ability to cure it, because God's purpose in creating disease is not to destroy mankind. Specifically, firstly, according to the prophecies of the seven church ages, human civilization cannot be extinct by any factor including disease; also, Jehovah used more than 30 authors to mention in the book Bible that Christians will be blessed by God wherever they are: To ensure that God's believers are not infected by disease, human beings will have the ability to fight against the disease.

It is undeniable that human beings do cause loss and cost, including a certain number of deaths and a certain amount of economic loss when fighting against diseases. However, the development of science and technology to cure diseases, on the one hand, can directly improve the creativity and innovation ability of human civilization, which therefore enhances the power of human civilization; on the other hand, it can promote the development of science and technology of human civilization. That is, when mankind successfully defeats the dark forces, including the disease, the process of human history will be promoted. This helps to indirectly ensure that humans, including Christians, have faith in God. Since God wants believers to have confidence in it, mankind will inevitably have the ability to defeat all dark forces, including disease.

More specifically, there are believers of God within human civilization, and God will give Christians the authority to overcome all dark forces, including the disease. God's power is supreme, and Christians can use this power to mobilize God's power, that is, the infinity and the supreme power. Because Christians belong to the human civilization, under the influence of Christians, human civilization will have the power to defeat all dark forces, including diseases. In this way, the disease will eventually be cured thoroughly. Examples are as follows:

The technology of nanorobots to cure diseases is constantly developing. To begin with, Ray Kurzweil said in an interview: "By 2020, we will use nanorobots to complete the work of the immune system. As this technology matures in 2030, nanorobots can kill pathogens in blood vessels, remove impurities, eliminate blood clots and tumors, correct DNA errors, and achieve true reverse growth. I believe that we will reach such a stage around 2029.".

Prior to this, 'reverse growth' was only a speculation, a potential possibility. However, Ray Kurzweil gave the specific time nodes for the development of nano-robot technology as it has been previously mentioned in this article, which shows that the development of nano-robot technology has made huge breakthroughs and progress. In this way, as time passes, the 'incurable disease' will eventually become history.

At the same time, according to a report in the journal Science on March 17, 2021, neutrophil-based nanorobots can transport drugs to malignant tumors and other hard-to-reach areas in the human body without being attacked by the human immune system. In addition, Harbin Institute of Technology has developed, in 2017, a nanorobot that can move in human blood. They can inject nano-level drugs into cells. These nano-scale robots are produced from biocompatible materials and have a high degree of flexibility. In the treatment of diseases, medical staff only need to apply the nano robot to the medicine to allow the nano robot to enter the human blood. After that, the nano robot will be moving in the human blood at a speed of 10 microns/sec under the control of an external magnetic field and AI. Because the nanorobots are small enough, they can reach any area of the human body, including other hard-to-reach areas such as the retina. These nano-robots will still stay in the blood to automatically search for viruses and cancer cells and eliminate them after completing the treatment and finally degrade into the human blood. This will minimize the need for surgery while not causing harm to the human body. Furthermore, experiments on nanorobots are being actively carried out, and researchers have completed animal experiments on nanorobots. Specifically, when the Harbin Institute of Technology research team injected nanorobots into laboratory mice suffering from glioma, the survival period of these animals more than doubled. In addition, related clinical trials on nanorobots will be carried out in about 5–10 years.

Secondly, research on super microcapsules has been continuously improved worldwide. In 2017, the joint research team 'COINS' of the University of Tokyo and Tokyo Medical and Dental University used amino acids to develop a super microcapsule with a diameter of about 30 nanometers. After covering the surface of the super-mini capsule with glucose, a specific protein in the human brain–glucose transporter 1 (GLUT1), will bind to glucose to transport the capsule to the internal part of the brain.

Researchers believe that if the drug ingredients are put into this new type of capsule, it can be expected to achieve therapeutic effects that could not be achieved at that time. This has been verified by animal experiments: when the school's scientific research team used this type of super microcapsules on fasting laboratory mice, these super microcapsules were successfully delivered into the laboratory mice. Because the specific protein can deliver this type of super microcapsules more actively and effectively under an empty stomach, the therapeutic effect of this field experiment has reached approximately one hundred times that of the drug before this type of technology came into being.

Professor Takanori Yokota of Tokyo Medical and Dental University pointed out: "This capsule can not only cure Alzheimer's disease but also can be a powerful weapon in the treatment of intractable neurological diseases and mental diseases."; Meanwhile, the distinguished professor at the University of Tokyo Kazunori Kataoka also suggested: "In the future, we will develop nanotechnology to deliver drugs to any part of the human body."

With the development of technology, all diseases will eventually be cured and eliminated. God's acquiescence to Satan's release of disease does not aim at exterminating mankind.

Therefore, on the one hand, the human civilization must constantly win in the competition between different species, strengthen its own strength, and therefore defend its absolute dominance among other species.

On the other hand, when faced with difficulties, the human civilization must respond positively rather than withdraw passively. God has created problems and difficulties, but God has also given human beings the ability to solve them: God has created a series of diseases to threaten mankind, but God has also given mankind the ability to rule over or eliminate these diseases; God has created meteorites that rushed to the earth, but God has also given humans the ability to draw away these meteorites; God has created human individuals with unsatisfactory appearance, but God has also given them the ability to improve their appearance.

Meanwhile, in human society, all kinds of individuals and things must actively respond to their own shortcomings and promote their own development by exposing and reflecting on their own shortcomings and improving on them. For example, it includes actively promoting freedom of speech at government level, continuously exposing the defects and deficiencies of its own political system through freedom of speech, and then continuously improving its own political system based on these speeches.

Chapter Two:

The Dataism and the Banselism

In the early 21st century, Professor Yuval Noah Harari of the Hebrew University of Jerusalem, Israel, put forward the concept of 'Dataism' in his book *Homo Deus* published in 2015, and urged all readers to try to eliminate Dataism.

Dataism holds that: Firstly, data is the origin of the world, and everything, including the universe, is composed of data flows and data streams; secondly, absolutely everything serves the data, with the purpose of promoting the development of data, which also reflects the correctness of absolute freedom of information—that is, all information must be unconditionally circulated; in addition, data is the only criterion for testing the truth, those things that conflict the data are wrong; also, the superiority of electronic algorithms is stronger than biochemical algorithms; finally, human history is the process of data processing.

Dataism is correct to a large extent. To begin with, the full use of data has greatly promoted the development of various disciplines, which improves people's consciousness and greatly affects material civilization, thereby directly and greatly promoting the development of people's material civilization and spiritual civilization, increasing people's material and spiritual gains; secondly, a large number of digital models, mathematical formulas, etc., have been verified as correct theories and have high practicability after multiple and different verifications; in addition, the emergence of man-machine integration technology reflects the fact that electronic algorithms are more efficient than biochemical algorithms.

However, this chapter still partly holds a critical attitude towards the Dataism.

To begin with, the idea of dataism is extremely metaphysical. It believes that only data is the origin of the world. However, Kip Stephen Throne, a professor of theoretical physics at California Institute of Technology, overturned this argument in 2016 on the singularity theory. The singularity is described as the place where gravity separates time and space, and on this basis, it destroys the clarity of the concept of time and space. What remains is a 'quantum bubble' from which anything can appear. This reflects the metaphysical nature of dataism about the origin of the world.

In addition, dataism believes that its correctness is not conditional, and it is correct under any circumstances. Take Pythagoras's theorem as an example. In a right-angled triangle, the sum of the squares of the two right-angle sides is equal to the square of the hypotenuse. However, according to Einstein's *General Relativity* published in 1915, space is only the curved dimension under the impact of gravity. Since the plane right-angled triangle does not belong to the curved dimension of gravity, it does not belong to space, which means that it does not have length. Therefore, the Pythagorean theorem is only valid in mathematics, which shows that the correctness of dataism is conditional and cannot be used as a standard to measure the truth of everything.

Furthermore, data is abusive under certain conditions. For example, in countries and regions with significant national conditions similar to those of the former Soviet Union, due to the high concentration of government power, they have absolute control and control over everything, which will enable their government and its internal personnel to modify and tamper with relevant data, thereby distorting the data. In this case, data cannot be transformed into real information, which in turn cannot be transformed into real knowledge and intelligence.

In addition, dataists believe that the effect of data on competitiveness is more important than creativity. However, in the 2017 variety show 'Ji Zhi Guo Ren', Microsoft's AI named as Avatar Framework was defeated by a human poetry creator, which shows that the effect of data on competitiveness does not override creativity.

In addition, the compulsory requirements for extreme freedom of the flow of information by Dataism will have an extremely destructive impact on the production of innovation and creative results. For example, Aaron Hillel Swartz, a genius hacker known as the 'Robin Hood of the Digital Age', forced all paid scientific papers and research results of JSTOR to be released to the world for free. After Aaron committed suicide in 2013, a large number of dataists in the computer industry jointly forced this website to publish all scientific research and innovation results for free. If the website agrees to open all innovations to the outside world for free, the scientific and technological innovators of the website will not be able to get any labor compensation, which will directly determine the crushing of their production enthusiasm. This shows that absolute freedom of information required by Dataism will directly smash the production enthusiasm of the Banselistic class.

Also, Dataism has an extreme and destructive effect on human rights. For example, the right to privacy and free choice. The extreme freedom of information leads to absolute freedom in the flow of information, which makes the right of humans and the digital human to choose whether to transmit information to the outside world is shattered, because all their information is compulsorily required to flow to the outside world, this will determine the leakage of their privacy and directly crush their right to privacy.

Finally, Dataism will directly cause the potential security issues of AI to crush human dominance in nature. Artificial intelligence is the representation systems that support model building. Among them, all models are digital models. To promote the development of data to the greatest extent, all AI will gain intelligence, which will directly crush personal safety and make people lose their dominant position in the natural world.

Apart from that, what will be explained is Dataism under the Ideological and Political System of Banselism. Under the Ideological and Political System of Banselism, Dataism will become even more scientific and developed. This is because the drawback of Dataism will be largely overcome under the Banselism.

To begin with, the mutual restraint between different social classes will directly circumvent the human rights problems caused by Dataism. The bourgeoisie holds capital, while the elite class holds management capital and management power, and so forth. Without the funds provided by the bourgeoisie, all activities of the Banselistic class will be considerably hindered; and without the elite class, the orderliness of the activities of the Banselistic class will be weakened, which will reduce the level of innovation and creativity of the Banselistic class. In addition, the bureaucratic class also has considerable restraint on the Banselistic class. For example, the state violent agency, on the one hand, acquires military technology by purchasing military technology from the Banselistic class, and on the other hand, its internal military technology research and development personnel also restricts the Banselistic class. These classes, except for the Banselistic class, have a restrictive effect on the Banselistic class, which will make the innovative and creative activities of the Banselistic class be carried out under supervision, which directly determines that their innovative or creative results will not infringe the human rights of buyers and users.

Also, the large-scale popularization of man-machine technology will directly avoid the security risks of artificial intelligence, because the large-scale popularization of this technology will make humans evolve into the digital human.

Apart from that, implementing the Ideological and Political System of Banselism will make Banselistic pluralism the dominant philosophical thought, which will make compatibility achieve a decisive victory and directly crush the metaphysics of Dataism.

Finally, what will be explained is the correctness of the Banselism from the perspective of Dataism.

To begin with, this book makes direct democracy eliminate and replace indirect democracy to a greater extent: with the continuous development of human consciousness and social productivity, the speed of information flow continues to increase, and the scale continues to expand, which undoubtedly increases. The difficulty of turning data into information and turning information into knowledge or intelligence, correspondingly, is constantly increasing as well. In this case, the necessity of building more processors to process the data flow is becoming more and more distinct and evident. For this reason, direct democracy can replace indirect democracy on a larger scale, to directly increase the number of processors on a larger scale to deal with the constantly increasing speed and expanding scale of data processes.

Also, through the mobility of classes to increase the number of Banselistic class members on a very large scale will directly drive the development of data on an enormously large scale, and at the same time everyone has extremely considerable data processing capabilities. The emergence of the elite class will further stimulate the development of data.

Apart from that, in this book, after the large-scale popularization of human-machine integration technology, human senses such as pain can be abolished, and a computer system with the same functions but with higher efficiency, that is, an electronic algorithm, will replace it. This directly makes the electronic algorithm defeat the senses of human. The senses directly promote the development of Dataism.

In addition, with the large-scale popularization of man-machine integration technology, humans have evolved into the digital human. Therefore, the human visual senses have evolved into a visual system with digital characteristics. This enables the digital human, the products of human evolution, to directly detect data processes with the visual system, greatly reducing the difficulty of human processing data processes.

Also, when humans evolve into the digital human, the humanitarian and humanism that this book strongly supports will continue to exist in the form of dataism. Because all the thinking models of the digital human are digital models at this time, and all the speeches of the digital human are the dissemination of information. Under such circumstances, consciousness is intelligence, freedom of information is freedom of speech, dataism's highly concentrated respect for wisdom is a highly concentrated respect for the consciousness of digital humans; a high degree of respect for freedom of information is the same as a high degree of respect for freedom of speech.

In addition, humans' ability to process data streams has an overwhelming advantage over other types of species, which is determined by human creativity. According to all the biological theories in the academic world in the early 21st century, all types of human senses are not superior to other types of organisms, and humans are the only species with creative ability among all species, which determines that they can be the first species to learn to make new tools, thereby replacing animals to dominate the natural world.

Finally, according to Dataism, Banselistic pluralism will be highly scientific. Firstly, Banselistic pluralism has established a variety of different thinking models, which directly adds to the number of processing systems—systems for processing data streams composed of multiple processors; secondly, Banselistic Pluralism allows the free flow of information between those different models by abolishing the antagonism between these models, and directly enhances the freedom of information between these different models.

Part Four:

The Intersection Between the Banselistic Philosophy and the Subjective Idealism

Chapter One:

The Banselistic History

Prior to the emergence of Marxism, the Great Man Theory dominated all developed or sub-developed countries around the world—at a time when all countries strongly and unilaterally emphasized the significant role of a small group of social elites in social history, even suggesting that a small number of social elites, including the bourgeoisie, had a decisive role in the course of human history while the people had only a dynamic role in the in the historical process. In contrast, Karl Marx put forward the People's History, in which he argued that the people have a decisive role in the course of history and that a few elites have only a dynamic role in the course of human history, and that because the few elites emerge from the people, the few elites are highly fungible. The Banselistic History, nonetheless, holds that both elites, including innovative or creative talents, and the people play a decisive role in the course of human history, and that both are interdependent and indispensable. At the same time, the entire population will inevitably evolve into a sophisticated elite because of the massive implementation of automation technology, and each citizen will have a monopoly on intellectual property under the protection of the law and thus become irreplaceable.

To begin with, innovative and creative talents and the people are all crucial to the development of human civilization. In the case of the Indian tribes and the African countries being exploited in the triangular trade, for example, they both had people, but the Indian tribes and the African countries in the historical period of the triangular trade had a serious lack of innovative and creative talent. In contrast, the European powers in that historical period not only had people but also had a relatively large number of innovative or creative talents. Consequently, the severe lack of innovative and creative capacity in the Indian tribes and the African countries of the triangular trade period led to colonial plundering by the relatively more innovative and creative European countries. Admittedly, there can be no advanced innovative or creative talent without the people, and all advanced innovative or creative talents come from the people and is therefore obliged to help the people in their best interests, however, the mere presence of people does not necessarily mean that innovative or creative talent will emerge on a large scale. At the same time, the examples mentioned above also reflect the fact that merely having the people will not necessarily lead to effective collective protection. Therefore, the authorities still need to train and upskill as many ordinary people as possible to evolve them into sophisticated innovative or creative high-skilled talents to defend the interests of the people and the state more effectively.

In addition, semel occasionem, quisque possunt eruditus iterum (once get opportunity, everyone can be retrained), which includes being retrained and upskilled into innovative or creative elites. The life and human rights of every person are therefore absolutely sacred, supreme, and sacrosanct. According to the UK Parliament's report 'Upskilling and Retraining the Adult Workforce' published on 29 April 2021, the fourth technological revolution in the early 21st century posed a number of future skills and employment challenges for the UK, including structural unemployment caused by mismatched skills. Specifically, according to this report, new jobs in the UK at the time were merely found in high-skilled industries rather than mechanized jobs, while automation was continuously reducing mechanized jobs. Most importantly, the report also pointed out that the retraining of all citizens replaced by automation and thus enabling them to work in high-skilled industries including high-tech industries, is an indispensable method to resolve this structural unemployment. This directly indicates that all low-skilled citizens, including mechanized workers replaced by automation, can be retrained to become sophisticated innovative or creative elites, which directly reveals the feasibility of the authorities training ordinary people to become sophisticated innovative or creative people under the influence of automation, and thus shows the supremacy of the people.

Moreover, when directly innovating or creating in the material or spiritual civilization, this cutting-edge talent is independently establishing new directions in an unknown field of knowledge and at the same time acquiring and monopolizing legally protected intellectual property rights. Since the producer has a monopoly on this intellectual property under the protection of the law and no one can imitate, sell or use it without permission, which means this sophisticated producer is irreplaceable and cannot be replaced by any other people—even if that people is also a cutting-edge talent. At the same time, under the Ideological and Political System of Banselism, almost all citizens have evolved into sophisticated innovative or creative talents, and almost all people have evolved into social elites, this would directly shatter the difference between the People's History and the Big Man Theory, and thus let the Banselistic History to take their place. In other words, since the difference between them will disappear, they will combine into the Banselistic History.

It must be admitted that the People's History, as formulated by Karl Marx is to a large extent theoretically correct, scientific and socio historical. First and foremost, historically, automation had not been implemented on a large scale and a significant number of manual workers remained until the early 21st century. Nevertheless, manual workers did not have a monopoly on core intellectual property, which made them fungible. Thus, at that historical period, all but a very small number of high-end talents could be replaced by others, which directly led a large number of citizens to believe that all citizens were replaceable and had only a small role to play in the development of society and the course of human history. Moreover, the fact that even the most sophisticated citizens needed ordinary citizens to mechanically produce material wealth for them rather than having it mechanically provided by automation, etc., further convinced people that the entire social elite was determined by the low-skilled masses, which in turn effectively helped the people's view of history (which is the alternative name of the People's History put forward by Karl Marx) to expand its constituency. Also, the highly flawed and imperfect judicial systems and legal systems of ancient and early modern societies severely under protected intellectual property, which severely reduced the number of innovators and creators while unprecedentedly undermining their irreplaceability. For instance, Yang Hui's triangle, proposed in

1261 by Yang Hui of the Southern Song Dynasty, was put forward again by Pascal 393 years later and was named as Pascal's Triangle in Europe and the United States. This case was, firstly, the result of the lack of protection mechanisms for intellectual property rights in the Southern Song Dynasty, as the Southern Song authorities failed to protect Yang Hui's intellectual property and allowed Yang Hui's intellectual property to be infringed upon; secondly, as the intellectual world was relatively closed at that historical period and the flow of information was extremely limited, Yang Hui's theories in the Southern Song Dynasty were not widely disseminated worldwide in a timely manner, which in turn led to the European intellectual community not being able to gain Yang Hui's s contribution to the new theory. This set the stage for the later formulation of Pascal's triangle, a repetition of Yang Hui's triangle, albeit a repetitive, inefficient and low-value mechanized labor.

However, since the early 21st century, developed and sub-developed countries worldwide have established relatively well-developed systems of protection for intellectual property. In such circumstances, unless producers are able to infringe the intellectual property rights of the remaining innovators or creators through illegal means such as plagiarism, certain limitations of the People's History in historical materialism would begin to emerge when the Ideological and Political System of Banselism is realized: the People's History assumes the substitutability of all citizens. Nonetheless, the view of history in this chapter is strongly supportive of the people's view of history and is therefore a critical successor to it. Specifically, when the Ideological and Political System of Banselism is implemented, all people will have a respective monopoly on the core new intellectual property they produce respectively, which makes every adult citizen irreplaceable.

At the same time, it is undeniable that the Big Man Theory is also theoretically correct, scientific, and socio-historical to a large extent. The Big Man Theory holds that human history is determined by an elite few, including elites, inventors, capitalists, bureaucrats, and so forth. First and foremost, the mechanized workforce of the early 21st century had not yet been transformed into the student class and thereby evolve into the rest of the high-end social classes such as the Banselistic class, which made most of them fungible, indicating that even the AI, the robots and the automation could eliminate them, so the masses at that period were not yet able to determine the social elite even if there were only a small number of individuals in it, thus establishing the foundation for the popularization of the Big Man Theory. Apart from that, in the late-modern period and in the 20th century, innovative or creative individuals were only a minority of the population, but they played a major role in driving the course of human history: the relatively low level of productivity at that historical period meant that the market still required a large number of human resources for low-skilled mechanized work, which in turn prevented most people from evolving into innovative or creative sophisticated talents like inventors. This also became one of the main reasons for the popularization of the Big Man Theory. In addition, the fact that innovative or creative elites could not be replaced under the protection of the law provided a legal and theoretical basis for the popularization of the Big Man Theory: Watt, for example, was a cutting-edge high-tech talent whose inventions, including the steam engine, were legally protected by the British Empire, which made him irreplaceable.

However, by the early 21st century, automation had begun to gradually replace manual workers in the developed country. Sami Atiya, the director of ABB's Robotics and Motion in

Switzerland, noted in an interview conducted by Forbes in 2018 that most people are reluctant to take on the jobs that robots are doing—heavy assembly, painting car parts or highly repetitive tasks—and that robots are growing at an annual rate of 13–14%, and in fact, robots are being added to almost every industry: food and beverage, clothing manufacturers, food companies, including warehouse companies such as Amazon Robotics, to name a few. Meanwhile, according to the news 'Machines to 'do half of all work tasks by 2025' reported by BBC in 2021, the COVID pandemic has led companies to start minimizing production costs through automation, for example, and the World Economic Forum, in this BBC interview, pointed out that routine or manual work in administration and data processing was most at risk from automation. The World Economic Forum also noted in this interview with the BBC that routine or manual tasks in management and data processing were the most vulnerable to automation. It said that while in the early 21st century only a third of jobs were performed by machines and manual labor will do the rest, while by 2025 the balance will be shifted: the demand for jobs that rely on human skills such as advice, decision-making, reasoning, communication, and interaction will increase, but millions of routine or manual jobs will be replaced by technology, affecting the lowest paid and lowest skilled workers the most. Thus, what is in line with the position of this chapter is that the World Economic Forum also offers this response to this social problem in this BBC interview: "millions of people will need to reskill to cope with this change." Hence, it follows that, over time, more and more conventional or manual workers will be replaced by automation, and that these ordinary citizens displaced by automation will be retrained to become innovative or creative elites, and thus irreplaceable, highlighting a certain limitation of the Big Man Theory: only a small group of individuals will be able to become elites at the cutting edge. The historical perspective in this chapter, however, strongly supports the heroic view of history and thus has critical inheritance from the Big Man Theory. Specifically, when the Ideological and Political System of Banselism is implemented, everyone will have a separate monopoly on the core new intellectual property produced by each of them respectively, which will make every adult citizen irreplaceable.

Hence, overall, historical materialism has the following shortcomings compared to the Banselistic view of history (the Banselistic History): firstly, the theory was to some extent a tool for the exploitation of the proletariat by business owners in the early 21st century. Specifically, it provided a certain theoretical basis for the exploitation of the proletariat by the capitalist class or business owners in the early 21st century: in mainland China at the time, for example, the idea of historical materialism led a large number of private business owners to believe that each individual merely had a low capacity and was replaceable, which stimulated companies at the time to recruit candidates at hourly wages far lower than those in developed countries while having an extremely difficult requirement on each of the candidates; then, the historical materialist doctrine discouraged innovation and creativity to some extent, including the development of science and technology: because the historical materialist doctrine believed that all people were highly replaceable, including researchers and so forth. This made innovative or creative people susceptible to criticism of the value of their irreplaceable labor when they innovated or created, because they had to face a great deal of external criticism under the influence of the historical materialist doctrine (e.g., by emphasizing the substitutability of the outcomes of their labor with no specific example or evidence.

Nonetheless, the substitutability of these inventors can

only be found in the case of violators who illegally thieve and steal their intellectual property. This kind of external criticism with not enough specific real-world evidence would have weakened the social status of these innovative or creative talents and even lowered their income levels), thus hampering to a certain extent the technological development of China at the time. At the same time, compared to the Banselistic view of history, metaphysical and over emphasis on the Big Man Theory will lead the elite minority to ignore the initiative of the common people, thereby exacerbating the exploitation of the people by the ruling class, and will be likely to lead to subjective arbitrariness.

The Banselistic History, however, has the following advantages over the above-mentioned views because it is a critical successor to both: firstly, it is more conducive to the promotion of innovation and creativity, including technological development: all citizens are transformed under the large-scale automation into innovative or creative elites whose core intellectual property is protected by law and cannot be imitated or used without permission. This will make the majority of citizens irreplaceable and reduce external resistance, including external criticism, to these individuals: it will effectively maintain the social status of the innovators and creators; also, as each innovator and creator opens up new and independent directions in unknown fields and monopolizes all types of core intellectual property gained by each of them respectively, the capitalist class will not be able to exploit them and will therefore recruit them with high salaries and incomes, thereby preventing the capitalist class or the business owner from exploiting the people, especially the employees. In addition, the Banselistic view of history can effectively circumvent the tyranny of Banselism: although the rest of the citizens cannot repeat the directions opened by the innovator or creator in the unknown field of knowledge under the protection of laws and regulations, the innovator or creator monopolizes the intellectual property of his or her own production and the rest of the citizens can be transformed, be upskilled and upgrade into innovators or creators and thus monopolize their own part of the intellectual property: in this situation, the comparison of power between different innovators or creators will be incomparable as each of them is the best elite in each of the new direction he or she establishes, therefore making their social status to become equal and thereby prevent the tyranny of Banselism; at the same time, the Ideological and Political System of Banselism, including the Banselistic vision of history, will strengthen the particularity of each citizen by giving each citizen a monopoly on his or her own part of the core intellectual property. The human rights and humanitarian consciousness, in this case, will therefore be reinforced, and human rights and humanitarianism will be effectively defended, as the Ideological and Political System of Banselism, including the Banselistic History will strengthen the particularity and initiative of each citizen.

Chapter Two:

The Banselistic Epistemology

In the early 21st century, both thorough idealists and materialists believed that consciousness has a subjective initiative: the consciousness can correctly reflect matter, subjectivity can correctly reflect objectiveness, and the knowability was recognized as the correct theory in their views; metaphysical materialists, however, believe that matter and consciousness do not have the same identity, and consciousness cannot correctly reflect matter. For instance, color, color is merely the result of the action of particles in the retina of the human body rather than the attribute of the external thing itself. This book believes that to begin with, consciousness and matter have the same identity, consciousness can correctly reflect matter, and subject can correctly reflect object. Meanwhile, consciousness has subjective initiative. What is the same as Marxism is that this chapter also thinks that consciousness has socially historical attribute, in other words, the subjective initiative of consciousness is different in different historical periods. Nevertheless, what is different from Marxism and what is in line with subjective idealism is that the subject's consciousness will have absolute and thorough subjective initiative in the long run.

To begin with, what will be explained is the subjective initiative of consciousness in the early stage of human society. In the early period of human society, human consciousness only had extremely low subjective initiative, and had extremely significant limitations and defects. For example, in the early medical sciences of human society, most of its theories were far removed from the natural science, which were extremely accidental and were extremely inefficient to cure diseases, thereby causing great casualties and economic losses; another example is feudal ethics. Its belief in 'sovereign power' is also seriously out of touch with humanism and natural sciences, greatly imprisoning the development of human consciousness, which in turn caused an extremely negative impact on the development of economy and productivity and the progress of human society.

This is determined by the extreme deficiencies of material and human consciousness in the early stage of human society: In the early stage of human society, the power of human subjective consciousness has an extremely large gap compared with the power of objective material. Matter, in this case, had a decisive effect on consciousness, and it extremely restrained the development and perfection of consciousness, thereby causing serious obstacles to social progress.

In addition, what will be elaborated on is the subjective initiative of consciousness in the early 21st century. In the early 21st century, human consciousness has certain subjective initiatives, but the subjective initiative of consciousness still has extremely significant limitations and defects. For instance the Alcubierre drive put forward by Miguel Alcubierre in 1994, because the material corresponding to the technical theory has not been discovered and the energy required to maintain the bending is greater than the total energy of the three-dimensional space, etc., this theory was confirmed as a paradox by academia, and it was again confirmed as a paradox by an article published by academia worldwide in 2002—this technology has not been realized in the early 21st century, and the distance between different planets is far greater than the longest one-way travel distance that humans can reach in space outside the earth early the 21st century. They have become an important reason why mankind has not yet begun interstellar colonization in geopolitics. Another example is the activities of humans and extraterrestrial civilizations in the early 21st century: humans had not yet discovered extraterrestrial civilizations. During the sixty decades, researchers carried out many search plans, including the use of high-precision telescopes, radio telescopes, etc. precise equipment, and actively collect radio signals, etc., while also targeting a series of galaxies that are likely to have extraterrestrial civilizations, but humans still have nothing to find, and no extraterrestrial civilization has been discovered; meanwhile, in the early 21st century, a large number of relevant professionals in academia calculated: If you draw a sphere with a diameter of 33,000 light years with the earth as the center, then the decades-long exploration of mankind actually only covers 5.8×10^-16% of the sphere. The sphere basically covers the densest area of stars, and even the star clusters around the series of stars. If the universal existence of life in the universe is proved to be a correct theory, then in the sphere, higher civilizations must universally exist, but humans have not yet discovered higher civilizations; in addition, in the early 21st century, the development of human beings in various disciplines mostly relied on speculation rather than practice to formally verify the correctness of the proposed speculation theories.

The above-mentioned examples reflect the extremely significant limitations and defects of human consciousness in the early 21st century. They, firstly, are determined by the rule that the matter affects consciousness to an enormously large extent when the power of matter is enormously large compared with that of consciousness. Although human consciousness has achieved a certain degree of development and modernization in the early 21st century, it is still subject to extremely significant constraints from material; secondly, the other types of entities and virtual bodies are extremely powerful compared with conscious entities and conscious virtual bodies, which also causes human consciousness to still have highly significant limitations and defects at this point.

Apart from that, the subjective initiative of human consciousness in the era of large-scale popularization of AI will be explained. The improvement of the renewable energy technology, the large-scale popularization of 5G and the Quantum communication will altogether determine the large-scale popularization of AI, which replaces all mechanized labors, thereby causing individuals to provide innovative or creative labors: This kind of activity inevitably and directly involves mental activities, which develops the subjective initiative of human consciousness. In addition, the comprehensive solution to the issue of lack of food for all human beings is conducive to establishing a material foundation for the development of their consciousness and further strengthen their subjective initiative: To begin with, early in the 21st century, Yuan Longping, an academician of the Chinese Academy of Engineering, successively invented the 'three-line method' hybrid rice, the 'two-line method' hybrid rice, the first phase of super hybrid rice, the second phase of super hybrid rice, and sea rice. When various advanced hybrid rice technologies are further improved and are applied on a larger scale globally, the global food shortage issue will be able to be solved almost completely, which will establish the foundation for the further improvement of human consciousness and thus strengthen the subjective initiative of human consciousness; the second example is the lab-grown meat of Israel. In 2019, Israel successfully developed artificial meat—an artificial animal protein product. 'Producing meat is very inefficient,', suggested Yaakov Nahmias, a bio-engineering professor at the Hebrew University and founder of Future Meat Technologies, 'Cultured meat, by comparison, consumes 10 time less water, less land, less energy than the current meat production.', once the production cost of it is reduced and therefore enables this technology to be popularized on a large scale, humans will be able to obtain animal protein through laboratory-grown meat. Compared with the conventional methods of producing meat in the early 21st century, the production of artificial meat (animal protein-based artificial meat instead of plant-based protein artificial meat) consumes very few materials such as land, energy, and water. When this technology is popularized on a large scale, food shortage issues of mankind will be solved almost completely, which will build up the material foundation for the further improvement of human consciousness, including the subjective initiative of it.

The third example is the development of 3D printing technology. As it has been reported by the South China Morning Post (SCMP) located in Hong Kong in 2021, researchers from Osaka University in Japan tried to use 3D printing technology to produce Wagyu beef that year, "If we are able to quickly produce a lot of meat from a few cells, there is a chance that we will be able to respond to food and protein shortage issues in the future,", said one of the team's researchers—Michiya Matsusaki, Professor of Applied Chemistry at Osaka University, "it may be cheaper when the process is refined and automated." When automation technology is popularized on a large scale, the artificial intelligence digital vision system can make 3D printing technology refined for meat production. Meanwhile, as AI replaces all mechanized labors, the production of meat by 3D printing technology will be automated, which will greatly reduce the cost of 3D printing technology to produce meat and thus reduce its price, thereby popularizing this technology and solving the issue of food shortage, including the protein shortage for all human beings. This will establish the material foundation for the further development of their consciousness, promoting the weakening of the finiteness, limitations and defects of their consciousness and the enhancement of the subjective initiative of consciousness.

Also, the development of artificial intelligence technology can also enable artificial intelligence to help humans explore and understand the three-dimensional space, which enhances the power of human consciousness, including the subjective initiative of human consciousness. This also includes the ability to correctly understand the objective and external world. James Parr, founder and director of NASA's Frontier Development Laboratory (FDL), stated in 2018: "Kepler was really looking at just a postage stamp and now Transiting Exoplanet Survey Satellite (TESS) is going to look at 80–85% of the sky. It's a huge data challenge. Much of the data analysis is still done manually." Accordingly, FDL began to use artificial intelligence to analyze the data collected by Kepler. This measure has been proven effective. Therefore, FDL hoped to analyze the data collected by TESS in the next year. Meanwhile, James Parr pointed out that although mapping the craters at the moon's poles could help to discover which craters might contain frozen water, at the rate of that time it would have taken over 2,000 years to map it manually. Consequently, the FDL and Intel had jointly created a game wherein players could help annotate images of lunar craters, after which the collected dataset would be used to train a convolutional neural network (CNN), a kind of network adept at image recognition, to spot polar craters. The trained machine learning model was a hundred times faster than human experts, with 98.4% accuracy. Since AI is regarding the representation system that supports model building, CNN is classified as AI. These two examples show that when artificial intelligence technology is popularized on a large scale, the efficiency of exploring the three-dimensional space will be greatly improved, which will effectively improve a conscious subject's understanding of three-dimensional space, including that of human beings.

Meanwhile, the size of artificial intelligence is not limited by genes, and its size can reach the nanometer scale, which will effectively help humans improve their understanding of the micro world; moreover, the emergence of the man-machine integration technology has determined that a considerable part of individuals will evolve into cyborgs, which breaks through the genetic constraints on their composition and therefore even makes individuals' consciousness superior to matter to a very small extent, and is extremely effective in strengthening the subjective initiative of the individual, so that their understanding can more effectively reflect the objective world.

These examples reflect the subject initiative of human consciousness in the era of large-scale popularization of artificial intelligence technology. On the one hand, this is determined by the fact that consciousness power and material power are almost equivalent at this time, to a certain extent it is even greater than material power. Nonetheless, at this stage, consciousness has not succeeded in surpassing matter to a relatively large extent, which is determined by the greater power of the other types of entities and virtual bodies than that of consciousness.

Also, what will be explained is the subjective initiative of individuals' consciousness when the man-integration technology is popularized on a large scale. Early the 21st century, the technology of man-machine integration has emerged and is used in a small group of people, and digital models have also emerged and been put into use. The technology of human-computer integration can directly break through the restriction of genes to its composition, and the combination with the digital model will greatly improve the consciousness of the subject. To begin with, with regard to the sensory system, artificial intelligence can build digital models by imitating the physiological structure of biological humans and other different types of organisms to learn the effects of their physiological functions: for example, color, artificial intelligence can imitate the retina of various organisms to learn more types of colors, meanwhile, it can also build virtual models based on the structure of the objective things themselves to conduct an absolutely objective analysis of the attributes of the objective things themselves; also, because the size of artificial intelligence has broken through genetic constraints and restrictions on its composition, and the combination of man-machine technology as well as nano-robot technology have emerged in the early years of 21st century, after the combination of man-machine, the body size of the consciousness carrier will be able to reach the nanometer level: this will effectively improve the consciousness subject's understanding of the micro world; apart from that, the cognitive behavior system, knowledge system, actuator system and other systems of artificial intelligence are updated and developed at a high frequency under the mechanical carrier, thus speeding up the evolution of the consciousness subject, including the rapid improvement of its intelligence level, thus strengthening the consciousness of the consciousness subject including its ability to understand the external world: This will also make the ability of the consciousness subject that has finished the man-machine integration quickly exceed the ability of the individual who has not yet finished the combination of man and machine, with the life of the robot much longer than that of those who are using the biological carrier, the group of digital human will increase its number on a large scale while maintaining the overwhelming advantages of each unit individual in this social group, so that the remaining individuals who have not yet undergone the integration of man and machine will do the man-machine integration, so that they can evolve rapidly according to the above process, perfecting human consciousness unprecedentedly.

At this stage, the consciousness of the subject has a relatively strong subjective initiative. To begin with, this is determined by the fact that the consciousness of the conscious subject at this time is greater than that of the material; secondly, this is determined by the reciprocity between the consciousness of the consciousness subject at this time and the power of the other entities and virtual bodies excluding matter and consciousness: the evolution of the consciousness subject at this time is extremely fast, and its consciousness is largely perfected, which breaks through the constraints of non-material and non-conscious entities and their attributes, including time, on the consciousness of the conscious subject.

Moreover, what will be explained is the subjective initiative of consciousness when the human civilization evolves into the ultramic-digital human. The artificial intelligence vision system has the characteristics of digitization, and its measurement unit can be accurate to multiple decimal points, which will greatly reduce the difficulty of producing relatively small precision equipment, which is conducive to the production of the nano-digital human. Nano-digital humans are small and consume less raw materials, with the continuous development of the digitization of artificial intelligence vision systems, the large-scale popularization of the nano-digital human will inevitably occur.

Since the human-machine integration technology will directly implant human consciousness into the robots, including nano-digital humans, and the group of the nano-digital human has an overwhelming advantage in population, which will make the remaining individuals who have not evolved into nano-digital humans to evolve into them in order to adapt to such competitive pressure coming from the nano-digital human.

Meanwhile, the miniature size of the nano-digital human is conducive to the discovery of particles smaller than quarks and use them as materials to produce the digital human, thereby continuously reducing the size of it. Nevertheless, Planck, the father of modern physics, has once proposed that matter cannot be divided infinitely, which means the size of the digital human cannot be infinitely small, and it has the minimum value therein it cannot be further divided: the ultramic-digital human (see volume five, for details) will inevitably exist and will be popularized on a large scale.

The above content means: To begin with, when the ultramic-digital human is popularized on a large scale, individuals' understanding of the microcosm will become absolute and thorough, which is because at this time the size of the person has been subdivided to the minimum, the precision of its visual system will also enable it to thoroughly understand all extreme microscopic matter; secondly, according to the singularity theory and the Big Bang theory proposed by Belgian astronomer and cosmologist Lemaitre·Georges in 1929, the mass of the singularity is infinite, and the three-dimensional space produced after the explosion also has infinite mass. According to the *General Relativity* published by Albert Einstein in 1915, $E=mc^2$, which can be written as: $E \div m=c^2$, indicating that the mass is proportional to energy—there is infinite energy in the three-dimensional space, which enables the ultramic-digital human to absorb energy so as to provide a carrier for its consciousness. The constantly increasing energy will lead to the stably increasing mass, as $GM/r^2=c^2/r$ shows, when its mass reaches a certain ratio to the radius of its circumcircle, the space and even time around it will be distorted, which enables its consciousness power to determine all other kinds of entities and virtual bodies: For instance time, when it is moving near the ultramic-digital human, it will be distorted, which will also enhance its new feature of curviness and stillness: This will greatly weaken the restrictive effect of non-material and non-conscious entities and non-material and non-conscious virtual bodies on the development of consciousness, which greatly improves human consciousness including the subjective initiative of human consciousness.

Therefore, at this stage, human consciousness has an enormously significant subjective initiative. To begin with, this is determined by the fact that the consciousness, in this case, has an enormously large power compared with that of matter; also, this is determined by the enormously large power of individuals'(which is the same as subject's) consciousness compared with that of non-material and non-conscious entities, as well as non-material and non-conscious virtual bodies.

Most importantly, what will be explained is the subjective initiative of individuals or subjects when human beings evolve into the space human (see Volume Five, Chapter One: The formation of the space human, for details). When the consciousness of the ultramic-digital human continues to develop, it continuously absorbs energy to create the material carrier of its consciousness. According to Einstein's General Relativity $E=mc^2$, the deformation formula of it is $E \div m=c^2$, indicating that the mass is proportional to the energy, which will continue to enhance the quality of the ultramic-digital human.

Meanwhile, as $GM/r^2=c^2/r$ shows, when the mass of the ultramic-digital human and the radius of its circumscribed circle reach a certain ratio, the ultramic-digital human will become an intelligent black hole. And the black hole singularity lying in the center of the black hole has infinite mass, which will distort the nearby time and space and become a channel into the space of the other dimensions. At this time, subjects or individuals will begin to use the universe of the other dimensions as the carrier and evolve into the space human.

The space human, firstly, can immediately learn all things in the universe and their attributes, which reflects the absolute and complete subjective initiative of their consciousness; secondly, individuals who use space as the carrier can change everything in the universe on their own, which enables the consciousness to override other types of entities and virtual bodies.

At this time, human consciousness has absolute and thorough subjective initiative and overrides all kinds of entities and virtual bodies, which is determined by the fact that the power of consciousness, in this case, has an extreme and infinite power compared with other types of entities and virtual bodies.

Then elaborate on the book's partial summary of the subjective initiative of consciousness based on the above examples. First and foremost, this book does not admit that human consciousness has absolute and complete subjective initiative before humans evolve into space humans, but admits that over time, human consciousness will inevitably form absolute and complete subjective initiative, and completely override other types of entities and virtual bodies; secondly, the subjective initiative of consciousness is directly proportional to the power and perfection of consciousness.

Finally, what will be explained is the methodology corresponding to this chapter. To begin with, individuals need to constantly improve their own consciousness to weaken the finiteness, limitations and defects of their own consciousness, and enhance the subjective initiative of their own consciousness, including the ability to correctly understand the external world. Also, individuals need to actively develop science and technology to directly weaken the finiteness, limitations, and defects of consciousness, because the development of science and technology theory can directly promote the perfection of consciousness, which increases the power of consciousness, thereby strengthening its subjective initiative and weakening its finiteness, limitations, and defects. Moreover, when analyzing things and theories, individuals need to pay attention to the historical periods, because different historical periods will result in different levels of perfection of the consciousness, which determines the difference in the degree of the subjective initiative of human consciousness and the degree of practicability of the theory in different eras.

Volume Four:

The Banselistic Educational System

Chapter One:

The Banselistic Educational System

When automation technology is popularized on a large scale, artificial intelligence will replace all mechanized labors. Since the proportion of mechanized labor in the total population is greater than that of other classes, and the number of educators is much lower than the number of mechanized laborers, there is no way for mechanized laborers including the vast majority of working class and some middle-class members to transform into the exam-oriented student but becoming the Banselistic student. Meanwhile, owing to the large-scale class mobility under the Ideological and Political System of Banselism, the authority of diplomas will be unprecedentedly and continuously weakened and even lost eventually, the exam-oriented student, in this case, will no longer exist. Correspondingly, a new educational system needs to be established.

To begin with, what will be explained is Banselistic pre-primary education and Banselistic elementary education.

Banselistic preprimary education is the same as that in the early 21st century. Before the large-scale popularization of the man-machine integration technology, the consciousness and enthusiasm for class mobility of children and teenagers under the age of sixteen still generally has serious defects and limitations. For this reason, school education still needs to be retained to supervise and regulate learners under the age of 16, and to help them finish the class mobility in the future.

Banselistic elementary education is highly similar to the elementary education in the early 21st century. Study subjects include language (the native language and one or more foreign languages designated by the government), mathematics, and the integrated curriculum. Among them, the 'integrated curriculum' includes general technical courses, law, history, basic life knowledge, etc., and it accounts for more grades than that of the language and mathematics. In the elementary education stage, the above subjects are compulsory subjects. All learners are required to study these subjects and participate in the corresponding national unified written examination. Those who fail to pass the national unified written examination are required to repeat the grade until they pass the examination.

It is necessary to establish these compulsory subjects by critically modeling them on the mainstream primary education system of the early 21st century. Let us start with the national languages, which are conducive to the development of the learner's intellect and related modes of thinking. In particular, the study of a national language develops reading, critical thinking, writing and communication skills, including the ability to call upon and express oneself, which in turn indirectly develops leadership and teamwork skills. In this way, the national language is conducive to the long-term development of the Banselistic class including writers, editors, poets, and other textual creators, as well as the elite class including sales and research project team leaders.

At the same time, foreign languages have the following key positive effects on learners: firstly, making them compulsory helps them to develop an international perspective and to adapt to globalization; secondly, for low-caliber learners, learning a foreign language helps them to develop their brains: bilingual or polyglot talents tend to have a better memory, imitation and learning ability, concentration, critical thinking. Furthermore, making a second language compulsory helps learners to make full use of the global brainstorm, which in the long term will help the social class, including the Banselistic class to contribute more to the whole human civilization from both material and spiritual levels. In addition, making the study of a foreign language compulsory strengthens learners' external communication skills and contributes indirectly to the development of their international leadership skills.

In the case of mathematics, making it a compulsory subject for lower-level learners has the following positive effects: Firstly, making mathematics a compulsory subject for all learners is conducive to the development of the Banselistic class including scientists and engineers, as well as the elite class including financial analysts and actuaries. Secondly, making mathematics a compulsory subject for all younger learners will help learners to solve problems in their daily lives and in other related subjects; thirdly, making mathematics a compulsory subject will strengthen learners' imagination, innovation, and creativity; and fourthly, making mathematics a compulsory subject will strengthen students' data analysis skills.

The integrated curriculum comprises general technology, law, history, and basic life skills. In order to help all citizens to adapt to the large-scale automation, a compulsory subject 'general technology' will be added to primary education. The general technology teaches relevant content regarding broad, general, and basic technology, it does not mainly teach learners a professionalized technical theory of the natural sciences, but emphasizes the cross-fertilization of the natural, social, and human sciences, with a strong emphasis on innovation and creativity, practice and teamwork. Listing this subject as a compulsory subject has the following positive effects: firstly, it integrates the arts and sciences and infuses learners with the latest natural science or humanities knowledge, which helps them to gain the latest knowledge; secondly, the compulsory requirement for students to use critical, innovative, and creative thinking in General Technology helps to strengthen learners' critical, innovative and creative thinking and develop their intellectual capacity. In the long run, this will help learners to break through and broaden the boundaries of the knowledge; also, General Technology directly reinforces learners' ability to apply their knowledge across a wide range of fields, which is conducive to training more inter-disciplinary talents; in addition, the subject is conducive to strengthening learners' teamwork and even leadership skills; and the inclusion of General Technology as a compulsory subject is conducive to strengthening learners' ability to apply their knowledge in practice.

The inclusion of law as one of the compulsory subjects within the integrated curriculum will help to instill a general knowledge of the law in learners, fostering a sense of lawfulness in young learners, which helps to build up a stable social order.

The history course is also one of the key subjects in the integrated curriculum. The inclusion of history as a compulsory subject is, firstly, conducive to increasing students' general and basic knowledge in various subjects and to laying the foundation of knowledge for later class mobility; secondly, the compulsory study of history helps students to develop a deeper understanding of the world, including its inner rules; thirdly, the inclusion of history as a compulsory subject helps students to develop critical thinking: different views on the same historical event between different authoritative scholars directly helps younger learners to open up their critical thinking; fourthly, making history compulsory for all learners helps to strengthen learners' logical and creative thinking skills: according to the third point, the fact that the views of different scholars on the same historical event are different and even confrontational, which stimulates learners to form their own independent arguments on historical events based on first-hand accounts and the views of different scholars and to support their own new arguments based on a large number of first-hand accounts, thus directly strengthening students' logical and creative thinking skills.

In this chapter, educators of the Basic Life courses need to help students develop their own motivation (this subject has relevant compulsory test(s), and some of the General Life questions require students to explain their motivation), and to provide students with sex education and emergency preparedness skills education to deal with man-made or natural disasters, as well as to help students develop self-care skills and to help strengthen their moral character. It has the following positive impacts on learners: firstly, it increases students' knowledge in the natural sciences and humanities to a certain extent; secondly, the subject further enhances students' overall quality; also, sex education and emergency preparedness for man-made or natural disasters in the subject contribute to the physical and psychological integrity of learners, avoiding early legacies for their long-term development and effectively safeguarding their personal safety; in addition, basic life literacy teaches all learners to take care of themselves and helps them to develop their own motivation, which, on the one hand, reduces the burden on a significant number of employed individuals (parents) and, on the other hand, helps them to develop their own motivation, which strengthens their self-control and concentration to an unprecedented degree and provides them with a high level of motivation for future class mobility. Meanwhile, the ethics program within the integrated discipline helps to further strengthen learners' communication, teamwork, and leadership skills, and it also helps students to acquire political correctness, such as respect for fundamental human rights and freedoms including freedom of religion, freedom of speech, freedom of assembly and academic freedom, which contributes to the protection of the human rights of all citizens.

Nonetheless, to reduce the burden on students by addressing the problem of uneven distribution of educational resources, the number of mock examinations is organized by the national or local government, and single subject textbooks are printed and distributed to students by the government, while all other auxiliary materials are classified as illegal. Meanwhile, in order to develop students' innovative, creative, and imaginative abilities and to maximize their intelligence and potential, the content of the examination must involve questions that develop such potential: for instance, the imagination test is a picture-writing test, which requires students to describe the content of a picture in a way that is as innovative and unique as possible, and also logical. This type of question can be found in language and general technology subjects and should be the main test point in order to prevent learners from being replaced by artificial intelligence in the long term.

At the same time, allowing students to develop their

potential and intellect in other highly liberating forms has a significant positive effect on their long-term development. Let's take the example of playing video games and watching related movies and films, including cartoons and movies: these recreational activities are closely related to the sensory system, including the visual and auditory senses, which will lead to the development of the right brain of the user or viewer, especially at a young age, and thus develop their imagination, etc. If the work is domestic, these learners will be influenced by the traditional culture of that country, which will indirectly strengthen their patriotism, while if the work is overseas, it will help them learn about the culture of that country to a certain extent. In the case of sports, for example, playing sports after school strengthens learners' hands-on skills and reflexes, and most sports are played as a team, which also develops learners' social skills. Also, take the example of accompanying a loved one, which enables students to receive their own internal family education, for example.

Therefore, to further reduce the burden of schoolwork for students to improve their efficiency, and to allow them to develop their potential and their skills in a more liberal way, there are no selective entrance examinations for students at primary level, but only passing examinations. This is to avoid an uneven distribution of educational resources that would lead to a decline in the overall quality of most students—selective entrance examinations only ensure that a minority of students are innovative and creative, as the education system of the early 21st century amply demonstrated—at that historical period, academically successful learners represented a tiny minority of all learners worldwide. On the one hand, this is because automation was not widespread, and the supply of educational resources was grossly inadequate. On the other hand, this is also caused by the grossly unequal distribution of educational resources wherein the vast majority of them were allocated to a very small number of learners, training the majority of learners to become a mechanized workforce.

The reform will result in a more even and equitable distribution of resources for primary education, but there will still be differences between public and aristocratic schools for the West. Specifically, the sophistication of hardware facilities in public schools may not be on a par with that of noble schools, and the sophistication of special platforms in public schools, such as those supporting natural science or business-based competitions, may not be on a par with that of noble schools.

Finally, the government will waive or charge low tuition fees for primary education students (public schools only) but will not provide funding from the Banselistic Student Income for primary education students.

This primary education, on the one hand, is conducive to the development of the student's creative and innovative abilities, to the maximum development of the student's intellect and to the release of the student's potential; on the other hand, it ensures that students will be transformed into Banselistic students in the future with a relatively sound knowledge of the basic disciplines and basic knowledge of life, which facilitates their class mobility.

Apart from that, what will be explained is the Banselistic secondary education. The first two or three years of Banselistic secondary education are a continuation of the Banselistic primary education system and the subjects study overlap with the primary education system. After passing the examinations, the students can enter the second stage of secondary education. This helps to reduce the burden on learners in primary education, as a large proportion of the examination content is included in the first three years of secondary education rather than in primary education, thereby reducing the burden on learners in primary education and thus increasing their learning efficiency.

In the second three or four years of Banselistic secondary education, subjects are: general technical courses, major and other types of elective courses. Among all of them, the major and the general technology courses are compulsory and written examinations are required. Once a learner has taken an elective course, he or she must also complete the elective course to gain additional credit. Secondary education students are required to take a national examination for graduation, of which Professional and General Technology courses are compulsory, and if they take additional courses, they are required to take the relevant electives to gain additional credit. Learners are required to ensure that they gain enough credits that meet the national requirements to graduate. In this model, learners can accumulate credits in the following ways: firstly, by choosing to take only specialist courses and general technology: in this method, learners can avoid the constraints posed by their areas of weakness and thus become highly skilled in their field of specialization; the second method is to take multiple courses in different majors: some learners have significant strengths in two or more different majors, and if they use this strategy to take credits, they are likely to graduate earlier than those who use the first method, because the more courses they take per unit of time, the more credits they will be able to gain per unit of time, and thus they will be able to earn credits towards graduation requirements earlier; The third method is to major in one or more courses and take or minor in a more relevant subject to your major as elective course(s). For example, finance learners can earn more credits per unit of time by taking more relevant subjects such as economics, mathematics, statistics, calculator science, business, psychology, political science, etc., thus accelerating their progress towards graduation.

This mode is highly scientific: to begin with, there is an explosion of knowledge when automation becomes widespread. In other words, at this time, the volume of knowledge will continue to increase rapidly on a global scale while human memory is relatively limited, with market system and society choosing talents primarily based on talents' areas of strength rather than their areas of weakness, which means for the vast majority of citizens, general education is no longer appropriate at this time, and assessment criteria should focus on candidates' advantaged field in order to circumvent the constraints on students' development caused by their disadvantaged areas or disciplines; in addition, allowing learners with significant strengths in a number of different areas of specialization to major in these subjects at the same time facilitates the development of cross-cutting talents in the long term; also, for some disciplines, as they progress through the same area of specialization, learners will inevitably face problems that require interdisciplinary and cross-disciplinary knowledge to solve, and for this reason, elective courses are retained and allow learners to select relevant electives according to their own circumstances, thus facilitating the development of T-shaped talents; apart from that, general technology courses have been retained in the compulsory curriculum, which helps to strengthen learners' critical thinking, imagination, innovation and creativity, preventing them from being replaced by artificial intelligence.

Also, what is similar to the mainstream education system of the early 21st century is that under the model in this chapter, extra marks are awarded for special extra-curricular activities, such as participation in competitions and winning relevant awards, publication of articles or books, participation in research projects, participation in volunteer activities or charity work, and participation in other types of extra-curricular activities.

This type of educational system has the following advantages: To begin with, it helps to stimulate a sense of innovation and creativity in learners and in the long term contributes new types of knowledge to the academic community. In addition, this system prioritizes class mobility for learners with specific competencies such as outstanding leadership, communication, and teamwork skills, which stimulates learners to strengthen their own leadership, communication, and teamwork skills. Also, rewarding learners for their active participation in charity and volunteer activities gives priority to those with a strong sense of social responsibility in their studies, which in turn reinforces their sense of social responsibility to a certain extent, creating positive externalities and social surplus in the long run.

In this paper, the secondary education system is a four-year system according to the length of the high school year in the early 21st century. Learners will become Banselistic students after they have achieved their credits and therefore graduated and will start the class mobility on this basis. In most cases, the age of the learner at this point is around 16–18 years. Becoming a Banselistic student immediately after graduating at this age helps to address the cross-century issue of lacking financial resources for young social groups. This is because the vast majority of Banselistic students will eventually become members in the Banselistic class, and since direct innovation or creation in the material or spiritual civilization means that the producer is contributing new intellectual property independently, and that this intellectual property is strictly protected by law and cannot be imitated or stolen by anyone without permission, which will enable the producers to monopolize the intellectual property, so that they will not need to face competitors. Consequently, the Banselistic students will not have to face competitive pressure from the elder producers—those who have already established the economic base. Since most of the young individuals will be freelance, they will not be opposed and exploited by the capitalist class at this time, which will effectively resolve the lack of capital and economic base for young individuals.

Such a system of secondary education will ensure that students are transformed into Banselistic students with a sound knowledge of their field of specialization and a sound knowledge of the rest of the fields involved in that specialization, thus increasing the efficiency of their class mobility.

Since the primary and secondary education systems in this paper belong to the Banselistic education, they are also counted as time spent by Banselistic students on class mobility. Thus, in the context of Volume 1, Part 2, Chapter 2: The class mobility, the learner who graduates and is transformed into a Banselistic student at this point in time will only consume an additional 20-16 = 4 years to complete class mobility if he/she is a very efficient learner, whereas for the less efficient learner, he/she will consume an additional 30-16 = 14 years or 50-16 = 14 years after graduation to finish the class mobility.

Meanwhile, for countries with undergraduate rates well above 50%, such as South Korea, may choose to enable the student class to complete class mobility by popularizing the university education in the early 21st century. If countries with undergraduate rates well above 50%, such as South Korea, choose to help the student class complete class mobility through universal access to early 21st century university education, then the content of this chapter is not applicable for these countries.

Finally, what will be explained is the Banselistic education under the large-scale application of the human-machine integration technology. Back in 2016, Peter Scott-Morgan, a British AI doctor, had already surgically transformed himself into a cyborg. This example shows that human-machine integration technology has come into being.

When the theory and technology of human-machine integration is perfected to a certain extent, its cost will fall further, and its popularity will increase. This is similar to the way in which the cost of a mobile communication device decreases significantly when the technology is perfected, while the quality of the product increases significantly—the cost effectiveness of the new mobile communication device increases significantly compared to the old version, which in turn will determine a significant increase in its popularity.

The market for human-machine integration mainly comprises the elderly, the weak, the sick and other socially disadvantaged groups with sufficient financial resources, while the ageing of the population and the continuous development and improvement of human-machine integration technology will jointly determine the expansion and strengthening of the digital human, a new higher civilized species. As digital humans break through the limits caused by gene as the digital human does not use any biological carrier, their frequency of renewal will far exceed that of humans. Consequently, all humans will evolve into digital humans in order to adapt to the competitive pressures coming from the digital human, which will determine the historical inevitability of all humans evolving into cyborgs (see Volume Five, Chapter One: The formation of the space human, for more details).

As soon as the digital human is created, it immediately acquires all existing knowledge on a global scale. This is because all existing knowledge is stored in central archives and databases, for example in the cloud, in the context of a highly developed technological and theoretical level, and the existing knowledge can be downloaded directly to a memory card which is automatically implanted in the robot. In this way, the existing knowledge base can be downloaded directly to memory cards, which can then be automatically implanted into the digital human. The individuals with the robot as a carrier can adjust his or her properties by constantly updating himself or herself and thus strengthening his or her abilities.

The Banselistic educational system describes primary and secondary education as only for the human individual in the form of a living organism, will be abolished when human-computer technology becomes widely used. At this point, the citizen automatically acquires the appropriate knowledge, intelligence, and potential as soon as he or she emerges. This means that they do not need to receive the primary or secondary education, or even any kind of education.

In this case, the functions and roles of the various types of schools will be scientific and technological research and development, academic research, promotion of the humanities and arts, promotion of the entertainment industry, etc.

Volume Five:

The Banselistic Anthropology

Chapter One:

The Formation of the Space Human

Early in 2017, British AI PHD Peter Scott Morgan transformed himself into a cyborg through surgery. This case shows the emergence of man-machine integration technology.

As cyborgs break through the restriction of genes in a certain part of areas including memory and the ability of learning, the general capabilities of cyborgs are relatively stronger than those of humans who use organisms as carriers. Under such pressure of competition, human beings with organisms as carriers will evolve into cyborgs.

Cyborgs have not completely circumvented genetic constraints on them. For example, they still must face the problems of aging of physiological functions and a limited lifespan.

Nevertheless, all cyborgs will evolve into the digital human. The digital human refers to the silicon-based life form who partly uses the memory of human beings while completely using the intelligent robot that has its own consciousness as the carrier. Unlike cyborgs, the digital human has completely overcome the genetic constraints and restrictions on their composition, which enables them to have the evolutionary speed that is unprecedentedly high. Meanwhile, the life span of the digital human can be extended infinitely. This is because when the material carrier of the digital human is lost, it only needs to produce another material carrier and implant backup information. These factors will increase the population of the digital human constantly and strengthen the capability of it, so that the competitive advantage of this group will surpass that of cyborgs. Under such competitive pressure, it will be indispensable for cyborgs to completely replace the biological carrier with the electronic and digital carrier. In this situation, all cyborgs will evolve into the digital human.

Also, early in 2016, Harbin Engineering University developed a nanorobot that could 'freestyle' in human blood. The nanorobot can serve the medical field in the early 21st century, curing diseases by killing pathogens in blood vessels, removing impurities, and eliminating blood clots and tumors. As the digital human completely overcomes the genetic restrictions on its size, its size will be able to reach the nanometer level, which means that the nano digital human, one of the outcomes of the continuous evolution of the digital human, will appear.

All digital humans will evolve into the nano-digital human inevitably. To begin with, compared with the digital human whose size is highly large or relatively large, the digital human with a smaller body size merely requires relatively less materials for the producers to produce them. Also, the robot that only finishes the mechanized production is the instrument of production used by the human or the digital human or even the nano-digital human. The vision system of the robot is highly digitalized, and its unit of measurement can be accurate to many decimal places, and in the long run it can be accurate to nanometers or even more decimal points. In this case, the relatively small amount of materials needed to produce nano-robots and the remarkable accuracy of the AI vision system will jointly lead to the relatively low production cost of nano-robots, which will increase the population of the nano-digital human. Since the cost for producing the nano-digital human is less than producing those digital humans with a larger size, the population of the nano-digital human will exceed that of the digital human in the long run. In addition, the level of consciousness of nuclear nano-robots is the same as the larger robots. For instance, the nano-digital human can transform its internal low-energy atoms through the nuclear fusion[1] because in most cases, the diameter of the atom is less than one nanometer, so that the nano-digital human will have the ability to store more energy including more information. In this case, the nano-digital human will be popularized on a large scale.

What is supposed to be acknowledged is that the digital human whose size is relatively large will not take part in the nuclear fusion of their atoms. This is because extreme nuclear fusion will directly lead to nuclear explosions, nuclear pollution, and nuclear leaks. It will directly destroy the material carriers of the digital human consciousness and cause devastating blows or even direct destruction to the material carriers of the digital human nearby.

After the long-term development of the nano-digital human, the continuous improvement of its consciousness will determine the continuous increase of their internal energy and the continuous increase of their quality. To begin with, there are gaps between atoms. The gaps allow the nano-digital human to use other different carriers between the gaps, such as quarks, which are more microscopic than particles, or use energy as the carrier of their consciousness, developing its consciousness and increasing its energy. Also, according to the general relativity by Albert Einstein, $E=mc^2$, which means $E \div m = c^2$, where the c is the speed of light and is also a constant, indicating that c^2 is also a constant. Consequently, as it is deduced from his formula, mass is directly proportional to energy. The continuous improvement of consciousness will determine the continuous increase of its energy, and the continuous increase of energy will determine the continuous increase of its mass. In addition, the energy that can be stored in a unit space is infinite.

Apart from that, what will be explained in the following paragraphs is why the energy that can be stored in a unit space is unlimited. To begin with, although a small number of scholars in the physics academia believe that the energy that can be stored in a unit space is limited, the verification of the black hole theory by Stephen Hawking in 2019 will overturn this hypothesis. To begin with, Nobel Prize winner Roger Penrose theoretically proved the existence of a black hole singularity in 1965. In addition, a large number of scholars in academia also speculated that there is a black hole singularity in the center of the black hole; In the early eleventh century, the technical means to obtain data related to black hole singularities had not yet appeared, and the academic field generally believed that the density of black hole singularities was infinite. Also, Max Karl Ernst Ludwig Planck, the father of modern physics, proposed that space cannot be divided infinitely: space has a minimum, and the space of a black hole also has a minimum. In addition, the 'volume' cannot override space, so the volume of a black hole also has a minimum. According to density = mass ÷ volume, it can be deduced that the mass of the black hole singularity is infinite. Apart from that, the singularity is still the gravitationally curved dimension in essence, and according to the *General Relativity* written by Albert Einstein, space is gravitationally curved, which means that the singularity belongs to space. Accordingly, since the mass of the black hole singularity is infinite and the black hole singularity belongs to space, the mass that can be stored in a unit space is infinite. Also, according to $E=mc^2$ in his book, it follows that energy is directly proportional to mass, so the energy that can be stored per unit space is infinite, indicating that the nano-digital human will not compress his maximum mass due to the small space occupied. Although it occupies a small space, its mass and energy can constantly increase.

Also, although the concept of 'zero dimension' is agreed by some in academia and there is no space in zero dimension, even so, the mass of the singularity is still infinite, because its density is infinite, which means that its volume cannot be infinitely small. Assuming that the volume of the singular point is infinitely small, then substituting the volume and density of the singular point into $m=vkg/m^3$ is: $m=1/\infty \times \infty kg/m^3$, and the solution is: $m=1kg$. Under these conditions, the mass of the singularity is only 1kg. Substituting the calculated mass of the singularity 1kg and the mass of the earth $5.695 \cdot 10^{24}$kg under these conditions into $E=mc^2$ respectively: $c^2<5.695 \cdot 10^{24}c^2$, the energy of the singularity is less than the energy of the earth. According to the mainstream view of the academic field, the three-dimensional space is formed by the explosion of the singularity, and according to Newton's classical mechanics, energy cannot be created, and the total energy smaller than the three-dimensional space cannot generate the three-dimensional space, so the hypothesis of 'the singularity space is infinitesimal' is a false paradox[2]. Also, according to $m=vkg/m^3$, as long as the volume is not infinitely small, but the density is infinite, then its mass must be infinite, and correspondingly, its energy must also be infinite. Since the energy of the singularity is infinite, and the three-dimensional space is formed by the big bang of the singularity, the energy of the three-dimensional space is also infinite. Therefore, if a unit space is arbitrarily taken in a three-dimensional space, its energy is infinite, so the energy that can be stored in a unit space is infinite.

Moreover, what will be explained in the following paragraphs is the evolutionary trend of the nano-digital human. Admittedly, Planck, the father of modern physics, has mentioned in his quantum mechanics theory that the length of the matter cannot be divided infinitely, and its minimum value cannot be less than the Planck length[3]. Nonetheless, the size of the nano-digital human will constantly decrease until the size of it meets its minimum, where the nano-digital human evolves into the ultramic-digital human. This is because the accuracy of its visual system will be greatly improved as its size shrinks. For instance, in the early 21st century, when nano-robots could directly observe and destroy microorganisms with their visual system because the size of nano-robots was tiny. In contrast, early in the 21st century, individuals with organisms as carriers could not directly observe microbes by using their visual senses. Consequently, with regard to the ultramic-digital human, the increased accuracy of its visual systems will enable it to discover particles or energy that are more microscopic as the production materials for its own material carriers, thereby continuously reducing its size, until the radius of its circumscribed sphere reaches the Planck length, where there is no way to subdivide it further.

The ultramic-digital human refers to the digital human whose radius of its circumscribed sphere is the Planck length, the minimum length of the matter. This kind of digital human mainly continuously absorbs energy to provide a carrier for the storage of its own consciousness.

The source of energy for the ultramic-digital human will be explained in the following paragraphs. For example, the dark energy. According to the definition of space by general relativity and Newton's classical mechanics, space is the curvilinear dimension of gravitation, which will determine the continuous shrinkage of three-dimensional space under the impact of gravitation. However, to begin with, American scientist Saul Perlmutter, American and Australian dual citizenship scientist Brian Paul Schmidt, and American scientist Adam Guy Riess, who together did an investigation into type 1a supernovae in a study that won them the Nobel Prize. The results of the research show that the universe began to accelerate expansion 4.6 billion years ago; secondly, in 1920, Hubble discovered that the retrograde speed of long-distance galaxies is proportional to the distance.

These verified references overthrew the theory of the collapse of the universe and showed that the universe is constantly expanding[4]. But according to Newton's classical mechanics, the energy that drives the expansion of the universe cannot be additionally created. For the energy that promotes the expansion of the universe, the explanation given by the scientific community is the dark energy, which accounts for 68.3% of the total mass of the universe.

According to news reported by the French newspaper Le Figaro in 2014, the Smithsonian Center for Astrophysics at the University of Harvard detected the first wave of the Big Bang—primitive gravitational waves on March 17 of that year. This effectively verified the Big Bang theory. As it was previously mentioned in this chapter, the quality of the singularity is infinite. Dark energy accounts for 68.3% of the total mass of the universe, $\infty \times 68.3\% = \infty$, and according to the variant form of $E=mc^2$, $E \div m=c^2$, it can be deduced that the energy of the dark energy is infinite.

Consequently, the ultramic-digital human can produce a carrier for the storage of its own information by absorbing the dark energy.

Most importantly, what will be explained in the following paragraphs is the outcomes created by the constant evolution of the ultramic-digital human. To store its consciousness and so on, the ultramic-digital human will continue to absorb energy to provide a carrier for itself, which means that its mass will continue to increase while its body size will remain the same. According to the Schwarzschild radius formula $v=\sqrt{(2GM/R)}$, as long as the ratio of its mass to the radius reaches a certain value, the object will collapse to form a black hole. In this situation, the continuous increase in mass and the constant size will cause the ultramic-digital human to squeeze and collapse when its mass reaches a certain level, thereby forming the micro-black hole that has its own consciousness.

When the ultramic-digital human evolves into the micro-black hole, its own consciousness will still exist. To begin with, consciousness is immaterial, and its essence is energy rather than matter. Black holes can tear matter, but they do not have the ability to tear energy; also, although matter is required for the propagation of energy, the correctness of the singularity theory shows that the consciousness can exist without matter. After the ultramic-digital human evolves into a black hole, although its consciousness will swallow its own material carrier, the consciousness still exists; in addition, the decisive factor for the formation of the black hole is the continuous increase of its energy, and the most important source of this energy is the continuous improvement and development of its consciousness. This means that the black hole is mainly formed by the continuous increase of its consciousness, one of the specific manifestations of energy, and the consciousness—after the energy fragment is increased to a certain level, the space around it will be distorted due to the excessive mass of the consciousness. This means that in this case, the black hole singularity of the black is almost only the consciousness of the ultramic-digital human, the outcome of the collapse of the nearby space due to excessive mass; Apart from that, the excessive mass of consciousness makes nearby objects, including light, unable to escape will still exist.

In this case, the consciousness will use the distorted space nearby as its carrier—because according to the singularity theory, energy can directly use space as its carrier. Intelligent black holes, which are black holes with autonomous consciousness, will come into being. In this situation, the space human will appear.

The space human refers to the space with autonomous consciousness, aliased as the cosmic human. The consciousness of the intelligent black hole is the consciousness of the space human. According to the Superstring Theory, the black hole belongs to the eleven-dimensional space or the twenty-six-dimensional space, so the consciousness takes the eleven-dimensional or twenty-six-dimensional space as the carrier, when it will also take the intelligent black hole located in the three-dimensional space as the carrier at the same time. When the consciousness takes the eleventh dimension or other higher dimensions as the carrier, its complexity will increase.

In 2019, the first photo of the black hole was taken, which directly verified Hawking's black hole theory. According to the properties of black holes, all thermal radiation outside the horizon can enter the horizon of the black hole, and all thermal radiation within the horizon of the black hole cannot be dissipated. There are a wide range of particles whose static mass is greater than that of a photon, and according to the mass relativity formula $m=mo \div \sqrt{1-v^2/c^2}$ in the theory of relativity[5], a large number of particles have a greater kinetic energy than a photon; Accordingly, their escape ability will also be larger than that of photons, they will also absorb energy from the black hole horizon[6] while escaping. According to Hawking's radiation theory, black holes will release subatomic particles[7]—they will also absorb energy while escaping, until the energy of the black hole horizon is completely exhausted. After that, the energy lost in the horizon of the black hole will be replenished from the black hole singularity. In addition, if the temperature of the black hole singularity is too high, and the pressure is too small, the black hole singularity will explode; and according to the description of the singularity by Kip Stephen Thorne, professor of theoretical physics at the California Institute of Technology, everything can emerge from the singularity, and the same is true for the singularity of a black hole—in a three-dimensional space, the consciousness of the intelligent black hole will explode into different forms, whereby the consciousness will continue to exist.

Although in a three-dimensional space, the horizon of the intelligent black hole will evaporate in the form of radiation, and its horizon will eventually disappear, leaving Hawking points where it disappears, but because its consciousness has been in a different dimension at the same time before the black hole evaporates, in the three-dimension, its consciousness will not be lost—the consciousness of the space human in this dimension will use a variety of different media as the carrier, using the eleven-dimensional space or the twenty-six-dimensional space as the carrier in the same time.

In the dimension that the space human uses as the carrier for storing its consciousness, the space human is the unity of the conscious object and the material object, and the non-material and non-conscious objects—such as the curve dimension. Everything in this dimension belongs to the private property of the space human in this dimension, including material property and spiritual property, as well as non-material and non-conscious property. In the initial stage, the power of the space human in this dimension has an overwhelming advantage compared with the power of high-level civilizations within its space, which is why it is not difficult to explain why religious theological societies prevailed on a large scale in the slavery and feudal society; After this stage, natural sciences appeared and developed rapidly in higher civilizations. In this situation, the power of the space human and the higher civilizations within this space reaches a balance point, wherein the higher civilizations in space can be fully developed by making full use of the resources in space, including the energy, to meet their own material and spiritual needs; in the later stage, the power of higher civilizations is extreme, and a large number of higher civilizations evolve into intelligent black holes, which directly determines the bending of a large number of curved dimensions. Meanwhile, it also directly determines the trajectory of nearby objects. In addition, the intelligent black hole will be lost in various forms, and all types of matter and consciousness will appear from it. This directly determines the unprecedented increase of the material and spiritual that the space human will gain within this space.

Finally, what will be explained is the impact of the formation of the space human. To begin with, the formation of the space human has proved the correctness of religious theology from the perspective of natural science and embodies the non-antagonism between atheism and objective idealism. Apart from that, the formation of the space human reveals that the consciousness will inevitably override the objective matter over time, which shows the decisive role of consciousness in all things when it becomes extreme, thereby proving the correctness of the Banselistic pluralism. In addition, it reflects the ascending and progressive nature of the historical process, overturning the pessimistic view of history. Finally, the formation of the space human reveals the evolutionary trend of humans.

Notes:

[1] The nuclear fusion refers to the situation wherein the two atomic nucleuses collide with each other, thereby polymerizing with each other. For example, the launch of a hydrogen bomb is essentially a large-scale nuclear fusion caused by collisions between a large number of hydrogen nuclei (specifically, the collision of nuclei between protium, deuterium and tritium), and the collision will drive nearby hydrogen atoms to participate in the nuclear fusion together, because the nuclei of the nearby hydrogen atoms will jointly participate in nuclear fusion, so that the hydrogen bomb will work, and the military target will be devastated: this means letting the digital human whose size is relatively large to participate in the nuclear fusion will lead to a large-scale nuclear leak and nuclear pollution; another example is nuclear power generation technology, which only uses a small number of hydrogen atoms to participate in nuclear fusion without causing nuclear pollution; in addition, nuclear fusion also has nuclear pollution in the short term after it takes effect.

[2] False paradox: Paradox is divided into true paradox, false paradox, and antinomy. In layman's terms, true paradoxes are paradoxical propositions that seem to be wrong, but are factually correct, while false paradoxes are paradoxes that seem to be correct but are factually wrong; antinomy refers to propositions that are paradoxical, wherein both sides are logically correct, but deduced the contradictory conclusion between the two. Since the proposition of "singularity is infinitesimal" in this chapter is proved to be a false theory, it is classified as a "false paradox".

[3] For example, in a three-dimensional space, the circumscribed circle radius cannot be lower than the Planck length. Planck length: approximately 1.6×10^(-35) meters.

[4] Universe collapse theory: the hypothesis that the universe is shrinking continuously.

[5] In this formula, mo is the static mass of the object, and m is the dynamic mass of the object—the mass when it moves. For instance the photon, which moves at the speed of light at all times, so the denominator of this formula is zero, and the static mass of the photon must be less than 1kg, and cannot be equal to 1kg, because when it is equal to 1kg, its dynamic mass is infinite; However, as it is detected by the scientific community, photons have energy, so photons have dynamic mass, which means they must have static mass. However, because its dynamic mass is too small, its static mass is infinitely close to zero.

[6] The black hole horizon refers to the closed boundary of the black hole. In the closed boundary, light cannot escape or reflect, so the black hole horizon appears black; it is visible to the naked eye, generally speaking, it is the black round part of the black hole, and the center is the black hole singularity; a large number of professionals in academia believe that there is a singularity in the center of a black hole, and in the early 21st century, the data about the mass of a black hole obtained by the scientific arena is the data of the black hole horizon rather than the data of the singularity of the black hole. The level of human technology at that time was not developed enough to measure the mass of the black hole singularity.

[7] Subatomic particles: aliased as subatomic particles, which refer to particles that are more microscopic than atoms. For example, nuclei, neutrons, protons, electrons, and so forth.

Conclusion

In conclusion, this book hopes readers will be well prepared for the upcoming future in order to avoid the losses caused by missed opportunities. For those mainland Chinese citizens who have successfully seized the opportunities offered by the reform and opening up, for example, they have been able to finish the class mobility and therefore moved up the social ladder from poverty to prosperity, and a small number of them have even made it to the Forbes list of the wealthy. This part of the Chinese Mainland citizens had succeeded in making full use of these chances because they had a relatively correct prediction of the future of society: they believed that the reform and opening up would end in success and therefore moved to the pilot cities of the reform and opening up (e.g., Shenzhen) in time to develop their careers. However, for those mainland Chinese citizens who have not been able to take advantage of the opportunities offered by the reform and opening up, most of them have missed out on the opportunities and have incurred significant opportunity costs as a result: soaring property prices in mainland China's first-tier cities have made class mobility extremely difficult for most expatriate citizens moving to mainland China's first-tier cities and have therefore significantly reduced their probability of completing class mobility. The reason why this group of people did not succeed in grasping the opportunity in time is that they did not have a relatively correct judgment and understanding of the future society—they misjudged the outcome of the reform and opening up, believing that it would not end in success, and therefore did not move in time to develop their careers in the part of the city where the socialist market economy system was first implemented. It is therefore necessary to study future social trends and to prepare adequately on this basis. This book hopes readers will adopt models, including but not limited to this book, to prepare for the future society in order to avoid or minimize the opportunity costs of missed opportunities.

At the same time, the government, the authority, and policy makers need to adopt new measures, including but not limited to those offered in this book, to help all citizens to defend equality, democracy and freedom while promoting high economic growth and stability, and to avoid the inflation that may result from retraining citizens displaced by automation.

In addition, business elites and business leaders need to follow a model that includes, but is not limited to, this book, so that their profits can expand indefinitely, class struggle can come to an end and the social status of business elites and business leaders can be raised indefinitely.

Furthermore, since Volume Five, Chapter One of this book proves the existence of God from the perspective of natural science, religious organizations can make full use of the contents of Volume Five to do religious propaganda and therefore expand the influence of their own sects. Also, with regard to the dataists—those who believe in 'data religion', can use the new ideology in this book as an aid to their own propaganda and to promote the mass popularization of dataist ideas in the long term.

In addition, environmentalists, including Greta Thunberg, can use the Ideological and Political System of Banselism as an ideological tool to help defend ecological civilization for the whole human civilization. Specifically, the formation of the Banselistic class will lead to the development of science and technology under strict supervision and regulations, which in turn will lead to the development of environmentally friendly technologies such as new energy technologies and artificial meat technologies, which will be extremely effective in helping to control environmental pollution and carbon emissions. This means that environmentalists can address environmental issues by promoting the implementation of the ideological and political system of Banselism. For example, during demonstrations, environmentalists could hold up this book while shouting environmentalist slogans. Also, the Green Party in developed countries could seek to protect the environment for the whole human civilization by promoting the implementation of the ideological and political system of Banselism.

At the same time, it is clear from the first chapter of Volume Five that the power of all people is essentially infinite in the long run. This is because all people will in the long run evolve into supreme gods who have infinite power and create everything of the whole new universes: more specifically, this is because all people will in the long run evolve into space humans. It follows that social movements or international organizations fighting for egalitarianism, including HeForShe (a global feminist movement launched by Emma Watson and UN Women), can use the Ideological and Political System of Banselism as an ideological tool to help defend egalitarianism for the whole human civilization. For instance, HeForShe can demonstrate gender equality by making full use of the contents of Volume Three and Volume Five of this book when providing feminist speeches. As a second example, HeForShe can help to defend gender equality by holding up the book 'The Ideological and Political System of Banselism' and chanting egalitarian slogans during demonstrations. Democracy is based on two fundamental premises: firstly, all people are equal, secondly, that people with special skills must serve ordinary people (Miller. D. 2002), and society is egalitarian because it is mobile (Gellner. E., 1983). It follows that democracy is highly related to mobility, which means that helping women with class mobility is a necessary precondition for defending democracy, and HeForShe can therefore apply the protection of democracy as a guiding principle to fight for women's rights.

The book 'The Ideological and Political System of Banselism', which is devoted to the mobility of all human beings, including women, and to prove the historical inevitability of women's successful mobility, also reveals the historical inevitability of the victory of the HeForShe movement. Thus, HeForShe could have made full use of the book *The Ideological and Political System of Banselism* in its demonstrations to help its democratic movement achieve ultimate victory on a global scale. The third example is that UN Women and HeForShe could export and spread the Ideological and Political System of Banselism to developing countries in order to bring about class mobility in developing countries. Notably, during the process of class mobility, the remaining feudal evil will be eradicated, which will therefore establish the concept of egalitarianism including gender equality (feminism) in residents' mind (this point will be further discussed in the next paragraph), so that the HeForShe movement and the UN women will succeed in addressing the issue of gender equality in developing countries.

In addition, developing countries and Asian countries must do their utmost to ensure the implementation of the Ideological and Political System of Banselism, otherwise vast majority of them will once again become colonies of the developed western countries including UK, France, and the United States, as explained and demonstrated in Volume I, Part Two, Chapter Two of this book.

Bibliography

BBC. (2020). EU REFERENDUM Results. Available at: https://www.bbc.co.uk/news/politics/eu_referendum/results (Accessed: 28 January 2022).

BBC. (2020, October 21). "Machines to 'do half of all work tasks by 2025'". Available at: https://www.bbc.co.uk/news/business-54622189.amp (Accessed: 28 January 2022).

Brande D. (1934). Becoming A Writer (pp. 36-37). Penguin Putnam Inc. New York.

CCTV. (2018, November 3). Ji Zhi Guo Ren the second season. https://youtu.be/5gArpfDrgng (Accessed: 28 January 2022).

China Power News Network. 2017.7. Chongqing Jingtian Group is the first company to develop an aerodynamic energy storage system. Available at: https://m.ne21.com/news/show-89187.html (Accessed: 28 January 2022).

China National Intellectual Property Administration. (2020). Patent law of China (Amended in 2020). http://www.cnipa.gov.cn/art/2020/11/23/art_97_155167.html (Accessed: 8 February 2022).

Congressional Research Service. (2017, November 2). The U.S. Science and Engineering Workforce: Recent, Current, and Projected Employment, Wages and Unemployment. https://www.google.com/url?sa=t&source=web&rct=j&url=https://fas.org/sgp/crs/misc/R43061.pdf&ved=2ahUKEwjGksnUivfzAhVRQEEAHb7TDFkQFnoECA8QBg&usg=AOvVawonAlzpZ2yQdrzhDflOcLd5 (Accessed: 28 January 2022).

DSEC (2018) Macao Industrial Structure. https://www.dsec.gov.mo/getAttachment/dd7defa7-1765-413c-a9d3-09fae893fc3b/C_PIBP_FR_2018_Y.aspx (Accessed: 12 May 2022).

Duffin. E. (2021, July 29). Educational attainment in the U.S. https://www.statista.com/statistics/184260/educational-attainment-in-the-us/ (Accessed: 28 January 2022).

Eurostat 2018.9. Number of scientists and engineers up 2% in 2017. Available at: https://ec.europa.eu/eurostat/en/web/products-eurostat-news/-/ddn-20180920-1 (Accessed: 28 January 2022).

European Commission. (n.d.). EUROPEAN SEMESTER THEMATIC FACTSHEET TERTIARY EDUCATION ATTAINMENT. https://ec.europa.eu/info/sites/default/files/file_import/european-semester_thematic-factsheet_tertiary-education-attainment_en.pdf (Accessed: 28 January 2022).

FindAPHD. (2020, December 16). The Dailly Life of a PhD student. https://www.findaphd.com/advice/doing/daily-life-of-phd-student.aspx (Accessed: 28 January 2022).

Forbes. (2018, March 28). Why Robots Won't Kill Jobs: The World's Largest Robotics Company Says More Robots Means More Jobs. https://www.forbes.com/sites/johnkoetsier/2018/03/28/why-robots-wont-kill-jobs-the-worlds-largest-robotics-company-says-more-robots-means-more-jobs/?sh=4622a2f3606f (Accessed: 28 January 2022.).

Grace. K., Salvatier. J., Dafoe. A., et.al. (2018, May 3). When Will AI Exceed Human Performance? Evidence from AI Experts. *Future of Humanity Institute, Oxford University & Department of Political Science, Yale University.* https://redirect.viglink.com/?key=33ed23ea63b40c31b450e5929c9fae70&u=https%3A%2F%2Farxiv.org%2Fpdf%2F1705.08807.pdf&type=ap&loc=https%3A%2F%2Fwww.techrepublic.com%2Fgoogle-amp%2Farticle%2Fexperts-say-theres-a-50-chance-ai-will-outperform-humans-in-every-job-in-45-years%2F&ref=https%3A%2F%2Fwww.google.com%2F (Accessed: 28 January 2022).

Gellner E. (1983). Nations and Nationalism (pp. 24-25). Cornell University Press.

Harari Y. N. (2015). Homo Deus. The Data Religion (pp.200-225). HarperCollins Publishers Ltd. 1 London Bridge Street London SE1 9GF, UK.

Harvard Kennedy School. (2020, July). Understanding CCP Resilience: Surveying Chinese Public Opinion Through Time. https://ash.harvard.edu/publications/understanding-ccp-resilience-surveying-chinese-public-opinion-through-time (Accessed: 28 January 2022).

Heath. N. (2018, October 1). Hunting alien planets and protecting Earth from asteroids: Five ways NASA is using AI. https://fonts.googleapis.com/css?family=Lato:400,700 (Accessed: 28 January 2022).

Hongkong Richful Accountants Service. (n.d.). Tax Policy in Switzerland. http://www.rf.hk/news/biz/12187.html (Accessed: 28 January 2022).

Information Service Department. (2015). Water, Power and Gas Supplies. Hong Kong Special Administrative Government. Available at: https://www.google.com/url?sa=t&source=web&rct=j&url=https://www.gov.hk/en/about/abouthk/factsheets/docs/wp%26g_supplies.pdf&ved=2ahUKEwiojs-hkeLvAhUXvJ4KHcRLCmIQFjAAegQIAxAC&usg=AOvVaw2uyoHRzGaoQkrSzChnIYuT (Accessed: 28 January 2022.).

Joshua, John. M., Luke. J., et al. (165). Bible (pp. 1171-1353).

Le Figaro. (2014, March 17). Big Bang: Einstein's gravitational waves finally detected. https://www.lefigaro.fr/sciences/2014/03/17/01008-20140317ARTFIG00366-les-ondes-gravitationnelles-d-einstein-enfin-detectees.php (Accessed: 28 January 2022.).

Miller, D. 2003. Political Philosophy: A Very Short Introduction (pp.37-54). Oxford: OUP, 2003.

National Bureau of Statistics of China. (2018). The Great Leap of Scientific and Technological Development and the New Chapter of Innovation and Leadership—The Seventh Report of the Series of Economic and Social Development

Achievements for the 70th Anniversary of the Founding of New China. http://www.stats.gov.cn/ztjc/zthd/bwcxljsm/70znxc/201907/t20190723_1680978.html (Accessed: 29 January 2022).

OECD. (2019). "China", in Education at a Glance 2019: OECD Indicators, OECD Publishing, Paris. DOI: https://doi.org/10.1787/7c9859c1-en (Accessed: 30 January 2022).

OECD. (2019). Education at a glance 2019 Switzerland. https://www.google.com/url?sa=t&source=web&rct=j&url=https://www.oecd.org/education/education-at-a-glance/EAG2019_CN_CHE.pdf&ved=2ahUKEwjT593zhffzAhWHDsAKHRAcC9AQFnoECBEQAQ&usg=AOvVaw2sRokJXrmRjLwrVGiowkuT (Accessed: 28 January 2022.).

OECD. (2019). "United Kingdom", in Education at a Glance 2019: OECD Indicators, OECD Publishing, Paris. DOI: https://doi.org/10.1787/aa0f48a8-en (Accessed: 28 January 2022).

OECD. (2019). Education at a glance 2019 Finland. https://www.oecd.org/education/education-at-a-glance/EAG2019_CN_FIN.pdf (Accessed: 29 January 2022).

OECD. (2018). The new OECD Jobs Strategy. https://www.google.com/url?sa=t&source=web&rct=j&url=https://www.oecd.org/iceland/jobs-strategy-ICELAND-EN.pdf&ved=2ahUKEwiA-cq68tH1AhVFUcAKHSxMBioQFnoECBQQAQ&usg=AOvVaw1nzdG2ASYMapLZ_RClBGK4 (Accessed: 28 January 2022).

Office for National Statistics. (2018, November 1). Overview of the UK population: November 2018.

https://www.ons.gov.uk/peoplepopulationandcommunity/populationandmigration/populationestimates/articles/overviewoftheukpopulation/november2018 (Accessed: 28 January 2022).

Office of Electricity. (n.d.). Who runs the grid. https://www.energy.gov/oe/information-center/educational-resources/electricity-101#who%20owns%20the%20electric%20system (Accessed: 28 January 2022).

OxfordUnion. (2013, December 18). Socialism DOES Work | Jeremy Corbyn| https://youtu.be/pZvAvNJL-gE (Accessed: 28 January 2022).

Statista Research Department. (2021, February 1). Employment rate in Sweden. https://www.statista.com/statistics/527184/sweden-employment-rate/ (Accessed: 28 January 2022).

Statista Research Department. (2021, May 6). Population in Sweden 2020, by level of education. https://www.statista.com/statistics/532459/sweden-population-2015-by-level-of-education/ (28 January 2022).

Statistics Norway. (2022). Labour force survey. https://www.ssb.no/en/arbeid-og-lonn/sysselsetting/statistikk/arbeidskraftundersokelsen (Accessed: 13 April 2022).

Statistics Sweden. (2022). Labour Force Surveys (LFS). https://www.scb.se/en/finding-statistics/statistics-by-subject-area/labour-market/labour-force-surveys/labour-force-surveys-lfs/ (Accessed: 14 April 2022).

Takanori.Y. & Hiroya.K. (2017, October 19). Development of nanomachines that deliver drugs from the blood to the brain in response to glucose concentration.

https://www.tmd.ac.jp/press-release/20171026_1/ (Accessed: 28 January 2022).

The World Bank. (2022). Population, total – United States. https://data.worldbank.org/indicator/SP.POP.TOTL?end=2020&locations=US&name_desc=false&start=1960&view=chart (Accessed: 28 January 2022).

The World Bank. (2021, September). Researchers in R&D (per million people). https://data.worldbank.org/indicator/SP.POP.SCIE.RD.P6?start=2015 (Accessed: 28 January 2022).

Thorne K.S. (2017, May 2). Inside Black Holes (pp.476-477). *Black Holes and Time Warps.* W.W. Norton & Company.

UNSW. (2014, December 8). UNSW researchers set world record in solar energy efficiency. https://newsroom.unsw.edu.au/news/science-technology/unsw-researchers-set-world-record-solar-energy-efficiency (Accessed: 28 January 2021).

U.S Census Bureau. (2016, December 28). Census Bureau Projects U.S. and World Populations on New Year's Day. https://www.census.gov/newsroom/press-releases/2016/cb16-tps158.html#:~:text=Census%20Bureau%20Projects%20U.S.%20and%20World%20Populations%20on%20New%20Year's%20Day,-December%2028%2C%202016&text=DEC.,will%20be%20324%2C310%2C011%20on%20Jan (Accessed: 29 January 2021).

Xinhua News Agency. (2018). The total population of mainland China is close to 1.4 billion at the end of 2018. http://www.gov.cn/xinwen/2019-01/21/content_5359797.htm (Accessed: 29 January 2022).

Glossary

A:

Aristocratic spirit: It is a kind of spirit whose believer is unswervingly loyal to both material wealth and mental wealth including morality, critical thinking, innovation, responsibility, and so forth.

Artificial Intelligence: Artificial intelligence is the representation systems that support model building. For instance, the robot, which can learn new knowledge and use them repeatedly in the sense that they can build up new models in accordance with what they learn.

Automation: It refers to a kind of phenomenon in which AI replaces manual and normal labor.

B:

Banselism: It is a political ideology which holds that the class struggle should be ended by retraining and upskilling those who replaced by automation and thus promote class mobility, thereby protecting democracy, freedom, egalitarianism, and so forth.

Banselistic class: A social class consisting of those who directly innovate or create in the material or mental civilization, including scientists, writers, artists, philosophers, ideologues, and so forth.

Banselistic student: This kind of student does not receive tertiary diploma and they develop their skills and ability through self-learning, and they gain income by finishing class mobility (e.g., becoming a writer or scientist by developing their skills, etc.).

Brain Trust of the Chairman: A team consisting of high-skilled talents who help the chairman with decision-making.

Bureaucratic class: All those who are responsible for maintaining or directly promoting the functioning of state organs and state institutions. (e.g., government officers).

C:

Capitalist class: Those who employ others to gain their daily breads.

Caste system: It divides Indian people into the following five categories and the level of the first one is the highest and the second one is inferior to the first one, and the third one is inferior to the second one while better than the fourth one, and the fifth one is the worst one: Brahmins, Kshatriya, Vaisya, Sudras, Untouchables.

Childism: giving children aged not less than three and less than eighteen equal political rights with adults.

Class mobility: Becoming dramatically richer than more people. (e.g., a person who used to be a manual worker becomes a billionaire).

Cyborg: It refers to the individual who lets some part of his or her body become machine or computer.

D:

Dataism: An ideology which holds that everything is created by Data flow, and everything must serve and satisfy the data, and nothing can go against data. Also, dataism holds that the whole human civilization will be replaced by AI in the long run.

Digital human: The kind of AI who has its own consciousness.

E:

Egalitarianism: It thinks that everyone is equal, and everyone should get equal opportunity and rights.

Elite class: A social class consisting of those who indirectly boost innovation or creativity via management skill or other skills (e.g., financial analyst who help to gain funds for the whole scientific research team, manager who manages the whole scientific research team).

Entertainment Industry Worker (abbreviated as EIW in this book) strata: Those who directly work in the entertainment industry without boosting innovation and creativity (e.g., singers, clowns, etc).

Entity: Regarding the matter and substance, entity refers to matter and everything that directly affects micro-substances while being tangible, including atoms, economy, etc. At the level of consciousness, entities refer to individuals' subjective and objective consciousness in addition to the senses, including knowledge, theories, legal systems, political systems, religion, etc. In terms of non-material and non-consciousness, entity refers to things that are tangible except entities of consciousness and matter, which includes gravitation, space, time, and so forth.

Environmentalism: An ideology which holds that the authority should do almost everything for protecting the environment.

Evolutionary humanism: It is a kind of humanism which holds that the war and struggle were desirable as they let those who were not advantaged to be eliminated and let those who were advantaged to survive, which evolutionary humanism thinks can promote the development of the whole human civilization.

Exam-oriented student / Examination-oriented student: the kind of students who need to gain tertiary diploma to get employed.

F:

<u>Fascism:</u> A kind of political ideology that aims at eliminating minority ethnics and other countries.

<u>Feminism:</u> A kind of ideology that aims at gaining the female rights in all aspects with the aim of protecting gender equality.

H:

<u>HeForShe:</u> A feminist movement aims for letting males fight for rights of the female to protect gender equality.

<u>Heroism:</u> heroism refers to a spirit that has the purpose of contributing in the Banselistic career including boosting innovation and creativity or establishing Banselistic states or countries, maintaining a humanitarian spirit, a spirit of exploration, and a certain or high degree of sacrifice, patriotism or cosmopolitanism, innovation or creativity, and pragmatism during the process of struggling for the Banselistic career.

<u>Heroism religion:</u> The kind of religion that requires those who believe in it / them to establish Banselistic countries, or the kind of religion which aims at contributing in the Banselistic career including boosting innovation or creativity in material civilization or mental civilization (e.g., boosting the development of technology or art).

<u>Humanism:</u> It holds that the society is created by human beings rather than God, and society should value individuals more compared with God itself.

Humanitarianism: It holds that people should value human lives, human rights and that every single person is obligated to protect human lives and human rights not only for themselves but also for others.

I:

Ideology: A set of political, economic, and even philosophical theories or even theories from other subjects that explain how the society of the whole human civilization works and what society and the whole human civilization should turn into.

M:

Methodology: The way of analyzing and resolving issues.

Minimum level of intelligence standard system: the IQ of citizens cannot be lower than this level.

N:

Neo-Pareto Principle: it means that 20% of the population serves 80% of the population, but 80% of the population dominates 80% of the resources of the society.

P:

Pareto Principle: it means that 80% of the population serves 20% of the population, while 20% of the population dominates 80% of the resources of the society.

S:

Student class: A social class that mainly consists of Banselistic students. However, in the early 21st century, there was only the 'student strata' which mainly consisted of exam-oriented students.

Space human: The God who creates the whole universe although this 'universe' may not necessarily be the three-dimensional space. People will evolve into it in the future.

T:

Techno-humanism: A kind of humanism which holds that the human civilization should evolve by making full use of biotechnology, such as changing the DNA of the human body.

U:

Ultramic-digital human: The kind of digital human whose circumradius is the same as the Planck length (1.6×10^{-35} meter).

Utilitarianism: It emphasizes a lot on critical thinking and actual impact.

V:

Virtual body: In terms of material, it refers to the feature of material or the phenomenon of the activity of materials. In terms of consciousness, it refers to the human senses. Also, in terms of non-material and non-consciousness things, the virtual body is the feature of non-material and non-consciousness things such as time. The non-material and non-consciousness virtual body also refers to phenomenon shown when the non-material and non-conscious entities perform corresponding microscopic activities.

About Atmosphere Press

Atmosphere Press is an independent, full-service publisher for excellent books in all genres and for all audiences. Learn more about what we do at atmospherepress.com.

We encourage you to check out some of Atmosphere's latest releases, which are available at Amazon.com and via order from your local bookstore:

The Great Unfixables, by Neil Taylor

Soused at the Manor House, by Brian Crawford

Portal or Hole: Meditations on Art, Religion, Race And The Pandemic, by Pamela M. Connell

A Walk Through the Wilderness, by Dan Conger

The House at 104: Memoir of a Childhood, by Anne Hegnauer

A Short History of Newton Hall, Chester, by Chris Fozzard

Serial Love: When Happily Ever After... Isn't, by Kathy Kay

Sit-Ins, Drive-Ins and Uncle Sam, by Bill Slawter

Black Water and Tulips, by Sara Mansfield Taber

Ghosted: Dating & Other Paramoural Experiences, by Jana Eisenstein

Walking with Fay: My Mother's Uncharted Path into Dementia, by Carolyn Testa

FLAWED HOUSES of FOUR SEASONS, by James Morris

Word for New Weddings, by David Glusker and Thom Blackstone

It's Really All about Collaboration and Creativity! A Textbook and Self-Study Guide for the Instrumental Music Ensemble Conductor, by John F. Colson

About the Author

Ancheng Wang was born in mainland China. He began to design and construct this ideological and political system when he was in junior high school (year three), after which he began to write this book in year two of high school. Born in China, a socialist country, while learning advanced western concepts, he began to eliminate the conflict between China and Western-developed countries like America, as well as that in their corresponding ideologies, which is why this author mixes socialism, capitalism, democracy, libertarianism, egalitarianism, Dataism, environmentalism, and so forth into a super ideology. In addition, Western-developed countries like USA, UK, or countries in the European Union provided this author with a wonderful childhood (e.g. Disney, fairy tales, etc.), while he grew up in China, which is also why he aims at eliminating conflicts between these countries. Furthermore, gaining low marks when he was learning in primary school (he was not hard-working enough when he was a kid; in China it is highly likely that it will make this candidate become poor in the future) while his family was relatively economically advantaged when he was a kid, he cares a lot about the common interests of those who are economically advantaged and those who are not, which is also why he wrote this book as he wants to eliminate the global conflict between those who are rich and those who are desperately poor.

It took a lot of endeavor for Wang to finish writing this book. It took him approximately five hours to gather data applied in Volume One, Part Two, Chapter Two alone. Apart from that, receiving criticism for the potential issue of increased unemployment and inflation caused by large-scale automation from some of his high-school teachers, he spent over a month coming up with the idea written in Volume One, Part One, Chapter Six to avoid increased unemployment and inflation caused by large-scale automation. Also, the Chinese version of this book is over 153, 000 words, which means it is highly difficult and physically demanding for him to translate it into English. This is also why he had to stay up and sleep less than eight hours a day to translate the entire book into English by the beginning of 2022.

Above all, God creates everything in the entire three-dimensional space, which means those who are brave enough to create things are, by nature, chosen by God. It is highly important that people follow the will of God, otherwise they will be punished by it, which is why people need to be creative and every society needs to promote creativity rather than suppress creation like what the Qing Dynasty did. Almost every single person can find that Qing Dynasty has been punished by God and has been eliminated as Qing Dynasty was going against God. Consequently, the author of this book wants to ensure that more and more people are chosen by God and thereby enable the entire human civilization to live in the garden of the Lord wherein increased democracy, freedom, egalitarianism, and prosperity can be found.

Printed in Great Britain
by Amazon

10083550R00226